ROUTLEDGE LIBRARY EDITIONS:
THE ECONOMICS AND POLITICS OF OIL AND GAS

Volume 5

# OPEC BEHAVIOR AND WORLD OIL PRICES

# OPEC BEHAVIOR AND WORLD OIL PRICES

JAMES M. GRIFFIN AND DAVID J. TEECE

Routledge
Taylor & Francis Group
LONDON AND NEW YORK

First published in 1982 by George Allen & Unwin Ltd.

This edition first published in 2016
by Routledge
2 Park Square, Milton Park, Abingdon, Oxon OX14 4RN

and by Routledge
711 Third Avenue, New York, NY 10017

*Routledge is an imprint of the Taylor & Francis Group, an informa business*



*British Library Cataloguing in Publication Data*
A catalogue record for this book is available from the British Library

ISBN: 978-1-138-64127-3 (Set)
ISBN: 978-1-315-62232-3 (Set) (ebk)
ISBN: 978-1-138-64683-4 (Volume 5) (hbk)
ISBN: 978-1-315-62735-9 (Volume 5) (ebk)

# OPEC Behavior and World Oil Prices

James M. Griffin

*University of Houston*

David J. Teece

*University of California, Berkeley*

with contributions from:

Morris Adelman George Daly William W. Hogan
John Lichtblau Theodore Moran Robert S. Pindyck
Henry B. Steele

London

GEORGE ALLEN & UNWIN

Boston Sydney

**George Allen & Unwin (Publishers) Ltd,**
**40 Museum Street, London WC1A 1LU, UK**

George Allen & Unwin (Publishers) Ltd,
Park Lane, Hemel Hempstead, Herts HP2 4TE, UK

Allen & Unwin Inc.,
9 Winchester Terrace, Winchester, Mass 01890, USA

George Allen & Unwin Australia Pty Ltd,
8 Napier Street, North Sydney, NSW 2060, Australia

First published in 1982

**British Library Cataloguing in Publication Data**

OPEC behavior and world oil prices.
1. Organization of the Petroleum Exporting Countries
I. Griffin, James M. II. Teece, David J.
338.2'3 HD9560.1.066

ISBN 0-04-338-103-0

**Library of Congress Cataloging in Publication Data**

Main entry under title:
OPEC behavior and world oil prices.
Bibliography: p.
1. Petroleum products—Prices. 2. Organization for Petroleum Exporting Countries. I. Griffin, James M.
II. Teece, David J. III. Adelman, Morris Albert.
IV. Title: O.P.E.C. behavior and world oil prices.
HD9560.4.06 338.2'3 82-6840
ISBN 0-04-338-102-2 AACR2
ISBN 0-04-338-103-0 (pbk.)

Set in 10 on 11 point Times by Typesetters (Birmingham) Limited,
and printed in Great Britain
by Biddles Limited, Guildford, Surrey

# Contents

# Preface

As economics professors, compelled to explain OPEC in the classroom, we have recognized serious weaknesses in the textbook treatment of OPEC and its cartel properties. Somehow, the textbook models of cartel behavior seem pathetically inadequate when it comes to explaining the structure and behavior of this intriguing organization. Using these models, many respected voices in the economics profession predicted that OPEC would go the way of all previous cartels, and collapse under the weight of competitive output expansion. This seemed all the more likely given the many differences of opinion and rivalries which existed among the members of OPEC. But it has not turned out that way, at least not so far.

We have also become concerned that formal modeling efforts are not paying sufficient attention to important subtleties of OPEC behavior. Those developing optimizing models seem to assume that their handiwork represents positive models of the oil exporting countries. This is not as self-evident to us as it apparently is to others, underscoring the fact that commonly accepted modeling efforts and price projections are built upon only very rudimentary and perhaps incorrect notions about OPEC behavior.

Because of these concerns, a conference was called in Houston on May 8, 1981, to discuss 'The Future of OPEC and the Long Run Price of Oil'. This book had its genesis at that conference. With the exception of Chapters 1, 8, and 9, draft versions of all of these chapters were presented at that conference, which was generously hosted by the Center for Public Policy at the University of Houston. We are especially grateful to the Director, George Daly, for his tangible support of this project. Special recognition is in order not only for those contributing papers, but the distinguished group of participants who added immensely to the dialogue. We wish to acknowledge the financial support of the Energy Laboratory at the University of Houston in the preparation of the edited manuscript. We are also indebted to Patricia Harrell for her careful assistance in the preparation of this manuscript.

As editors, we have accepted the challenge of weaving these proceedings into a unified monograph. This was not as difficult as it first appeared, because there turned out to be a large degree of commonality among the various views put forward. However, we believe that the subject matter is sufficiently important to warrant our labors on a rather lengthy introduction, which lays out some concepts and basic facts necessary for the understanding of subsequent chapters. We have tried to accomplish this task using only the most simple of economic concepts since it is our objective to make this material accessible to audiences without a specialized background in economic theory.

However, in attempting to summarize and unify, we suspect that we have occasionally distorted the views of some of our contributors. This is to some degree unavoidable given our desire to make the findings and conclusions as stark and provocative as is reasonably possible. Accordingly, we have labeled the individual chapter contributions as to authorship since we do not wish to overtly implicate the contributors in the rather heterodox conclusions to which we find ourselves drawn.

JAMES M. GRIFFIN
DAVID J. TEECE

## Contributors

MORRIS ADELMAN
Professor of Economics,
Department of Economics
Massachusetts Institute of Technology

GEORGE DALY
Dean, College of Social Sciences
University of Houston

WILLIAM HOGAN
Professor of Economics
Kennedy School of Government
Harvard University

JAMES M. GRIFFIN
Professor of Economics,
Department of Economics
University of Houston

JOHN LICHTBLAU
President
Petroleum Industry Research Foundation
New York

ROBERT S. PINDYCK
Professor of Economics
Sloan School of Management
Massachusetts Institute of Technology

THEODORE MORAN
Professor and Director,
Program in International Business Diplomacy
Georgetown School of Foreign Service

HENRY B. STEELE
Professor of Economics,
Department of Economics
University of Houston

DAVID J. TEECE
Associate Professor
School of Business Administration
University of California, Berkeley

# 1 Introduction

JAMES M. GRIFFIN and DAVID J. TEECE

## I INTRODUCTION

The decade of the 1970s ushered in a new epoch in the history of the world petroleum industry and in the economic power of the oil exporting nations. The price of oil at the end of the decade was about twenty times higher than it was at the beginning, with profound economic, political, and social consequences for consumers and producers.

The principal purpose of this book is not, however, to recount the tumultuous events of the 1970s; rather, we wish to gain insights into the price path for oil over the next two decades. Since this depends significantly on the production decisions of the oil exporting countries, we seek insights into the economic and political factors which will shape future crude oil production and export decisions.

Interest in the Organization of Petroleum Exporting Countries (OPEC), already awakened by the quadrupling of crude prices in 1973–74, surged dramatically in 1979 when oil prices doubled, but despite the enormous flurry of research activity occasioned by these events, OPEC behavior still elicits considerable puzzlement. Debates erupt over very basic matters, such as the degree to which OPEC is a cartel responsible for propping up the world price, or whether OPEC simply ratifies prices determined in an environment which is approximately competitive. It appears to us that OPEC behavior is not well understood, either by politicians, professional analysts, or the OPEC members themselves.

Indeed, professional analysts need little reminder that their understanding of OPEC and the world petroleum market has sometimes been wide of the mark. Professor Adelman reflected the views of many experts when he predicted in the 1960s that the world price of oil would approach the long run cost of extraction, which he estimated at just cents per barrel.[1] The events of 1973–74 took almost everyone by surprise, partially discrediting the earlier projections. However, for the most part, industry economists viewed the quadrupling of prices in

1973–74 as temporary. There were good theoretical and historical reasons to believe that cartels collapse under the weight of cheating,[2] and economists of no less renown than Nobel Laureate Milton Friedman predicted that prices would fall to competitive levels.[3] If these dogma were not sufficient, an army of energy modelers came forth with energy models showing that OPEC had reached or overstepped the limits of its monopoly power.[4] Instead of collapsing, prices rose dramatically once again in 1978, and had reached $35–40 a barrel by 1981.

The events of 1978–79 seemed to fundamentally transform the views of many professional economists. The new orthodoxy of the early 1980s is that prices will continue to rise at a rate 3–4 percent faster than the rate of inflation, once the temporary glut evaporates. This view has become embedded in government policy and in the planning assumptions of the major petroleum companies.[5] The new orthodoxy is set forth in the Stanford Energy Modeling Forum's 1981 study of ten world oil price models. To summarize the findings of the forum, 'The unmistakable overall message is that the world price of oil, in real terms, can be expected to rise during the next several decades.'[6]

Admittedly, the above characterizations of the pre- and post-1978 orthodoxies do not do justice to the works of individual researchers who have either rejected or added important caveats in their endorsement of the conventional wisdom. But our purpose is not to berate the profession of which we are members. Rather we wish to emphasize the complexities and uncertainties of the world petroleum market, together with the specialized and often unrecognized assumptions of economic models. It is this last matter which is of critical importance. As Graham Alison demonstrated in his classic study of the Cuban missile crisis, analysts tend to use the conceptual lens of a particular analytic paradigm without being fully cognizant of its specialized characteristics.[7] The unrecognized assumptions of a particular analytic perspective nevertheless often have important ramifications for the frame of reference which is adopted, the type of evidence which is considered relevant, and the predictions which are advanced.

This monograph enables the reader to compare, contrast, and synthesize various paradigmatic views of OPEC behavior. Too often researchers utilize a conceptual lens of a particular paradigm without recognizing its specialized characteristics. By assembling and integrating the writings of a group of distinguished scholars with backgrounds in economics, operations research, the petroleum industry, and political science, with known differences in views,[8] we hope to highlight elements of commonality as well as disagreement.

While we feel compelled to set forth our own views on the future of OPEC in the concluding chapter, we believe that the analytical process by which one reaches such conclusions are as essential as the conclusion itself.

Before discussing the future of OPEC and the path of oil prices, we must first consider: What is OPEC? Essentially four theories of OPEC are considered by three leading scholars of OPEC. These three include two economists, Professor Morris Adelman and Professor David Teece. The third is Professor Theodore Moran, a prominent political scientist specializing in the Middle East. Each sets forth a different perspective on the question: What is OPEC? Our thesis is that depending on how one characterizes OPEC, the implications for future oil prices are quite different. Thus Chapters 2, 3, and 4 are essential reading.

After the reader has formed an opinion on this fundamental question, he is then prepared to examine the market environment within which OPEC is likely to be confronted in future years. In Chapter 5, Mr John Lichtblau, a leading petroleum industry consultant, offers his characterization of the market OPEC will face in the years ahead. In Chapter 6, Professors George Daly, James Griffin, and Henry Steele apply modeling techniques to simulate oil demand, and OPEC and non-OPEC production for the period 1980 to 2000 under a variety of assumptions regarding economic growth and the price elasticity of oil demand.

In Chapter 7, Professor Robert Pindyck offers his own assessment of the future price path of oil as well as the importance of treating explicitly the large uncertainty that must be attached to any forecasted price path. Chapter 8, by Professor William Hogan, emphasizes that irrespective of the economic power attributes of OPEC, the consuming nations will continue to face serious security problems. Chapter 9, by Professors Griffin and Teece, summarizes the diversity of views on the important questions of the future of OPEC and the long run price path of oil. Particular attention is given to the policy implications arising from this analysis.

But before embarking on a demanding and, we hope, rewarding trip through the remaining eight chapters, the reader will need certain background information on the historical origin and development of OPEC, the economic theory of the pricing of nonrenewable resources, and a summary statement of four competing theories of OPEC. We now turn to each of these.

## II OPEC: AN HISTORICAL OVERVIEW OF THE PERIOD 1960 TO 1980

In 1960, when five major oil exporters - Iran, Iraq, Kuwait, Saudi Arabia, and Venezuela - joined together to form the Organization for Petroleum Exporting Countries, certain observations were no doubt fresh on the founders' minds. First, they were aware that there were substantial economic rents in the world oil market. The gap between the marginal production cost of oil of $.10 to $.20 per barrel and the price consumers paid for refined petroleum products was indeed large and only a small portion could be explained by transportation, refining, and marketing costs.[9] In 1960, retail gasoline prices exceeded $30 per barrel in numerous European countries, owing to the large gasoline excise taxes collected by the consuming countries. The hefty taxes on petroleum products were rather revealing, at least to OPEC. Thus, rents were spread quite unevenly between the consuming country's treasury, the international oil companies, and the oil producing countries.[10] The existence of these rents, with a large portion accruing to the consuming countries and the international oil companies, no doubt created considerable resentment in the producing countries. Thus, an initial goal of OPEC was to wrest some of these economic rents from the international oil companies and the treasuries of the consuming nations.

Second, OPEC founders were quite disturbed that producing-country taxes per barrel had been declining systematically since 1957. The decline in these revenues could be traced to the declining world price of oil, which in turn resulted from the increasingly competitive nature of the world oil market due to the entry of many new firms. Table 1.1 shows the market shares of the largest four, the largest seven, and other companies. In 1950, the 'Seven Sisters' consisting of Esso (now Exxon), British Petroleum, Shell, Standard Oil of California, Mobil, Texaco, and Gulf accounted for virtually all of the oil production involved in international trade. As Figure 1.2 (later on) reveals, the difference in 1950 between the market price of $1.80 per barrel and the payment to the host country of $.60 per barrel left a margin of about $1.20 per barrel, reflecting production costs and profits. With such large profits, entrants explored for oil in areas not controlled by the original concessions. The effect of this new entry was evident by 1957 when the market shares of the seven largest producers had declined from 98 percent to 89 percent. As this trend continued, prices gradually declined until 1970, when the companies' margins had fallen to a level consistent with long run competition. The demise of the 'Seven Sisters' would not have been a serious concern to OPEC except for the fact that in the mid-1950s exporter government taxes were based on 50 percent of the profits of the concessionaire. Thus, declining world oil prices posed as serious a threat to OPEC as it did to the international oil companies. Moreover, the declining per barrel taxes only exacerbated pressures for still lower prices. Host governments recognized that the only way to increase total tax revenues was to increase production. Thus during the 1950s, history is replete with examples of host countries pushing their concessionaires to increase production. This, of course, only put further downward pressure on prices.

A third reality facing the OPEC founders was that 1960 world supply/demand conditions greatly limited its set of possible actions. The decade of the 1950s had witnessed the discovery of numerous giant fields, increasing reserves far faster than the ability of oil consumption to reduce existing reserves. World productive capacity substantially exceeded demand and the reserves were sufficient to quickly expand productive capacity still further. In contrast to present conditions whereby OPEC supplies two-thirds of non-communist oil demand, in 1960, these same countries supplied less than half of such demand. In addition, the geographic and political diversity of countries possessing spare productive capacity meant that no one country or group of countries could appreciably affect the world price of oil. With reserve productive capacity of over 2 million barrels per

Table 1.1 *Percentage Market Shares of International Oil Companies in World Oil Market*

| | *1950* | *1957* | *1969*[a] |
|---|---|---|---|
| Exxon | 30.4 | 22.8 | 16.6 |
| British Petroleum | 26.3 | 14.4 | 16.1 |
| Shell | 13.8 | 17.5 | 13.3 |
| Gulf | 12.1 | 14.8 | 9.8 |
| Largest four | 82.6 | 69.5 | 55.8 |
| Standard Oil of California | 6.1 | 7.6 | 7.5 |
| Texaco | 5.7 | 6.9 | 8.0 |
| Mobil | 3.9 | 5.0 | 4.8 |
| Largest seven | 98.3 | 89.0 | 76.1 |
| All others | 1.8 | 11.1 | 23.9 |
| TOTAL | 100. | 100. | 100. |

[a] First half of 1969.

*Source:* M. A. Adelman, *The World Petroleum Market* (Baltimore: Johns Hopkins University Press, 1972) pp. 80–1. Note this excludes production from North America and communist countries.

day, the United States stood ready to supply its allies in the event of emergency. At the same time, Soviet oil productive capacity was expanding rapidly and oil sales to Western Europe offered a mechanism for earning much coveted foreign exchange. Facing a potentially serious revenue problem and aware of the limitations on its actions, OPEC moved cautiously, but yet purposefully.

## 1960 to 1973: A Period of Rapid Change

The period 1960 to 1973 marked a substantial change in the environment facing OPEC. The 1960s witnessed very strong economic growth in the key oil consuming countries which was manifest in rapidly expanding oil consumption. Gradually, there was a shift from a market characterized by oversupply to one characterized by excess demand with the virtual disappearance of excess productive capacity outside the OPEC countries (see Figure 1.1). In the late 1960s, US oil production peaked, sending the United States increasingly into world oil markets for new supplies to fuel its own rapidly expanding economy. By 1970, oil forecasters were astounded to conclude that

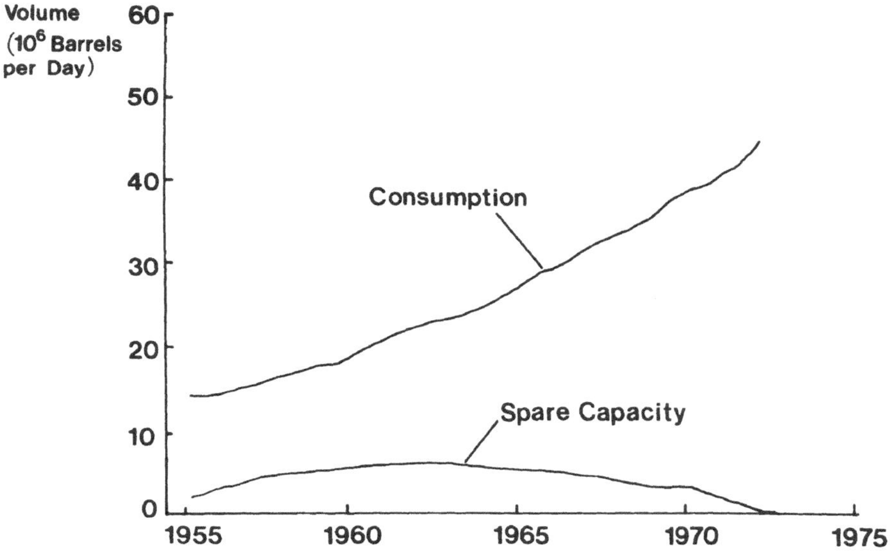


Figure 1.1 *World crude oil spare capacity and consumption (excluding communist countries).*

*Source:* Statement of G. T. Piercy, Exxon Corporation, before the Senate Foreign Relations Subcommittee on Multinational Companies Hearing, Washington D.C., February 1, 1974.

their trend-line projections showed only Saudi Arabia would have reserve productive capacity by the 1980s and even that would be predicated on a capacity expansion to 20 million barrels per day. Over the period 1960 to 1973, Saudi production had already grown from 1.25 MMB/D to 7.6 MMB/D. Statistics such as these only strengthened the credibility of the trend-line projections.

During the period 1960 to 1973, OPEC was involved in three processes: (1) tax system changes, (2) production controls, and (3) steps toward nationalization of concessions. The two latter areas bore little fruit in the 1960s. Attempts to set annual growth rates for each member's oil exports were undertaken in 1965, only to be abandoned in 1967. The exercise floundered since individual OPEC members could not be persuaded that their oil production decisions were not a sovereign domestic matter. With respect to nationalization, OPEC issued in 1968 a declaration of goals including not only the maximization of oil revenues but also the ultimate achievement of effective control of oil company operations. Under the doctrine of 'changing circumstances', concession agreements could be cancelled, tax reference prices could be unilaterally changed, company profit rates controlled, and so on. Even though this doctrine was not taken seriously at the time, the events of the early 1970s prove it was an accurate blueprint for events to come. Following the Algerian nationalization in 1971, new timetables were announced calling for the gradual transfer of ownership in the local concession from the oil companies to the host governments. Most of these transfers occurred after 1973, however.

During the 1960s, OPEC achieved its greatest successes in tax systems changes. Note that Figure 1.2 indicates steadily rising tax revenues per barrel, in contrast to the pattern over the period 1958–60. The major accounting change involved the price on which a concessionaire's income taxes were based. Since they were based on market prices, tax revenues were subject to the same forces which were eroding company profits. To circumvent this problem, the OPEC nations instituted fictional prices for calculating company tax liability. Even though the market price continued to decline throughout the 1960s, taxes were based on a tax reference price, which did not decline. In effect, by basing taxes on a tax reference price which exceeded actual market prices, OPEC succeeded in abandoning a 50 percent profits tax and replacing it with what amounted to an excise tax. The excise tax had the virtue of being unaffected by the declining market price and profitability of world oil markets. For the most part, these gains were won over only mild company objections. Initially, foreign earnings were sufficiently large for US companies that a dollar increase in host country taxes produced a dollar tax credit to apply

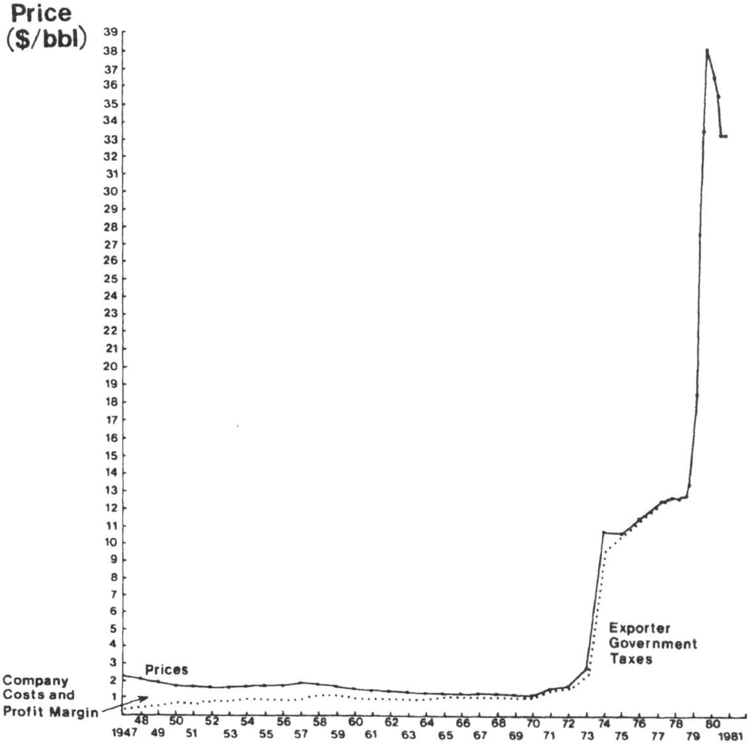


Figure 1.2 *Actual market prices and exporter government taxes.*
*Source:* J. M. Griffin and H. Steele *Energy Economics and Policy* (New York: Academic Press, 1980), p. 96; and *Petroleum Intelligence Weekly*, October 20, 1980, p. 11.

against US tax liability. As long as the foreign tax credits did not exceed foreign tax liability, the oil companies had no incentive to resist these tax changes as the real losers were the national treasuries in Washington, London, and the Hague.

Even though OPEC was unsuccessful in raising the tax reference price during the 1960s, market conditions in the late 1960s signaled new possibilities. In 1969, the Libyan monarchy was overthrown by Arab radicals who were less than enamored with the international oil companies. The closure of the Suez Canal since 1967, coupled with the sabotage of the trans-Arabian pipeline, and the unexpectedly big increase in world oil demand, resulted in a serious tanker shortage and extremely high tanker rates. Libyan oil, requiring only a short trip to Europe, became quite profitable for the oil companies producing in Libya. The Libyan leadership demanded an increase in the tax reference price. Initially, the oil companies resisted these demands, but following threats of nationalization and reductions in allowable production for 'conservation' purposes, the smaller companies acceded to the demands in September 1970, setting in motion a remarkable set of events. If Libya, standing alone, could force an increase in oil prices, what might OPEC accomplish if it acted in unison?

In early 1971, negotiations between OPEC and the oil companies began in Teheran and Tripoli with the aim of establishing a five-year price pact for the period 1971 to 1976. Threatening to embargo any company not acceding to its demands, OPEC forced through an initial increase in the tax reference price from $1.80 to $2.18, coupled with a tax rate increase from 50 to 55 percent. The tax reference price was pegged to escalate by 7½ cents per year through 1976.

The Teheran Agreement was short-lived as it soon became evident OPEC had left money on the table. Strong market conditions led to a world price which suddenly began rising toward the posted tax reference price and by early 1973 surpassed it. At the same time, the devaluations of the dollar, the unit for crude payment, and the accelerating inflation rate in the United States left OPEC in the position of receiving declining real taxes per barrel. In October 1973, the Persian Gulf OPEC members met with oil companies to proclaim the necessity of raising tax reference prices from $3.01 to $5.12. The motivation behind the increase was not to raise the actual market price of oil, but rather to raise tax references above current market prices to give OPEC members a larger share of oil company profits. Before this meeting could reconvene, Arab-Israeli hostilities erupted, opening a new era.

## 1973 to 1981: A Period of Dramatic Price Changes

Whereas up until the 1973 Arab oil embargo, OPEC had largely been concerned with capturing a larger fraction of the economic rents that would otherwise accrue to the oil companies or the consuming nations' treasuries, this event marked a turning point whereby the return to OPEC members arose largely from higher prices to consumers. With the outbreak of Arab–Israeli hostilities in October 1973, the Arab OPEC members announced a unilateral increase in the tax reference price, instituted production cutbacks, and embargoed oil to the United States and the Netherlands. Soon panic buying of oil sent prices in special auctions to over $15 per barrel, but market prices consolidated in the $10 range, creating large profits for the concessions and oil companies. In November 1974, Saudi Arabia adjusted its tax rates and royalties so as to increase tax receipts from $7 to $10.50 per barrel, absorbing the large differential earned by the

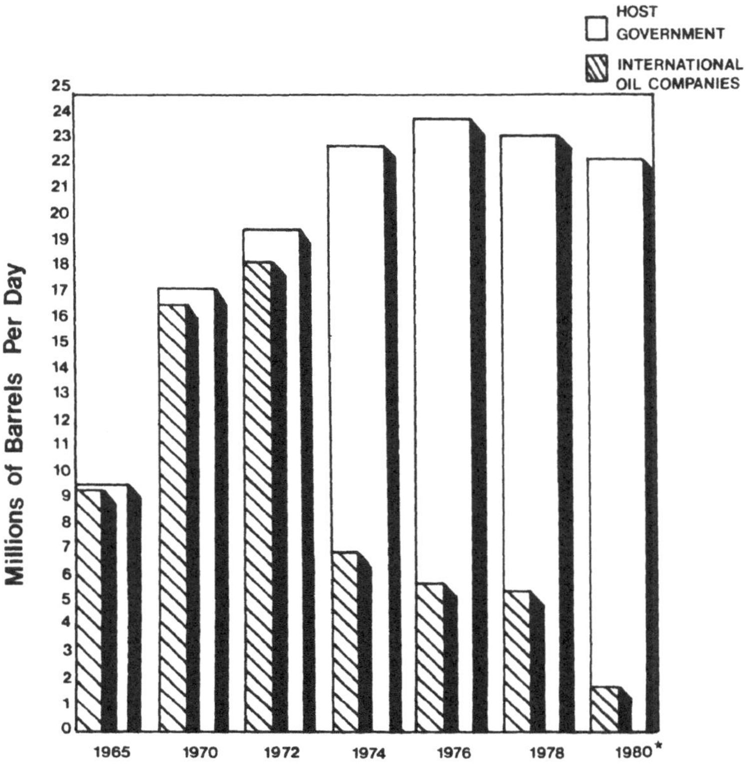


Figure 1.3 *International oil companies' equity interest in Middle East crude oil production.*

*Source:* OPEC Statistical Yearbooks for 1965–78. 1980 estimate based on earlier announced plans of producing governments.

companies. Thus, by setting the tax floor at $10.50, a new lower bound for future crude oil prices was established.

During this same period, the major oil companies' interests in the concessions were *de facto* nationalized with the concessions becoming essentially nationally owned companies. As illustrated by Figure 1.3, the oil companies' role was transformed into that of service contractors and crude oil buyers. This change enabled a great simplification in crude pricing as the national oil company simply announced the price of crude oil. Typically, partners in the old concession are granted small discounts off this price.

The period 1975 to 1978 was one of relative tranquility. Price increases of 10 percent were recorded in September 1975, 5 percent in December 1976, and 5 percent in June 1977. When measured relative to inflation, crude prices declined in real terms over this period. It is interesting to note the diversity of price preferences over this period. OPEC production and exports declined sharply in 1975 and recovered gradually in 1976–77. Particularly in 1975, this was a period of substantial production cutbacks by the Saudis. Saudi production for the first three quarters of 7.1 MMB/D represented a 17 percent cut, compared to the same period in 1974. At the same time that the Saudis reduced production to historically low levels, the Iraqis increased production significantly. Also, there was widespread price discounting by Abu Dhabi, Libya, Nigeria, Iraq, Algeria, and Ecuador. Interestingly, in the face of these conditions, there was considerable disagreement over the extent of price 'increase' preferred. A compromise of 10 percent was reached in Vienna in 1975. The subsequent price increases of 5 percent in December 1976 and 5 percent in June 1977 occurred as the major consuming countries recovered from recession and OPEC production returned to 1973 levels.

Just as the 1973–74 price increases were triggered by political instabilities, the Iranian revolution and the subsequent Iran–Iraq War sent prices to over $32 per barrel by late 1980. Civil disorders in the fall of 1978 resulted in a roughly 50 percent decline in Iranian production - from 6.0 MMB/D to 3.0 MMB/D. Subsequently in 1979 and 1980, Iranian production dropped still further as hostilities with Iraq broke out. Even though some other OPEC producers expanded production during this period, a substantial shortage persisted until the price rose to the $32 range. Table 1.2 provides a brief chronological summary of important events.

A closer look at this period emphasizes the considerable differences of opinion on the appropriate price increase among the OPEC members. For example, in the December 1976 increase of 5 percent, Iraq, Qatar, and Venezuela had initially called for a 25 percent increase while Iran proposed a 15 percent increase. Still another example of pricing disputes was evident in the August 1981 OPEC meetings in Geneva. With prices ranging from Saudi Arabia's $32 to prices of $40 per barrel for Libyan, Algerian, and Nigerian crude, the countries were unable to agree on a unified pricing schedule. Ultimately, Libya, Algeria, and Nigeria were forced to cut their prices.

In addition to disagreements as to price, individual OPEC countries' production policies remained under the sovereign control of each member. Table 1.3 indicates the market shares of OPEC producers as each country set its own production levels. Over the 1973–80 period, significant increases in market shares were attained by Saudi Arabia, Iraq, and to a lesser extent Indonesia. Saudi Arabia's market share increased quite sharply, particularly in 1980 due to the military action in Iran and Iraq. Conversely, the tremendous drop in

Table 1.2 *Chronology of Important Events*

| *Year* | *Month* | *Event* |
|---|---|---|
| 1981 | October | Assassination of Anwar Sadat |
| | | Saudi Arabia sets price for Arab Light at $34 |
| 1980 | May | Saudi Arabia sets price for Arab Light at $28 |
| 1979 | December | Arab Light raised to $24 after breakdown of OPEC price unity and series of individual member increases |
| | November | Spot price eclipses $35/bbl |
| | April | Saudi Arabia sets 8.5 MMB/D ceiling |
| | March | Iran gets new revolutionary government and resumes exports at lower levels |
| | January | In wake of the loss of Iranian crude, Saudi Arabia sets temporary production allowable of 9.5 MMB/D |
| 1978 | December | Iranian exports suspended |
| | Sept.-Dec. | Political unrest in Iran |
| | March | OPEC telescopes total 1978 increase of 14.5 percent into first quarter, raising price to $14.56 |
| 1977 | July | OPEC prices reunified at $12.70; with realignment of OPEC prices, Saudi Arabia returns to 8.5 MMB/D ceiling |
| | January | With two-tier prices in effect, Saudi Arabia suspends production ceiling |
| 1976 | | Recovery from recession in the United States |
| 1975 | October | OPEC prices increased by 10 percent |
| | June | Suez Canal reopened |
| | March | Kuwait Oil Company nationalized |
| 1974 | March-June | Several governments acquire 60 percent interest in oil production |
| | March | Embargoes and production cuts ended |
| 1973 | Oct. 1973-Jan. 1974 | OPEC quadruples the posted price |
| | October | With the fourth Arab-Israeli war, Arab governments order production cutbacks and embargo of the USA and the Netherlands |
| | September | Libya nationalizes 51 percent of all oil properties |
| | January | Saudi government requires 25 percent interest on producing properties |
| 1972 | | Several governments require 25 percent interest in oil operations, effective 1973, under General Participation Agreement |
| | June | Iraq nationalizes IPC |
| 1971 | February | Income tax raised to 55 percent from 50 percent and posted price raised 38¢ under Teheran Agreement, signalling new era in which governments take role in setting oil prices |
| 1967 | June | Suez Canal closed by third Arab-Israeli war |
| 1960 | September | OPEC formed |
| 1956 | July | Suez Canal nationalized |

Iranian production beginning in 1979 can be traced to the revolution and subsequent hostilities with Iraq. Other countries exhibiting appreciable declines in market share are Venezuela and Kuwait.

The effects of higher prices, particularly the large jump in 1973–74 and in 1979–80, have resulted in a far different path of oil consumption than forecasters envisioned in the early 1970s. Virtually all groups found it necessary to reduce their demand projections in the late 1970s. Table 1.4 proves convincingly that the demand curve facing OPEC is indeed price responsive. Following the initial price increase in 1973–74, oil consumption in the non-communist world dropped from 45.9 MMB/D to 41.5 MMB/D in 1975. Part of this decrease must be attributed to the worldwide recession. Even as the economies resumed growth in the 1976–80 period, oil consumption reached only 45.6 MMB/D in 1980. Lagged effects of the 1973–74 price increases were no doubt substantially offsetting the demand growth associated with economic development.

Still another important implication of Table 1.4 is that non-OPEC oil supplies have exhibited a modest expansion, rising from 14.1 MMB/D in 1973 to 18.7 MMB/D in 1980. Given that substantial lags exist in the exploration and production process, the huge price increases in 1973–74 and in 1979–80 are likely to result in still further production increases in the years ahead. The early 1980s have been characterized by historic records in drilling activity in the non-OPEC countries. Thus, OPEC has found itself in a world of relatively flat to declining production levels, resulting from conventional forces of supply and demand.

Table 1.3 *Percentage Market Shares of OPEC Members: 1973–80*

| | *1973* | *1974* | *1975* | *1976* | *1977* | *1978* | *1979* | *1980* |
|---|---|---|---|---|---|---|---|---|
| Saudi Arabia | 23.9 | 26.8 | 25.1 | 27.1 | 28.4 | 26.9 | 29.8 | 36.8 |
| Kuwait | 9.5 | 8.1 | 7.4 | 6.8 | 6.1 | 6.9 | 7.8 | 6.2 |
| United Arab Emirates | 4.8 | 5.3 | 5.9 | 6.1 | 6.2 | 5.9 | 5.8 | 6.4 |
| Iran | 18.4 | 19.1 | 19.0 | 18.5 | 17.5 | 17.0 | 9.5 | 6.2 |
| Iraq | 6.4 | 6.2 | 8.0 | 6.8 | 6.1 | 8.3 | 10.8 | 9.3 |
| Libya | 6.9 | 4.8 | 5.2 | 6.1 | 6.4 | 6.4 | 6.5 | 6.6 |
| Nigeria | 6.4 | 7.2 | 6.3 | 6.5 | 6.5 | 6.1 | 7.2 | 7.6 |
| Venezuela | 10.6 | 9.4 | 8.3 | 7.2 | 6.9 | 7.0 | 7.4 | 8.1 |
| Indonesia | 4.2 | 4.4 | 4.6 | 4.7 | 5.2 | 5.0 | 5.0 | 5.9 |
| Other | 8.9 | 8.7 | 10.2 | 10.2 | 10.7 | 10.5 | 10.2 | 6.9 |

## III ELEMENTS OF THE CRUDE OIL PRODUCTION DECISION: IMPLICATIONS FROM ECONOMIC THEORY

Before proceeding to consider alternative models of OPEC behavior, the reader should be aware of the economic theory describing the production and pricing of nonrenewable resources.[11] The fundamental assumption underlying this theory is that resource owners are wealth maximizers attempting to produce the resource in a manner that will maximize the present value of the asset. Our purpose in presenting this theory is not to argue that producers are strict wealth maximizers, but only to show how they would react if they indeed followed such an objective. The problem of understanding OPEC is complicated, because crude oil is a nonrenewable resource. Knowing that price equals marginal cost in a competitive market, one might be tempted to reason that OPEC is a wealth-maximizing monopolist based purely on the observation that the market price grossly exceeds the marginal cost of producing crude oil in the OPEC countries ($.10 to $.25 per barrel

Table 1.4 *World Crude Oil Production (in MMB/D)*

| *Year* | *Total* | *Non-communist world* | *OPEC* | *Non-OPEC* |
|---|---|---|---|---|
| 1973 | 55.8 | 45.9 | 31.8 | 14.1 |
| 1974 | 55.9 | 45.2 | 31.6 | 13.6 |
| 1975 | 53.0 | 41.5 | 28.2 | 13.3 |
| 1976 | 57.4 | 45.1 | 31.7 | 13.4 |
| 1977 | 59.6 | 46.6 | 32.4 | 14.2 |
| 1978 | 60.2 | 46.5 | 30.9 | 15.6 |
| 1979 | 62.4 | 48.4 | 31.9 | 16.5 |
| 1980 | 59.5 | 45.6 | 26.9 | 18.7 |

*Sources: 1979 International Energy Annual* USDOE/E1A-0219 (79). Released September 1980.
*Monthly Energy Review* DOE/E1A-0035 (81/08). Released August 20, 1981.

in most Persian Gulf countries). This fallacy arises from an inadequate understanding of marginal costs. In the standard textbook case of a firm using renewable inputs, the decision to produce today in no way affects the costs of producing in the future. Thus marginal costs ($MC$) consist entirely of the marginal production cost ($MC^p$), that is, the capital, labor, and material costs of producing the last unit of output. In cases involving the use of nonrenewable products, the decision to produce a barrel of oil today precludes the possibility of producing it at some time in the future. In effect, the decision to produce today results in an opportunity cost or a user cost, since production today precludes its production in some future period. Even though there is no tax collector present to collect this charge every time a barrel is produced, resource owners should recognize this component of costs in their decisions. Thus, in the nonrenewable case, marginal costs ($MC$) in period $t$ are modified to include the conventional marginal production costs ($MC^p_t$) and user costs ($U_t$)

$$MC_t = MC_t^p + U_t \tag{1}$$

The method of calculating the user cost is predicated on wealth maximization (i.e. setting marginal revenue, $MR_t$, to marginal costs, $MC_t$). User costs, which show the opportunity cost of forgoing producing today, are obtained by simply subtracting marginal production costs ($MC_t^p$) from marginal revenue ($MR_t$):

$$U_t = MR_t - MC_t^p \tag{2}$$

Since $U_t$ represents the opportunity value of selling the last barrel in period $t$, the producer may elect to switch production to some other period $t'$ where user costs are higher. In fact, if the producer maximizes its long run profit, it should be indifferent between producing the last barrel now or at any future time period.

$$U_0 = U_1 = U_2 = U_3 = \cdots = U_T \tag{3}$$

But equation (3) overlooks the fact that a dollar today is worth far more than a dollar in ten years. Thus wealth-maximizing agents must in reality discount future user costs at the rate of discount ($r$):

$$U_0 = \frac{U_1}{1+r} = \frac{U_2}{(1+r)^2} = \frac{U_3}{(1+r)^3} = \cdots = \frac{U_T}{(1+r)^T} \tag{4}$$

This means that the user costs must rise by the rate of discount if the net present value of the resource is being maximized, that is:

$$\begin{aligned} U_1 &= U_0(1+r) \\ U_2 &= U_1(1+r) \\ &\vdots \end{aligned} \tag{4a}$$

In effect, if the discount rate is 10 percent ($r = .10$) and $U_0 = \$1$, the user cost ($U_t$) must be \$1.10 in period 1, \$1.21 in period 2, \$1.33 in period 3 and so forth, in order for the discounted user costs to be equal over time. If, for example, $U_3 = \$2$, the producer has not chosen an optimal production strategy since the *discounted* value of oil produced in period 3 would be \$1.50 ($U_3/(1.1)^3$) and yet the discounted value for all other periods is \$1. The producer can increase the value of its oil reserves by allocating more production to period 3 and reducing production in the other periods. Thus, the problem facing the wealth-maximizing producer is to schedule production over time such that equation (4) holds for the last barrel produced in any period.

User costs introduce a fascinating aspect because they are conditioned on future supply and demand conditions. Even though nothing may affect demand or productive capability in the present period, if producers revise their expectations of the future, resulting in a new discounted user cost, the price in the current period can rise sharply or decline sharply depending upon the extent of changed perceptions of the future. In fact, a crude oil producer may find in retrospect that mistakes were made and that some other production profile would have generated greater profits. The reason for the mistakes arises because the nature of future conditions is seldom predicted accurately in advance. Invariably, the producer's assumptions about future demand and supply conditions are in error, rendering inaccurate estimates of future user costs. The point is that once the producers recognize that a mistake has been made, they will revise their future outlook, set a new production profile, and compute a new set of user costs which will differ from the old set.

As long as perceptions of the future are not revised, equation (4) yields some straightforward predictions about the rate at which oil prices will rise. Harold Hotelling, in his now famous 1931 article in the *Journal of Political Economy*, first articulated this model. In view of the trivial marginal production cost of most Persian Gulf oil, it is remarkable that Hotelling chose to simplify his analysis to a case where marginal production costs ($MC^p$) are zero. Under competition, price equals marginal costs, which in this case include only the user costs ($U_0$). Substituting prices ($P$) for user costs ($U$) into equation (4) yields:

$$P_0 = \frac{P_1}{1+r} = \frac{P_2}{(1+r)^2} = \frac{P_3}{(1+r)^3} = \cdots = \frac{P_T}{(1+r)^T} \qquad (5)$$

Or equivalently, prices will rise by the rate of discount:

$$\begin{aligned} P_1 &= P_0(1+r) \\ P_2 &= P_1(1+r) \\ &\vdots \end{aligned} \qquad (5a)$$

Thus, under competitive market conditions, the price of oil should be expected to rise at rate $r$, the rate of interest (assuming the social discount rate and the market interest rate are equivalent).

For the monopolist facing zero production costs, Hotelling notes that marginal revenues, which will be less than price, will rise over time at the rate of interest:

$$MR_0 = \frac{MR_1}{1+r} = \frac{MR_2}{(1+r)^2} = \frac{MR_3}{(1+r)^3} = \cdots = \frac{MR_T}{(1+r)^T} \tag{6}$$

This result follows directly from equation (2) where $MC^p = 0$. Obviously with marginal revenues rising, prices will rise, but the rate of increase depends on the nature of the demand curve. In the usual textbook case of the linear demand curve, the initial price will be higher under monopoly and rise at a slower rate than under competition. Figure 1.4 contrasts the competitive price path with the monopolist's price path facing a linear demand schedule. Thus, the monopolist's high initial price promotes more initial conservation, enabling relatively more production and lower prices in the future. This example supports the claim, 'the monopolist is the conservationist's best friend'. While this may be true, we simply note that the monopolist exacts a huge fee for performing this rationing function and that the monopolist's price path distorts intertemporal resource allocation.

Still another intriguing aspect of Hotelling's 1931 paper was that he explicitly considered the case of the monopolist facing a demand curve which had a constant elasticity at every point. Hotelling demonstrates that the monopolist's price path is identical to that of the competitive market! Some scholars have accepted Hotelling's result as if it were a prophecy. To them, the question of whether OPEC is a cartel is moot – the price of oil would be the same under either regime!

To reach this conclusion based on Hotelling's simplistic model would be to commit an egregious error, for two reasons. First, the demand for oil is not a static function with constant elasticity. It is an empirical fact that the long run demand schedule is much more price elastic than its short run counterpart. Since it may take ten to twenty years to achieve long run adjustment, a monopolist can exploit the short run inelasticity of oil demand by charging an initially high price. Thereafter, prices may even decline for a substantial period as consumers react to the price jump. Thus, the nature of the demand for oil suggests that the monopolist's price path is likely to be more like Figure 1.4, with an initially higher price and slower rate of price increase than would occur under competition. A second and more fundamental objection is that Hotelling's model assumes a fixed and homogeneous stock of oil reserves available at zero cost. When one recognizes that the stock of oil reserves is expansible at higher prices as

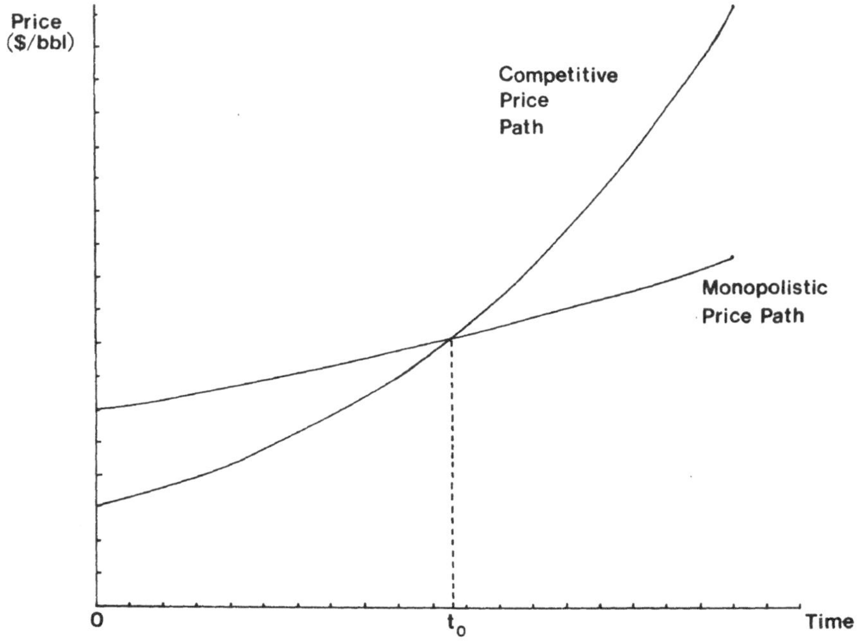


Figure 1.4 *Possible monopolistic versus competitive price paths.*

submarginal reserves become supramarginal, monopoly and competitive solutions will differ dramatically.

Notwithstanding these objections, some may argue that even if the two price paths are not identical, the period of time $t_0$ in Figure 1.4 during which the monopolist's price exceeds the competitive level is relatively short and the period thereafter of lower prices under monopoly is relatively long. Applying this logic to today's situation, one might argue that OPEC's prices may exceed that of a competitive market, but within five years we will reach a time when the price of oil will be actually lower, thanks to OPEC. Obviously, it matters greatly whether $t_0$ is 10 years or 50 years. Unfortunately, our ability to pinpoint $t_0$ is indeed problematic. Furthermore, it matters greatly whether some 'backstop' fuel will be present to place a ceiling on future price increases. If a backstop fuel exists, the high future prices, which would occur under competition, would not materialize. Later we explore in more detail the implications of a backstop fuel.

The important point to be grasped is that user costs play an influential role in oil price determination, irrespective of whether one posits monopoly or competition. Since user costs are based on expectations of present and future supply and demand conditions, it is instructive to look in greater detail at five such factors which influence producers' perceptions of user costs.

### The Size of the Reserve Base

Oil producers must first form expectations about the magnitude of the underlying oil reserve base, in order to attribute a scarcity premium to oil. Existing oil reserves may be a poor indicator, since these are only the reserves found to date and surely future exploration will result in new finds. If the new discoveries matched expectations, producers will not revise their estimates of user costs. Figure 1.5 illustrates a Hotelling-type competitive market with zero production costs. Over the period that producers' expectations of user costs remain unchanged (period 0 to $t_0$), the oil price rises at the rate of interest. Suppose, at time $t_0$, geologists sharply increase their estimate of the reserve base. The scarcity value of oil being thus reduced, user costs will be revised down sharply. Following the revision, as long as expectations are unchanged (period $t_0$ to $t_1$), prices again rise at the rate of interest. Now assume, in period $t_1$, oil producers become convinced the ultimate resource base is much smaller than they had ever thought. Prices will immediately shoot upward and thereafter rise with the rate of interest until expectations are revised again. Figure 1.5

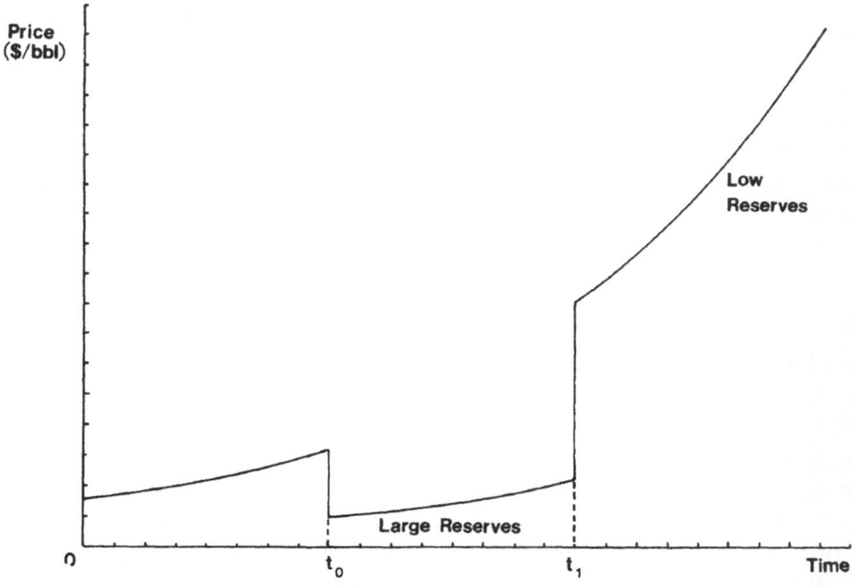


Figure 1.5 *Price paths under alternative resource base assumptions.*

illustrates the interesting point that prices need not follow a smooth price path since changing expectations will cause switching to alternate price paths.

## The Presence of a Backstop Fuel

In view of the vast potential supplies of crude oil from tar sands, oil shales, and coal, economists have been prompted to consider what their impact will be on the price of petroleum. For simplicity, let us assume that the reserves of these oil substitutes become infinitely elastic at some price $P^*$. Obviously, these resources are nonrenewable, but the reserve base is assumed so large that their user costs are effectively zero. Thus at price $P^*$, virtually unlimited supplies will be available. As Figure 1.6 indicates, the price paths of oil are substantially altered over time. No longer does the price continue to rise indefinitely at the rate of interest. The solid line price path depicts a world of perfect foresight. The price increases at rate $r$ until it reaches $P^*$, at which time the backstop fuel would meet all demand at the price $P^*$. Presumably, backstop fuel producers watch the price rise and correctly anticipate that the backstop fuel plants should be ready in year $t_0$ with sufficient capacity to meet demand. Also according to this view, oil producers would want to dispose of all their oil before $t_0$, since after $t_0$ the user cost would not rise. In reality, conventional oil production will continue past $t_0$ as oil fields cannot be exhausted instantaneously. Also, it seems plausible to conjecture that oil prices might even overshoot at $t_0$ if the introduction of the backstop fuel is initially insufficient to meet market demand. The dotted line occurring after $t_0$ shows how prices might overshoot while the backstop fuel industry is adjusting to meet demand (period $t_0$ to $t_1$). After $t_1$, oil prices are constrained to price $P^*$ whether or not there is a price overshoot.

## Rates of Discount

To Hotelling, the choice of the appropriate discount rate was obvious – the market rate of interest. Since inflation was not a problem in 1932, Hotelling was content to state his results in nominal or noninflation adjusted prices. Today, inflation rates are perhaps more uncertain than oil prices, causing practitioners to favor stating oil price forecasts expressed in dollars of constant purchasing power. Thus, the preference is to forecast the real price of oil, that is, the future price of oil is deflated by the general price index to give the real price of oil. Hotelling's framework, nevertheless, remains valid. We simply substitute the real rate of interest for the nominal rate of

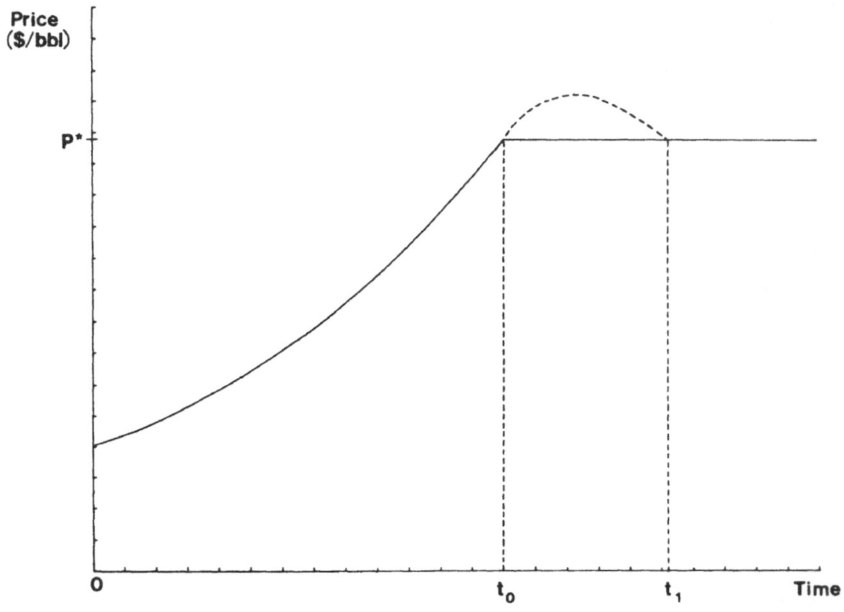


Figure 1.6 *Oil prices with a backstop fuel.*

interest and interpret oil prices in dollars of constant purchasing power.

Having resolved the inflation confusion, one must ask whether the real rate of interest, usually estimated at 2 to 3 percent per annum, is the appropriate real discount rate. If oil reserves were a riskless asset, private investors would utilize the real rate of interest since it reflects the real, long run return on a risk-free bond. Oil producers may argue that geologic and political risks require using a much higher real discount rate. On the other hand, to the degree usury is condemned as morally repugnant, resource owners may deviate from the wealth-maximizing rate and select a lower discount rate.

To illustrate the effects of changes in the real discount rate, Figure 1.7 describes price paths under three alternative discount rates. From period 0 to $t_0$, producers employ a very high discount rate of 25 percent in anticipation of nationalization. Now suppose the risk of nationalization abates and the discount rate is reduced to 5 percent. Finally, in period $t_1$ the state obtains control and adopts a zero discount rate. With a zero discount rate, the user costs are equal over time. In the case of a backstop fuel at $P^*$, the competitive price would jump to $P^*$ and remain forever at that real price level.

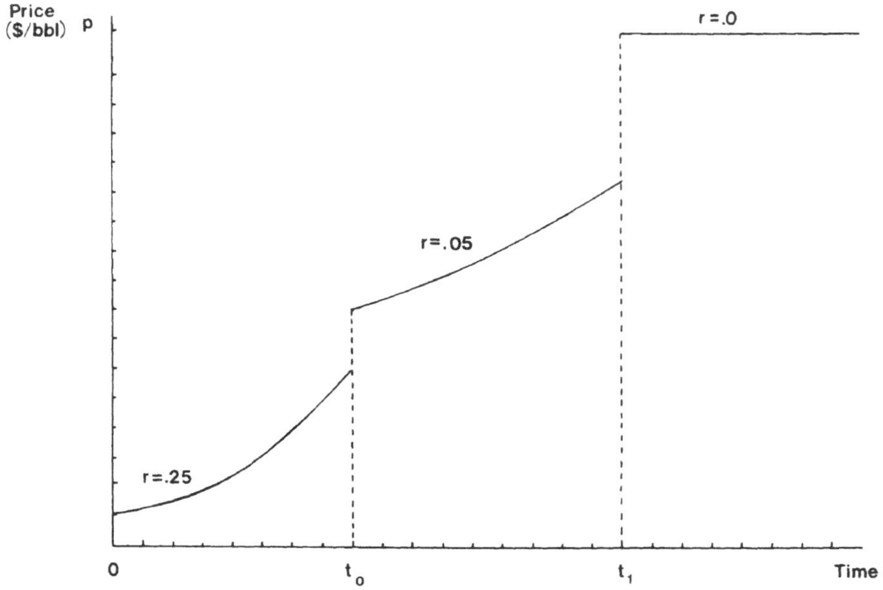


Figure 1.7 *Price paths under alternative discount rates.*

## The Magnitude of the Long Run Price Elasticity of Oil Demand

Since demand conditions affect marginal revenues and thereby the user costs, the price path even in a competitive market depends on the price elasticity of demand. In the short run, the price elasticity for crude oil is generally known to be quite inelastic. The magnitude of the long run elasticity is known with much less certainty since previous history provides little evidence for estimating consumer responses over current price ranges. The problem is exacerbated by the fact that a substantial adjustment period is required to alter the energy efficiency of the existing capital stock. Long lags, combined with unprecedented price levels, imply much uncertainty on the long run price elasticity question. Figure 1.8 contrasts two price paths, a high elasticity and a low elasticity path. In the low elasticity case, the price path begins at price $P_0$ and rises thereafter at the discount rate. Suppose in period $t_0$ producers come to believe long run demand is much more price elastic than believed. Clearly, at projected prices, consumers will not demand the projected production. This revision forces an abrupt downward adjustment in the user cost. Even though after $t_0$ the price rises at the discount rate, the base from which it rises is much lower and the price path always lies below the original price path.

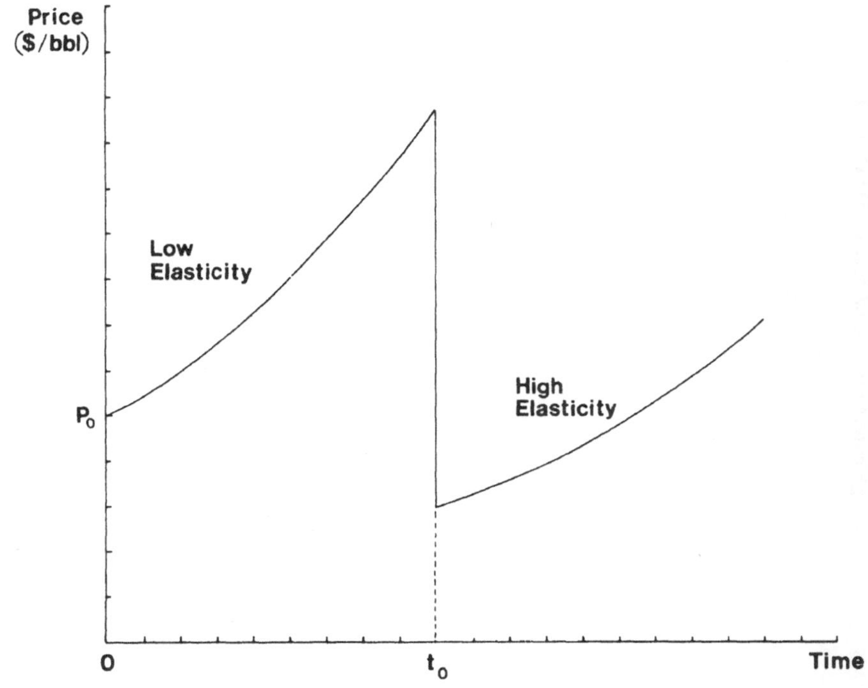


Figure 1.8 *The importance of the price elasticity of demand.*

**The Rate of World Economic Growth**

Still another factor influencing the calculation of user costs is the growth in oil demand resulting from world economic growth. Besides price, the major determinant of oil consumption is the rate of economic activity. Figure 1.9 plots per capita energy consumption with real per capita income for eighteen OECD countries in the year 1973. Note the strong positive correlation between standard of living and energy consumption. The point is that if producers expect rapid long run growth rates, *ceteris paribus*, user costs will be higher. Just as Figure 1.8 illustrated the case of low and high elasticities, it could just as easily represent the effects of assumed economic growth rates. The period 0 to $t_0$ is representative of expectations assuming high economic growth rates while the period $t_0$ into the future would signal a period in which economic growth projections had been scaled down.

**Interactions Among Five Factors: Increased Uncertainty**

From the preceding discussion, it is clear that any one price path

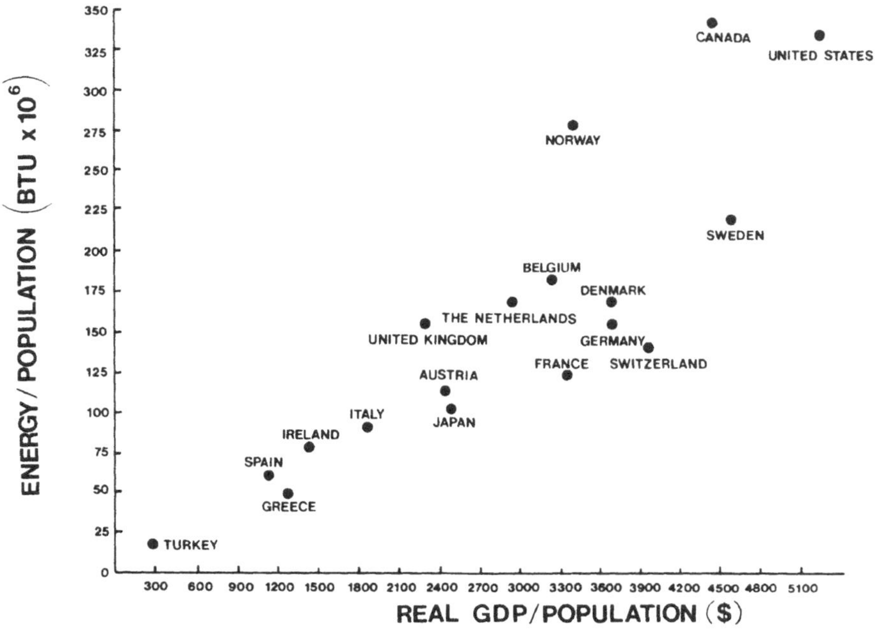


Figure 1.9 *The relationship between per capita energy consumption and GNP.*

*Source:* J. M. Griffin and H. Steele, *Energy Economics and Policy* (New York: Academic Press, 1980), p. 215.

requires explicit expectations regarding the resource base, backstop fuel prices, discount rates, price elasticities of demand, and economic growth. The usual presumption is that changes in expectations regarding any one of these five factors occur independently; therefore, the effect on the price path from changing expectations would be presumed small. In fact, changes in any one of the five factors can cause substantial shifts in the price path. Moreover, changes in expectations regarding one of these factors are seldom made independently. For example, downward revisions of oil reserves are frequently associated with a period of rapid economic growth, which places pressure on existing reserves and productive capacity. These effects may also be coupled with falling real interest rates. In effect, to the extent that revisions in one factor are correlated with reinforcing revisions in other expectations, price uncertainty is exacerbated. Natural forces suggest the price of oil is likely to be highly unstable, with the effects of switching to alternative price paths possibly dominating the more systematic movements along a given price path.

### A Brief Recapitulation

Even though 'user costs' do not show up in a resource owner's accounting statement of a firm, wealth-maximizing resource owners must implicity recognize the scarcity premium emanating from the nonrenewable nature of the resource. User costs, like extraction costs, constitute a component of costs which in turn affect prices and the movement of prices over time. The intriguing aspect about user costs is that they are not directly observable, unlike a firm's labor or capital costs. Rather they depend on the producer's expectations about present and future supply/demand conditions. These supply/demand conditions are enumerated in the previous discussion of expectations regarding the size of the reserve base, the availability of a backstop fuel, the rate of discount, price elasticities of demand, and world economic growth. For each set of expectations regarding the above factors, there is a unique user cost and an associated price path over time. Changes in expectations regarding any of these factors can produce substantial changes in the market's valuation of these user costs and, in turn, substantial shifts in the price path.

## IV MODELS OF OPEC BEHAVIOR

### Introduction

The analysis in Section III focused on the extraction decision of a single producer under monopoly conditions or of many producers under conditions of competition.[12] However, the monopoly problem is considerably more complex if the extraction of monopoly rents requires cooperative behavior among a number of producers. Coordination mechanisms are needed to control production and/or pricing decisions. Cartels provide the organizational structure within which the necessary restrictive agreements are executed and enforced.

The organizational architecture of a fully profit-maximizing cartel can be described as follows: the cartel will maximize profits by making each producer a member, and then allocating production among producers so that the marginal production costs are equalized among producers.[13] The cartel will then produce that output at which the common level of marginal cost for each producer equalizes the marginal revenue derived from aggregate industry demand. Since this solution may involve shutting in production in various periods for some producers, it will usually be necessary to arrange payments from one member of the cartel to another. This may have to be accomplished through a centralized headquarters function within the cartel. The headquarters unit will obviously need powers of audit and enforcement if the cartel is to be completely successful. Generally side-payments are difficult to negotiate, and cause tremendous problems for cartels, even when the cartels are legal and government supported.

As a practical matter, cartels do not develop as fully as they might because of the transactional difficulties involved in writing, executing, and enforcing the set of contracts among members that would be needed to achieve complete monopolization. More often, cartels simply involve price fixing and/or division of the market. But even these activities require some degree of coordinated behavior. For instance, a market sharing arrangement requires a quota system of some kind. This may be specified in terms of criteria such as percentage market share, units of output, customer identity, or some combination of these.

When user costs are large, and where discount rates differ among producers for political and cultural reasons, a perplexing problem arises in attempting to identify whether an exhaustible resource market is competitive or monopolistic. The problem arises because it is not clear whether there exists an objective standard for determining the competitive price. As explained in Section III, above, the nature of competition cannot be assessed simply by examining the relationship between price and marginal production costs, because of the user cost phenomenon. One possibility is to compare the market price to the level that would be optimal were producers competitive-type, wealth maximizers using reasonable discount rates. As we indicate in the concluding chapter, every contributor to this volume appears to agree that by this standard there are large economic rents in the crude oil market today. However, if it is the case that resource owners eschew wealth maximization, then we are left without a clear-cut criterion for differentiating competitive from monopolistic regimes. For example, if for some internal political reason, current production is held below the wealth-maximizing level, then prices will exceed the competitive levels. Given that this outcome need not depend on collusion or monopolistic intent, it is purely a matter of semantics whether this is labeled as monopoly or competition. Since the outcome involved no collusion, some may argue that the price is competitive even though it exceeds the true Hotelling-type competitive price. Others may argue that the outcome is monopolistic since the price exceeded the Hotelling-type competitive price. As we indicate below, some of the confusion over how best to characterize OPEC stems from this problem.

However, there is a difference between the two outcomes which is likely to matter for the purpose of assessing future OPEC behavior. If the monopoly rents, which have been captured in the past, depended on OPEC achieving coordinated behavior, then prolonged soft markets in the future would seem less likely to result in significant weakening of the price since OPEC has already demonstrated (in 1975) that its members can band together when the market is soft. If this were not so, then a prolonged period of soft markets could be expected to generate pressure for additional production, and, in the absence of cartel mechanisms to block output expansion, the price might very well tumble. For these reasons, assessing the appropriate descriptive model by which to characterize OPEC is not an idle task.

In the remaining sections of this chapter, various monopolistic and competitive models of the world oil market are surveyed. As shown in Table 1.5, these models can be first categorized along two dimensions: models which assume oil producers follow wealth maximization and those which posit nonwealth-maximizing behavior. In turn, there are theories predicated on wealth maximization which posit either monopolistic or competitive behavior. Among nonwealth maximization theories, there are economic models based on a country's target revenues and noneconomic models predicated on political factors.

Table 1.5 *Models of OPEC Behavior*

| | |
|---|---|
| Wealth-Maximizing Models | Monopoly: Dominant Producer Model |
| | Competition: Property Rights Model |
| Nonwealth-Maximizing Models | Target Revenue Model |
| | Political Models |

**Wealth Maximization: The Dominant Producer Model – A Monopolistic Interpretation**

One interpretation of OPEC is that the dominant producer, Saudi Arabia, sets the price, allows the other OPEC producers to sell all they wish, and supplies the remaining demand. Saudi Arabia is thus the 'balance wheel' or 'swing producer', absorbing demand and supply fluctuations in order to maintain the monopoly price. Such an arrangement creates no cartel problems. However, it does run the risk of inducing sufficient new production, outside of Saudi Arabia, to make the strategy nonviable for the Saudis. The stability of OPEC turns, therefore, on whether world supply and demand at the monopoly price results in sufficient demand for Saudi oil to satisfy Saudi objectives. Put another way, the world price does not necessarily depend upon the strengths and weaknesses of cartel cohesion.

In the simplest version of this model, the dominant producer chooses the best price from its own viewpoint, taking into account both present and future demand and supply of the competitive fringe at whatever price the dominant producer may choose. The problem facing Saudi Arabia is to choose a price path which maximizes its wealth over time. If the price set by the dominant producer is high enough to let fringe producers earn monopoly rents they will have an incentive to expand their capacity. Also, new entrants will be attracted into the fringe. This causes a reduction in the residual demand confronting the dominant producer. If Saudi Arabia adopts a high discount rate, implicitly setting a low value on future profits, the dominant producer selects a high initial price and makes room for an expanded competitive fringe, earning much higher profits initially than later on. Its high prices and profits in the current period set into motion a chain of repercussions reducing the dominant producer's market share in the future years.

In many instances there is only one way for the dominant producer to avoid this outcome: it must adopt a lower discount rate, reducing its current price to a level at which new entry and the expansion of fringe members are discouraged. An overly simple but useful first approximation is to view the dominant producer's decision problems as dichotomous. Either it sets high prices and accepts declining future market shares and profits, or it sets low current prices to deter all entry and expansion by fringe competitors. The latter strategy is commonly referred to as limit pricing, in that a price is selected which limits entry to zero.[14] In reality, depending on the rate of discount, intermediate outcomes between these two extremes may well be chosen.

The case of limiting entry is particularly germane with reference to synthetic oil production from shales, tar sands, and coal liquefaction. Since these fuel sources can be likened to a backstop fuel, available in more-or-less infinitely elastic supply, a wealth-maximizing dominant producer with huge reserves would probably choose a price path below the price at which large quantities of synthetic fuels would be produced.

A principal objection of this model is that if it were applicable solely to Saudi Arabia, Saudi production would be a smaller fraction of total OPEC production today than it was in 1973. The Saudi Arabian share of OPEC's production, however, increased in the post-1973 period reaching 36.8 percent in 1980. The general stickiness of Saudi Arabia's share as well as the shares of other OPEC members appears to be evidence against the short run validity of the dominant producer view of the market. The fringe members of OPEC would have every incentive to adjust their market shares so that their marginal costs including user costs are equal to price. Market share variability ought to result, with the Saudi's market share falling during periods of declining OPEC demand and rising during periods of growing demand. This would not be the pattern for other producers who, as price takers, have every incentive not only to produce at sustainable capacity levels, but also to develop new reserves. Evidence is difficult to obtain on these variables, but several sources indicate that excess or shut-in capacity has been found to be widespread throughout OPEC including, at various times, Saudi Arabia, Kuwait, the UAE, Iran, Qatar, Iraq, Libya, and Nigeria. In contrast, outside of OPEC, producers have had, since 1973, little excess capacity and exploration and drilling activity has increased substantially. Thus the non-OPEC behavior is consistent with the behavior of the competitive fringe, but the behavior of OPEC countries other than Saudi Arabia seems inconsistent with competitive fringe behavior.[15]

To introduce collusive elements into the model, a number of variants of the dominant producer model have emerged with a group of OPEC producers acting essentially as the single dominant producer. One popular view is that there is a 'cartel core', variously defined (e.g. Saudi Arabia, the UAE, Kuwait, Qatar, and Libya) which behaves like a dominant firm. Analytically this model is basically the same as what we have just described. The only significant difference is that the 'cartel core' version depends for success on cooperative behavior within the core; the dominant producer version, on the other hand, does not depend on collusion, either explicit or implicit, for the generation of rents. This difference is important for assessing the stability of the cartel arrangement.

Models of this genre represent accepted dogma among most economists. Professor Adelman, an influential disciple of this traditional view, sets forth in Chapter 2 the factual argument in support of this genre of models. Chapters 3 and 4 offer critiques of this model from the perspective of Professor Teece, an economist, and Professor Moran, a political scientist and specialist on the Middle East.

### Wealth Maximization: The Property Rights Model – A Competitive Interpretation

Another view of OPEC sometimes advanced to explain the quadrupling of prices in 1973–74 is what can be labeled as the property rights interpretation. According to the view advanced by Johany (1978) and Mead (1979), the price regimes prevailing before and after 1973–74 are best explained by appealing to the change in ownership patterns which transpired in the early 1970s. Until that time, the concessions granted by the producing countries to the oil companies permitted the companies, in essence, to make unilateral production decisions. Accordingly, since production policies were essentially the prerogative of the companies, discount rate assumptions were made on the basis of the companies perceptions of the future. Since expropriation risk was nontrivial in many countries in the 1960s, the wealth maximizing strategy for the companies involved a high discount rate and rapid depletion. This was fueled by forever escalating royalty and tax demands by producer countries which further served to reinforce expectations that profits would decline in the future. The result, according to Johany, was that the companies 'produced as if there were no tomorrow', depressing world crude oil prices in the process.[16]

According to this view, the events of 1973–74 marked a watershed in the world oil market, principally because of the transfer of control over production policies which occurred at that time. As Johany explains it,[17]

> the oil producers decided to determine the price of their oil unilaterally rather than through negotiations with the oil companies as had been done in the past. Once the host countries became the ones who decide the rate of oil output and its price, the role of the companies had been essentially reduced to that of contractors. That amounted to a *de facto* nationalization of the crude oil deposits.

This reassignment of property rights was significant because 'the companies and the host countries have different discount rates and that implies different rates of output'.[18] These differences can be traced to intrinsic differences in the discount rate as well as to differences in risk evaluation. With lower discount rates, current production will fall, thereby driving up the world price. For example, Figure 1.7 shows the effect of switching from a world with a 25 percent discount rate to one with a 5 percent discount rate. At the time of the transition, production will drop sharply causing a switch to the higher price path. According to this line of reasoning, 1973–74 represented such a transition period and switching to a higher price path.

The property rights interpretation of the transformation of the world oil market is consistent with the observation that the world price during the 1970s was not threatened by cheating – such as the granting of secret price concessions by some members of OPEC in order to capture market shares from the others. Furthermore, there is plenty of evidence that the companies considered the expropriation risk in the 1960s to be real. In fact, significant episodes took place in Algeria, Iraq, Egypt, Iran, Libya, and Peru. These episodes illustrated the latent power of governments over the companies and the reality of the political risks inherent in the industry. The nationalization of foreign oil companies was an appealing way for governments to develop government owned enterprises and to win popular support. Implicit threats of expropriation stood behind many less extreme forms of regulation.

It is instructive to set forth the major inadequacies of this theory, some of which are elaborated in Chapters 2 and 3. The most obvious inadequacy is that most oil producing countries in the 1950s and 1960s were demanding that the companies expand production. The Shah of Iran pushed especially hard on the companies to expand production. This is completely at odds with the property rights model. However, Iran might be considered an exception, as the Shah's lust for current revenues was legend. Unfortunately, one is never likely to be entirely sure as to the relations between the companies and the countries, as 'behind the doors' manipulation is likely to have been of some importance. Still another objection is that while this theory could presumably explain a portion of the 1973–74 price increase, it offers no obvious interpretation to the doubling of prices in 1978–79. The transfer of ownership had long since occurred, so that further reductions in the discount rate are not apparent. Similarly, the rationale for changed expectations in other factors, which could allow competitive prices to double, is not apparent. It is not obvious that producers altered their long run expectations in 1978–79 regarding future reserves, future demand growth, the price of the backstop fuel, and so forth. Rather, following the rationale of a competitive model, one would expect that following the 1978–79 price rise due to short run supply constraints, the price would return to the initial price path, with an easing of these constraints. Additional elaboration on the property rights model is given in Professor Adelman's Chapter 2 and Professor Teece's Chapter 3.

### Non-wealth Maximization: The Target Revenue Model

In its pure form, the target revenue model elaborated in Chapter 3 depicts OPEC, or at least its principal members, as a collection of nation states whose oil production decisions are made with reference to the requirements of the national budget. Budgetary needs are in turn a function of absorptive capacity, which is limited where the economy is small in relation to oil revenues, or where the infra-

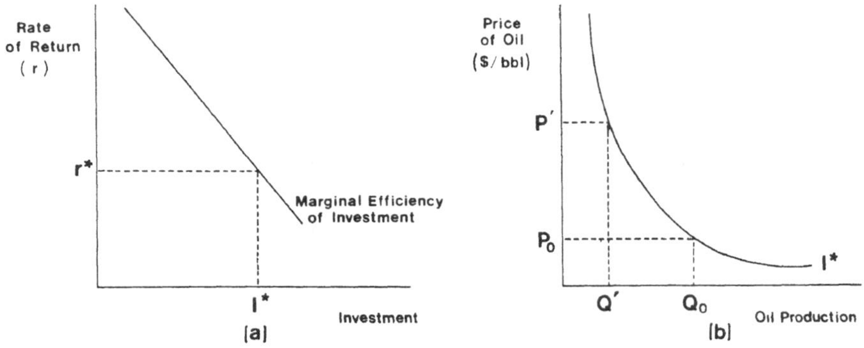


Figure 1.10 *Target revenue model. (a) Investment determination. (b) Oil output determination.*

structure is inadequate to support rapid escalation in consumption and investment levels.

More formally, oil revenues can be considered as the source of funding for potential investment projects, which can be arrayed along a representative marginal efficiency of investment schedule (see Figure 1.10a). If a country is unwilling to invest for returns less than $r^*$, then investment needs are limited by $I^*$. In Figure 1.10b, if oil production decisions are made in order to meet the investment objective represented by $I^*$, then increases in the world price (from $P_0$ to $P'$) in the current period will tend to result in reduced production ($Q_0$ to $Q'$) in the current period, and conversely. The supply schedule thereby generated will have the 'wrong' slope; that is, it will be backward bending, at least over the relevant range.

An intertemporal dimension can be readily added: Economic development can be viewed as expanding investment opportunities and thereby raising the revenue target. Consequently, any specific backward bending supply curve is dependent on a given level of infrastructure. Given adjustment time, the target revenue can rise substantially, so the target revenue model might be thought of as a more adequate description of OPEC behavior in the short run than in the long run. However, it can be argued that the target revenue model has long run predictive implications for countries with more limited potential for expanding domestic investments. Earnings from current investment activity may generate sufficient returns to partially finance future investment plans, enabling a lower dependency on oil revenues for domestic investment programs.

A challenge can be mounted to the target revenue approach on grounds that it is unrealistic to assume that foreign investment is not a viable alternative to domestic investment, for this is the assumption implicit in the analysis. One reply is that for various periods of history, OPEC producers have perceived foreign investment to be unattractive, not only on account of the perceived low returns (generally when the dollar was depreciating in relation to other key currencies and producers held dollar denominated assets), but also because of political risks. These risks are of several kinds. One is the risk that the nation in which the funds were deposited might confiscate, freeze, or otherwise manipulate financial assets for political reasons. The other is that the existence of huge external liquid assets may facilitate the survival of revolutionary regimes, which if successful in displacing existing governments, would have command over liquid assets which could be used to placate friends and buy off enemies. While admittedly such risks exist, it seems highly implausible that wealth maximizing agents, in selecting a portfolio of assets, would limit those portfolios to oil in the ground and domestic investments. As the Iranian experience proves, the latter are not devoid of their risks. A portfolio including foreign debt and equity securities would presumably both increase the expected return and reduce the overall risk of the portfolio. In view of these considerations, our interpretation of the target revenue model is that it eschews wealth-maximizing behavior.

An important implication for OPEC, as explained by Professor Teece in Chapter 3, is that prices can rise above the Hotelling competitive price path even in the absence of coordinated action by OPEC members. If an event, such as the embargo, brings current oil revenues into the target revenue range, there is no desire for individual producers to cheat by expanding production.[19] Conversely, if demand reduction or rapid expansion in absorptive capacity creates a situation in which revenue needs are not met, then the producer in question will expand production until revenue objectives are satisfied. With these characteristics of instability, the model allows for behavior by a number of producers which could lead to a collapse of the cartel price. In Chapter 3, Professor Teece elaborates on this model and sets forth the arguments in support of it. The reader also should be aware that in Chapter 2, Professor Adelman rejects this model on several grounds.

### Non-wealth-Maximizing: Political Models

Students of the sovereign nation state posit that while economic wealth is important, it is not the sole factor guiding decisions. Twentieth century history is replete with examples of the important security and political ramifications of oil. Thus it seems likely that nation states are simultaneously concerned with extending their political influence, assuring their own security, as well as maximizing the wealth from their oil reserves. The critical question is the degree to which these goals are mutually compatible or in conflict.

If these goals are mutually compatible, or complementary, there is really little need for political models of OPEC behavior. Even though 'wealth maximization' is merely serving as a surrogate for security and power goals, the predictions of the model should be accurate. Moreover, since wealth-maximizing behavior does involve an empirically measurable phenomenon and economic theory has isolated the factors influencing the choice, the model gives neat, explicit interpretations of the present and predictions of the future. In contrast, once political scientists begin to talk of security or political influence, the model necessarily becomes qualitative instead of quantitative. The predictions necessarily become more ambiguous. Thus, in this case, explicit political models may provide more intuitively pleasing assumptions, but a much weaker predictive model.

The more interesting case is one in which wealth maximization, security, and political influence, etc., are substitutes to one degree or another. Thus the decision to choose, for example, more security necessarily implies less wealth and/or influence. In this case, political models and wealth maximization models offer divergent interpretations and predictions. The obvious question is 'how diverse'. Clearly, if the goals are not close substitutes, then the divergence may not be great. In 1978, this seems to be the position from which Professor Pindyck reasoned:[20]

> OPEC's pricing behavior is surprisingly predictable, since the cartel is most likely to take only those actions that are in its best economic interest. Considerations other than economic ones may, of course, influence pricing decisions, but economic interests have dominated in the past and are likely to dominate in the future, and they provide the best basis for predicting oil prices. One must therefore put himself in OPEC's position and ask what is the best price to charge for oil.

Thus one might think of the wealth-maximizing price path of the dominant producer as being subject to minor revisions of $\pm 10$ percent due to political factors.

In the political model set forth by Professor Moran, this is clearly not the interpretation he would prefer. In Chapter 4, for instance, Moran asserts that political and security concerns 'wag the economic tail and where they have conflicted, the former have prevailed'. Professor Moran takes the view that Saudi Arabia's wealth-maximizing price path is in practice an empirically elusive concept and, therefore, of dubious predictive value. With respect to Saudi

Arabia, it is his view that the evolution of world oil markets merely defines the limits within which the Saudis can exercise their considerable discretion on pricing matters. This discretion is exercised to advance political priorities while minimizing hostile internal and external pressures.

Thus while the former view treats political factors as exercising dominance within very narrow limits defined by economic realities, the political model set forth by Professor Moran says that economic factors may place some limits on the bounds within which political factors dominate, and the bounds are sufficiently large and unknown as to render purely economic, wealth-maximizing models of little value.

## NOTES

1 See Adelman (1972).
2 For a review, see Stocking and Watkins (1946).
3 See article by Friedman (1980).
4 See review article by Fischer, Gately, and Kyle (1975).
5 For example, see *World Energy Outlook* (Exxon Background Series: December 1980).
6 See Sweeney (1981).
7 See Allison (1971).
8 As noted in the preface, this book is the outgrowth of a May 1981 conference in Houston sponsored by the Center for Public Policy at the University of Houston.
9 Any scarcity premiums owing to the finite nature of the resource base were perceived as trivial in 1960. The concept of scarcity premium or 'user' cost is discussed in Section III of this chapter.
10 For example, for 1961 it has been calculated that the following percentage revenues accrued on sales of finished petroleum products in Europe: 6 percent to producing governments, 52 percent to consuming governments, and 42 percent to oil companies. Note that the 42 percent received by the oil companies covered production, refining, and marketing costs as well as profits.
11 For a systemative treatment, see Dasgupta and Heal (1979).
12 The monopolist's problem, in simplest form, would be to choose an optimum quantity of (homogeneous) oil to sell in each unit of time $t$ in order to

$$\max_{q} \pi = \sum_{t=0} \left[q_t p_t(q_t) - c_t(q_t)\right] \frac{1}{(1+r_{\mathrm{m}})^t},$$

where the maximization is subject to feasibility conditions which we shall not enumerate. Discounted profits, $\pi$, are to be maximized, dependent on the demand function, $p_t(q_t)$, with $(dp/dq) < 0$ and the cost function $c_t(q_t)$ with $(dc/dq) > 0$. $r_{\mathrm{m}}$ is the monopolist's discount rate.
13 This assumes that the cartel members have homogenous discount rates and beliefs about the future so that user costs are everywhere the same.
14 For a good discussion, see Modigliani (1958).
15 However, the dominant producer models outlined above do not capture important aspects of the intertemporal monopoly problem when an exhaustible resource is

involved. Behavior is likely to be different if the monopolist in question is an extractor rather than a producer, because of user cost considerations. Gilbert (1978) has advanced a dynamic limit-pricing model of this genre, which takes strategic interactions among exhaustible resource producers into account. The cartel is represented as the price maker while all other producers are price takers. However, unlike the classical dynamic limit-pricing models outlined above, where the residual demand of the dominant producer depends only on its current rate of output, the response of the competitive fringe in Gilbert's model is a function of the entire sequence of output determined by the dominant extractor. The model is of the von Stackelberg variety, in which the dominant producer (extractor) takes the reaction of other firms into account in its pricing policy, while all other producers (extractors), collectively termed the competitive fringe, take prices as given. Gilbert suggests that this is the most natural description of the world petroleum market since OPEC claims over 70 percent of Free World reserves.

Under realistic demand assumptions, it is possible to show that the existence of a competitive fringe in a market dominated by a cartel leads to allocations that differ dramatically from those that characterize a pure monopoly on the supply side of an exhaustible resource. The model shows that the response of the competitive fringe to a cartel production plan depends on production costs in the fringe. Two different functional forms for costs are examined. In the first case, marginal production costs are independent of the rate of output, while in the second case marginal costs are constant up to a capacity constraint. For the demand function specified in the model, the optimal cartel strategy in the first case is independent of the cartel's production costs and rate of time preference. Until the reserves in the competitive fringe are exhausted, the profit-maximizing strategy of the cartel is governed by parameters specific to the competitive fringe, that is, the competitive firms' production costs, total stocks, and rate of time discount. After the fringe is exhausted, the cartel maximizes profits by pricing marginally below the cost of a substitute source of supply (e.g. synthetic crude).

The optimal policy of the cartel replicates the strategy of a conventional limit-pricing monopolist if the production capacity of the fringe is sufficiently small relative to remaining reserves. In this event the response of the fringe is determined by its level of capacity and, at least in the near term, the cartel may ignore the effect of its future actions on the current price and simply maximize the rate of profits given the capacity-constrained response of the fringe. The optimal price will eventually rise to the substitute price.

16 Johany (1978).

17 Johany (1978), p. 107.

18 Johany (1978), p. 107.

19 This is despite the fact that there is an incentive to do so if net wealth maximization is the goal.

20 Pindyck (1978), p. 37.

# 2 OPEC as a Cartel

M. A. ADELMAN

## I INTRODUCTION

The organization OPEC is no more than a convenient forum for the constituent nations. They have formed a loosely cooperating oligopoly – or cartel, if you prefer two syllables to twelve. But no two cartels are the same. They are all historical individuals, who change over time, and the OPEC cartel has changed greatly.

I wrote in 1973, before the embargo:[1]

> The monopoly ceiling is set by the competition of more expensive sources of crude oil, or by consumers' reducing their expenditures on oil products. This ceiling is very far above even the current price, and hence we must expect the cartel to keep raising the price throughout the 1970's. But for the longer run, the crystal ball becomes clouded, because there are factors working both to strengthen and to weaken the cartel. The net effect is a residual, which is basically unstable. Small changes can produce large effects. But at least we can try to set out what forces are worth watching carefully.

The 1970s are past. The ceiling on energy prices, we can now see, is set by opportunities to invest in greater thermal efficiency more than by new sources of crude oil. The question is whether the cartel is approaching the ceiling, whether they can keep raising the price. I will try to set out how the cartel arrived at its present position, as a place from which we can attempt to look into the future.

I cannot claim (as many do) to know what motivates the OPEC members, but we can recognize what is to their economic advantage. The reader must judge for himself whether noneconomic motives are superfluous in explaining their actions.

## II A REVIEW OF ALTERNATIVE THEORIES OF OPEC BEHAVIOR. OPEC AS A WEALTH-MAXIMIZING GROUP

Management, in conventional economics, tries to maximize the present value of an enterprise. Present value consists of all estimated future revenues and costs, discounted down to the present. Estimating and discounting are two kinds of forecasting procedures, which the human race carries out imperfectly. Inside any given firm, even under pure competition, there will be different visions of what is possible or inevitable. One man's prudence is another man's folly.

Uncertainties and clashes of opinion within the individual firm are magnified in a collusive group. Not only are there more possible viewpoints, but also real clashes of interest. Firms have different costs; hence the best price for one is not necessarily the best for another. In mineral production, this is particularly noticeable, because differences in reserve positions represent differences in cost.

So operating a cartel is often a complicated business of reconciling various objectives, patching up compromises, following rules of thumb, and revising bargains once made. Some years ago,[2] I suggested that the best approximation to a model of the OPEC cartel was somewhere between two polar cases. One case was the residual-firm monopolist, or the large seller who lets everybody else maximize profits individually, choosing their own production levels. The large seller then makes up the difference, varying his production to control the price. This is what Texas and Louisiana state prorationing systems did in the United States during 1935–70. The larger the market share of the residual seller, the easier for him to carry the load. At the other extreme, one could think of all the nations getting together to agree to some kind of price and output combination which suited nobody perfectly, but was accepted as the best compromise.

The two models are the horns of the sellers' dilemma. The residual-firm monopoly is easy to operate. One firm tailors its output to set the price, which the rest take as given. But the price, and the aggregate profit to the group, is less than what could be achieved by all sellers cooperating.

The firms or sellers may wobble from one model to the other in trying to escape as many of the rigors of competition as possible. The number of expedients is almost infinite. It is dismaying and amusing to see people brandish a particular cartel model, and proclaim that because this particular model does not describe reality, there is no cartel, and everything is done by the individual actions of the sellers. Of course each seller acts individually in his own individual interest. But his own individual interest is served by as close an approximation to a monopoly as he and his fellow members can manage.

## Low Discount Theories

One version of the noncollusive thesis of the OPEC nations can be stated succinctly. The producing governments have much lower discount rates than oil companies, particularly oil companies that knew in the 1960s that in the Middle East and elsewhere there was always a good chance of expropriation. The lower the operator's discount rate, the lower his preferred production rate, since he will be willing to leave oil in the ground longer. Hence, when governments gained control of their own resources in the 1970s, they produced less, raising the price.

We first test this against the historical record. During the 1950s and 1960s, governments grew ever more powerful relative to the companies. This can be measured very nicely by the proportion of profits which they took in taxes, which went from 50 percent in 1950 to over 80 percent in 1970. Hence, over this period there should have been a gradual tightening up of production and an increase in prices. In fact, real oil prices fell.

Let us try another test. In 1950–70, there was constant disagreement over production levels. *Countries always wanted more production than companies*. The quarrel was annually publicized in Iran, but the whole period was summed up very well by Mr Howard Page of Exxon.[3]

> The Iranian government was, as every other government, always trying to get more than their agreement called for. If I were in their position, I would do the same, but you have to realize this is like a balloon, push it in one place, it comes out in another. So if we acceded to all these demands we would get it in the neck.

The companies knew what the market would take, and knew they could not produce and sell more without driving prices sharply down. They might 'get it in the neck' too, by refusing demands. Iraq was a leader; for example, in June 1972 it kicked out the Iraq Petroleum Company for not producing at high enough rates. Since then, Iraq has increased capacity, from 1.7 MMB/D to about 4 MMB/D.

During 1970–71, the control swung completely to the side of the producing countries. So here at last one might have seen a growing scarcity in the market and rising prices. In fact, prices rose in 1971–73 only by the amount of higher taxes collusively fixed, and there was a growing surplus. When the Arab countries cut production during the so-called 'embargo' of 1973–74, this was a deliberate collusive act, not the gradual every-country-for-itself tightening of production schedules implicit in the low discount theories.

Thus the noncollusive theory of lower discount rates is in conflict with the historical record through 1973–74. We will see later that it does not perform any better for more recent years. But it is time now to ask whether the major assumption is justified: that lower discount rates will bring about lower production levels.[4] Let me ask a simple question: why does not every owner of a mineral reserve deplete it all in the first year? The reason is obviously that if he pushes the rate of depletion too high, he will be confronted by swiftly rising marginal costs, to the point where faster depletion will lose money. Therefore, every mineral operator from the beginning of time has been forced to solve this problem of the optimum depletion rate by trading off the higher present value of faster depletion against the higher cost. If the depletion rate is below optimal, the incremental money in the bank from additional output is worth more than the incremental mineral in the ground. At rates above optimal, the additional money in the bank is worth less than the additional mineral in the ground, and output should be cut back.

Yet public opinion and policy has been ruled by an empty dogma that 'oil in the ground is worth more than money in the bank'. Such an unqualified statement does not even rise to the dignity of error. It is gibberish.

Suppose now that oil depletion in some lease is optimal. Under competition, the operator cannot affect prices and costs, he takes them as given. He may expect increased prices or anything else,[5] but he has made what he thinks is the best possible adjustment to them. Now introduce one change – a lowering of the discount rate. On the one hand, it encourages a lower rate of production because the present value of a barrel left in the ground is now higher. On the other hand, it raises the present value of the cash flow of any project. The operator must revise his previous tradeoff. But there is absolutely no reason to suppose that the new optimal depletion rate must go up *or* down. Thus, depending on the magnitude of the discount rate, a lower discount rate can bring about higher production, and over other ranges a lower discount rate results in lower production.

In Figure 2.1 the horizontal axis represents the depletion rate, while the vertical axis represents the investment and the present value of gross revenues. Both are given as a percentage of the maximum value, that is, proved reserves times price (net of operating costs). The assumed cost function has a fixed component: the operator must pay 5 percent of the maximum value of the deposit (price × reserves) just to get started. The other restriction is that if he were to deplete the deposit at a rate of 50 percent per year, he would need to invest that same ultimate value.[6] So the limits of the possible outcome lie between zero and 50 percent annual depletion. The tradeoff between getting more present value by accelerating output, and paying more for that present value, can be 'eyeballed' by recalling that for maximum present value the slope of the investment line must equal the slope of the present value curve. (See Appendix I.) At a 1 percent discount

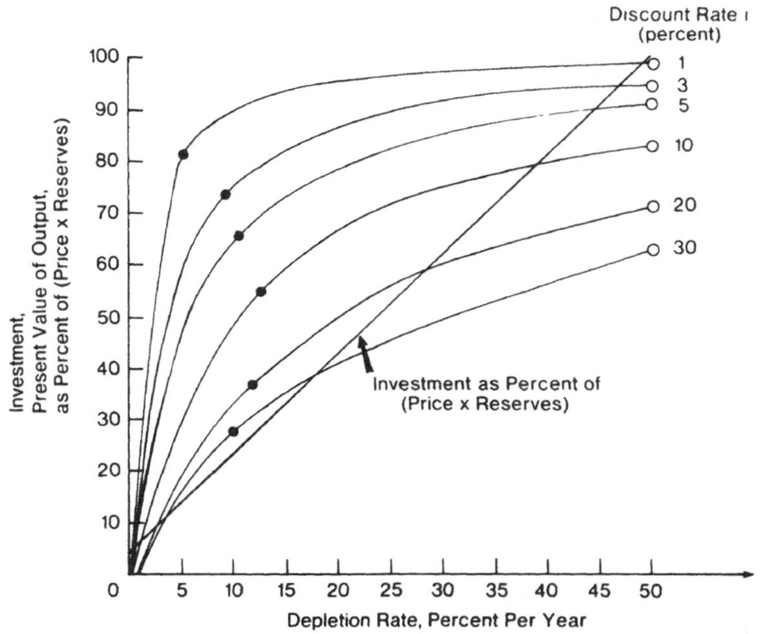


Figure 2.1 *Relation of discount rate, investment, and optimal depletion. Solid circles: optimal for given discount rate.*

rate, the optimum depletion rate is slightly over 6 percent per year. As one gets into the world of commercial reality, discounting at 5 percent, the optimal depletion goes to 12.4 percent. It varies little thereafter, but drops slightly on reaching 20 percent discount. And above 31 percent discount, there is a shutdown.

The discount rate applicable to any expected return from an investment depends on the risk, which is an objective fact. It has nothing to do with any individual's subjective time preference or risk preference. An individual will prefer one risk-return package to another, but this has nothing to do with the risk, the return, or the market value of the package. An individual who prizes safety of capital before all else buys short-term Treasury Bills. In theory and practice they track the inflation rate to yield approximately a zero real return. A more venturesome person will choose a diversified portfolio of seasoned common stocks and accept the risk in order to realize a real return, a little over 6 percent.[7] An oil property, large or small, is undiversified and (except under circumstances too special to detain us) inherently more risky than the common-stock portfolio. Hence our remark that discount rates below the neighborhood of 6 percent, real, are not relevant.

Although our example shows depletion rates rising with discount rates, it is only a special case, the result of our assumptions about the relation of prices to costs. In general, a changed discount rate can work either way. *But as risk becomes greater, and pushes up the discount rate sharply, depletion rates must fall, even to zero*, because fresh investment ceases. If that is happening in many places, then of course prices will rise.

But we need to consider risk, over and above normal commercial risk, to allow for the probability of an irreversible expropriation. A little algebra (Appendix II) will show that the risky rate is somewhat greater than the sum of the normal commercial rate plus that probability. In 1970, when I wrote my book on world oil, I used a 20 percent after-tax rate, which company personnel told me they were using. (A few years later they were using 40 percent in some places.) If a 'normal' commercial discount rate was 9 percent, this was an implicit prediction of a 50–50 chance of expropriation in 7.2 years. But perhaps 9 percent was too high because of the absence of geological risk in many countries. Accordingly, if a normal commercial rate was 6 percent, then in the middle and late 1960s the time to a 50–50 chance of expropriation was about 5.4 years. With hindsight, one concludes neither estimate can be called unreasonable.

Again our best example is in Iraq. Because of unfriendly relations between company and government, and the 1962 expropriation of the whole concession outside the fields actually being operated, Iraq had in effect told the companies that they must reckon with a very high rate of discount. Accordingly, they invested very little in that country, and capacity stagnated. This led, in turn, to expropriation, as already noted.

What would be a reasonable discount rate for a government, above the normal commercial rate in oil? The owners of the oil, whether a party, a junta, a family, a dynasty, etc., must know that they can be overthrown at any time by violence, their usual form of political argument. Suppose you think that your family or party has, say, three chances in four of still being in power in 1991. Then the chance of being overthrown during this year are just under 3 percent, and if 6 percent is a commercial rate, your discount rate should be 9.1 percent. Of course, reasonable persons will disagree on chances of survival, just as they do in private business. But the notion that Third World governments discount oil revenues at abnormally *low* discount rates is in conflict with the facts.[8]

The distinction between the *fact* of risk and the varying *attitudes* to it helps us dispose of another legend: that the Saudis or Kuwaitis or others are naturally reluctant to trade their solid black gold for 'depreciating paper', or depreciating dollars. First, as to denominating the price in dollars, this is a nonissue. They can be paid in any currency they choose, or if paid in dollars it takes a computer a fraction of one microsecond to convert into any other currency.

Saudi Arabia has apparently emphasized security, and bought low-risk low-yield assets. Kuwait has bought real estate and equities. Both of them, and other OPEC nations, have also invested heavily in real assets at home, many ultra-risky. But their preferences are not relevant to the risk and return on any given asset, only on their choice among assets.

With this in mind, we can trade off current against future receipts from oil reserves. Let us suppose that higher prices are expected. (In truth, those higher prices are not determined independently; they are the result of monopoly restriction. But we can overlook that.) The supposed Saudi Arab target is 8.5 MMB/D, and proved-plus-probable reserves total 175 billion barrels. The country is hardly explored, and an allowance of another 75 billion barrels is highly conservative. Hence a production rate of 8.5 MMB/D means that a barrel not now produced would not be produced for eighty years. This is much too simple a calculation, of course, but the errors work on both sides, and can be disregarded.

A discount rate around 9 percent is conservative, for the Saud family is no more immortal than the Pahlavi family. If one discounts at a rate of half of that, which is so 'conservative' as to be reckless, then a dollar to be received in eighty years is worth only 3¢ today. I do not know the price eighty years from now, but will take the highest prediction I have heard, which is $90; that would give us a present value of $2.70.

## III OPEC PRICING: ECONOMIC VERSUS POLITICAL FACTORS

In one respect, a group of governments should conform more closely to a cartel model than a group of private companies. A group of price-fixing companies may be restrained not only by anti-trust laws but by the disapproval of their fellow citizens, and the power of a government to make life unpleasant for them. But nobody dares oppose a sovereign state, and the OPEC nations have become accustomed to the anxiously deferential tone of all the consuming countries. Hence they fit the model well.

But companies exist only to make money; governments do not, but then neither do private owners. Governments and stockholders want money for many purposes, some of which they do not know themselves. But the more money they have the better, whatever they want to buy, whether it be investment, consumption, influence, armaments, or anything else. Getting should not be confused with spending, just as the risks on various assets should not be confused with various attitudes to risk. There is no conflict or tradeoff between more wealth and other purposes.

In 1973, the Arab 'embargo' against the United States and the Netherlands was a political failure, at least for a time, and had to be called off without any of its objectives being accomplished. The impact upon the target United States was less than upon the 'favored' and 'friendly' British and French. But it was a stunning economic success, in raising the basic price from about $2 per barrel in early October to $7 on January 1, 1974.

Some have argued that the Arabs knew this was going to happen, and that they 'really wanted' the extra money and did not care about political goals. That is unwarranted and unnecessary. Their political goals were helped by their enrichment, while their economic goals were in no way lessened by the hope of political gains. King Faisal was like the Spanish conquistador explaining why he came to the New World: 'to serve God, and get rich.' No conflict there.

Let us note just one possible exception to the rule that the more wealth, the better. Where oil revenues are a very large part of a nation's income, a government may slow down - or speed up - oil production because of its effects on the whole economy. This is certainly a possible difference between companies and governments, but it must be investigated, in any given case, to see how important it is in practice.

## Revenue Target Theories

Instead of any such questions, we are ruled by a set of dogmas to the effect that some at least of the OPEC governments set production according to their 'revenue needs'. Any production in excess of what they 'need' to sell is against their interests and done only as a favor to us. The higher the price, the less governments need to produce to satisfy those fixed 'needs'. The less they produce the higher the price will be. We have a backward bending supply curve. I will indicate later a different sense in which backward bending curves really do apply. But with some exceptions, revenue 'needs' explain only short run phenomena.

Saudi Arabia has for years been telling us that for the sake of the world economy they produce more than they want to produce. Thus they are making a 'sacrifice'. They say so without a smile. No wonder: American officials had been telling them this for some time. Back in 1973 their revenue 'needs' were $4 billion. For 1981, their projected expenditures state their 'needs' at $88 billion per year. Allowing for higher prices, the increase in their 'needs' has been by a factor of ten in seven years. So much for 'needs' which – common sense ought to tell us – are what people think they can get.

Twist and turn as we will, there is no way of explaining the Saudi output level by 'needs' or by the desire to conserve oil for future use. But there is a simple and straightforward explanation: if they produced more, they would wreck prices. So instead of installing 20 MMB/D capacity, as they once planned, they hesitate over going to 14 MMB/D. They operate fifteen fields out of a known fifty, and instead of drilling 177 oil wells (1973) they are down to 55 (1979).

## IV OPEC PRICING: AN HISTORICAL INTERPRETATION

From our long investigation of what the cartel is not, let us look at the cartel as it really is, an association of countries with similar but not identical interests. For twenty-one years their horizons have expanded as they started small and succeeded on an ever grander scale. The whole decade 1960–70 was spent just increasing their share of a price that was slowly dropping. By 1968, they felt confident enough to issue a set of resolutions which should have been carefully read. The bottom line: they would not be bound by any contract or agreement. Invoke the magic phrase of 'changing circumstances', and all commitments are dissolved. In 1970 and 1971, they learned to their delight that when they tackled the bigger and more rewarding task of raising the price level itself, there would be no resistance from the consuming country governments. The five-year agreement of January–February, 1971, of which our State Department was so proud, lasted about five months, and by late 1973, before the war broke out, it was simply torn up. As one oilman put it: perhaps the OPEC nations had 'grown tired of the charade of negotiations'.

At this point, and almost inadvertently, the cartel raised prices from $2 to a little over $7 a barrel (as of January 1, 1974), by a three-stage process: (1) restrict output, leading to (2) swift increase in spot prices, followed by (3) a catch-up increase in official or contract prices.

In January 1974, the first system was resumed, with greater success. From the $7 on January 1 the amount per barrel due the producing governments was raised to about $10.50 by November of that year. Contrary to official legend, the public record shows that the Saudis were the price leader throughout this period. The Iranian hawks talked big, but were price followers. The Saudis did talk in favor of lower prices, before, during, and after they raised prices. Along the way, they promised in July to have an auction in August, which would bring down prices; then they cancelled the auction. An October promise: they would not permit output to be reduced, and thereby would put pressure on prices. By March 1975, American officials were complaining that the Saudis had 'pulled the rug out from under them' by permitting output to be reduced.

But in 1975–77, the first price-raising method did not work well. Prices were raised from time to time, but not by much, and soon the world inflation cancelled the increases. The deterioration of the dollar after 1977 made things worse for them. They felt inhibited in raising prices for a time because the enormous surpluses which they were accumulating were a danger to the world monetary banking system, since all the surpluses came from consuming countries, but were only invested in a few. But the current account surplus went effectively to zero in a matter of four years. It should not have happened. Remember the official truth: the OPEC nations' expenditures were limited by their 'needs', so they would keep saving the surpluses. In fact, the Saudis even had a budget deficit in 1978.

The other obstacle was in the machinery of price increases. Up to this point, the OPEC nations had used the producing companies as their collectors when the revenues were in the form of a tax. Although the concessionaires had been reduced to the status of producing contractors and customers, they could still be used to match production with market demand. There was no collusion among companies, since they had no market power. But each producing company would lift only what it thought it could sell, and their total purchases equalled their total estimated sales.

This was an odd haphazard way to set market shares, but it was effective. The producing nations did not get into the difficult divisive task of trying to carve up the market. Instead they left it to a mechanism which was outside their control and which they did not need to control. The companies all bought at prices fixed by the cartel, and then sold as much as they could at those prices, plus the cost of transport, refining, and marketing.

But this system allowed small amounts of competition to seep into the marketplace. The trouble was that the relative values of crude oils were (and are) constantly changing, moving around because of constant changes in relative demands for the various petroleum products. But since the crude oil prices were rigidly set out in advance, crudes yielding higher fractions of some products became unexpectedly good buys, while other crudes became bad buys. Thus, fixed prices meant fluctuating market shares. The more the oil companies are cut loose to become buyers, the more of this we will see. Here and there some countries who were slow to reduce premiums and differentials suffered sharp losses in sales. Since there was a chronic surplus, as is usual in a cartel, some governments were seriously embarrassed. The best example is Nigeria, which in 1976–77 thought it had an arrangement with its neighbors and fellow producers of light sweet crudes, Algeria and Libya. By the spring of 1978 they realized that their fellow Africans were undercutting them by shading prices, and Nigeria was in serious financial straits, having overspent its declining income.

Millions of dollars and many hours of computer time were spent in the attempt to arrive at a 'right' set of differentials, all in vain. The failure was, I think, generally acknowledged by 1978. Now attention began to be directed at direct production control, which would keep market shares, if not completely stable, at least predictable. Of course, all these tensions could have been avoided if the Saudis had really been producing more than they 'needed'. They would have let everybody else sell all they wanted and would themselves have only made up the difference. They did nothing of the sort. But the Saudis as senior partners led the way in direct production control by establishing the system of fixing light and heavy crude proportions. This, it was hoped, would stabilize the differentials and keep them from being the subject of too much competition. But the 65–35 requirement was as everyone knew only a step in the right direction. Despite it, the oil glut worsened.[9] Then the Iranian revolution burst on the scene.

The Iranian revolution is generally considered as the cause for the price jump of 1979–80, from about $12 to about $32 per barrel. But this cannot possibly be true. Over the period October 1978–March 1979, the loss of Iran output was perhaps 2.5 million barrels daily. Unused capacity outside Iran was more than three times as great.[10]

In late 1978, there was a noticeable increase in spot prices, but this was regarded in December as anticipating an OPEC price increase.[11] After a relapse, prices again rose in January, to not quite $20. Then on January 20, 1979 – a day to remember – Saudi Arabia cut production from 10.4 to 8.0 MMB/D. The cut was only partly restored, to 9.5 MMB/D, on February 1, and by mid-February the price had jumped to over $31.

'It's one thing for the Saudis to use the 8.5 million allowable in normal times to create a nice tight supply situation,' said an oilman, 'it's another to use it to create a world crisis.' In aiming at the 'nice tight' market, they achieved the crisis.

The Saudi cut in production had a double impact. It reduced supply, but, more important, it made demand surge. The intense *uncertainty* of supply pushed every prospective buyer into panic. The value of a product is the loss suffered by not having it. (The economist's old friend consumer surplus is Dr Jekyll turned Mr Hyde.) The penalty for running dry is so great that, to ward it off, oil will be pursued at even the most extravagant price. For this reason, and not any actual shortage of oil, the spot price went through what was then considered the roof. The producing governments started to raise their contract or official list prices, either by charging premiums, or simply by finding reasons to withdraw from the contract market and sell at spot themselves.

No end of abuse has been heaped upon the spot market, and time and expense lavished on trying to keep companies out of it or to get into it. No public figure had the good sense to point out that spot prices merely register current excess demand, and that the cuts in output and the complete uncertainty of next month's output had precipitated the excess demand.

At the end of March, the spot price had declined from $31 to around $24. Indeed, a glut threatened. The Gulf nations met to determine what to do next. Sheik Yamani chastised the Iraqis for producing too much oil (half a million barrels daily) and trying to cover it up, causing the glut. Prices kept declining - until it was realized in mid-April that Saudi Arabia had again cut production. Again, prices soared because of the loss of supply and the renewed uncertainty and panic.[12]

We may oversimplify a little to say that by the middle of 1979 the spot market had gone about as high as it was to go. From early 1979 to mid-1980, government selling prices caught up with spot prices, first by a rich variety of devices and subterfuges, then by raising of official list prices. Saudi Arabia 'led the regiment from behind,' keeping its own official price usually $2 or so below the price for equivalent crudes sold by others.[13] Yamani reassured all, toward the end of June, that 'Saudi Arabia would never allow [OPEC] prices to rise to $20 a barrel'.[14] From consumer countries there were repeated hallelujah choruses of congratulations on Saudi statesmanship and forbearance. But in January 1981, when the Saudi official price was $32, Yamani called the price explosion 'another corrective move', that is, deliberate and intentional, as it truly was.

In October 1979, the glut again threatened, and by summer 1980 it was in full force. The OPEC nations made a 'gentlemen's agreement' to cut production by 10 percent, that is, by approximately 2.7 MMB/D. Whether this was greater or less than the existing glut we will never know, for the Iran–Iraq war broke out before we could find out. The war may have been a blessing in disguise (to consumers) because the gentlemen's agreement was cancelled, and there was increased production almost everywhere.

The loss of Iraq output, and of the remains of Iran's, did not much disturb the market, because of higher inventories and because the Saudis had raised the price about as high as they wanted it. They kept it from rising further by keeping output around 10 MMB/D. The big worry for all remains how to cut back to accommodate Iran and Iraq when and if they return to the market. It all sounds very familiar to the student of collusive price fixing:[15]

> The Gulf producers are carefully monitoring limited resumption of oil exports by Iraq and Iran . . .
> A market crunch between OPEC members themselves as soon as Iraq and Iran resume substantial exports is their preoccupation. Iran especially . . . won't find it easy to persuade others to move over and make room in the market. Saudi Arabia carried the burden of a previous market shift in 1975, when it reduced production from 8.5 to 7 mbd. But Yamani has indicated that Saudi Arabia is not ready to repeat anything along these lines . . .

It is time to sum up the new cartel method of raising prices before turning to the question of the ultimate ceiling. Members control production by each government, stating in advance the amount each will be producing in the next month. This, they hope, avoids the danger of supply fluctuations, and unexpected embarrassing losses of market share. In fact, it drastically destabilizes the market.

**Short Run Stabilization Problems**

The trouble is, nobody can fine-tune a market with such coarse instruments. We should contrast it with the system of production control that existed in the pleasant city of Austin, Texas. The Texas Railroad Commission controlled output to prevent it from exceeding market demand at the current price.[16] From time to time the price would be increased, and the Commission would validate that increase by not letting excess supply drive the price down. This was done very efficiently and smoothly, as acknowledged even by those who pointed out that the whole system was after all nothing but a domestic cartel. The Commission had the companies' demand forecasts for the next month, and they also had excellent inventory data, with a lag of only about a week or two. When stocks appeared to be accumulating, production would be cut back. If inventories appeared to be falling below the amount needed to support current production, production allowables would be increased. Everybody knew that stability was the Commission's object, and therefore nobody worried about small changes up or down.

There is a painful contrast between production management by the Texas Railroad Commission and by the OPEC core nations, where production figures are about a month behind. Consumption data even for the OECD nations are six months out of date. Inventory information is about seven months out of date, even for the International Energy Agency, which gets reports from about three dozen companies, and extrapolates for the rest. There is enough noise in the data for short-term movements to be quite misleading. Nobody knows the inventories in the hands of consumers (see Table 2.1). And outside of the IEA nations, there is mostly statistical darkness.

Accordingly, the decisions of the Saudis and their colleagues are made in ignorance. This in itself might not be so bad if they were equally willing to overshoot or undershoot, and to compensate promptly for error. But that is not the case. Their choice is a biased choice. They will not risk a glut, and they are willing to risk a shortage. Everybody in the trade knows this, and is slow to sell with the appearance of a glut, quick to buy with the fear of a shortage. So even the fear of shortage produces a shortage, and sends up the spot price, as refiners and consumers scramble for every available barrel: not because they want it, but because they fear to be caught without it.

This system of brinksmanship by the OPEC core magnifies any real shortages that might come about, and makes supply very insecure everywhere. Events like the Iranian revolution, which should produce at most a ripple, have produced a series of convulsions and may do so again. But for the OPEC nations, their response to the Iranian revolution has been a tremendous success, even greater than in 1973–74. At that time, the so-called 'embargo' raised the price from about $2 to $7 a barrel. The recent increase, from $12 to $32, was in real terms much greater than the 1973–74 hike. It can happen again almost any time, because the only defense against short-term fluctuations is a large inventory. Private inventories have accumulated and will probably stay at a permanently higher level than before 1979. But the consuming nations have been slow to stockpile. Partly, it is misinformed stinginess, but partly also the slogan of 'cooperation not confrontation' with the OPEC nations.

## V LONG RUN PRICING POLICY

Now in mid-1981, it is time to ask: how high can the price go ultimately? The market response to price increase is so slow and uncertain that it will be hard to tell even in retrospect when the monopoly maximum has been reached. It may have happened already. My own belief, before 1978, was that the OPEC nations would (and should in their own interest) be much more cautious about raising the price toward the ultimate ceiling, and not risk inflicting fresh damage on the world economic system, and possibly arousing defensive reactions from the consuming nations. I overestimated their caution.

*Synthetics as a constraint?*
The long-run objectives of the OPEC nations are well stated in the February 1980 report of the Committee of Ministers headed by Sheik Yamani: keep raising the real price of oil to the region of the cost of synthetic fuels, but not so fast as to severely restrict economic growth in the OECD nations. This is a sensible policy for a group monopoly, which would not wish to raise the price so high and lose so many sales as to diminish net revenues. I would have only the reservation that massive synthetic production is so far off in the future that it is no binding constraint today.

## Lower Consumption – the Binding Constraint

Something stronger has intervened. In the non-communist world, and omitting the OPEC countries where oil is not a normal commodity but a handout, oil consumption for the first half of 1981 is hardly above 1972.[17] Nothing like this has ever happened before. In 1930–33, the American GNP fell by a third, and other countries fared almost as badly. But world oil use decreased by only 5 percent, and by 1935 it had set a new high record. In the 1970s there has been a nine-year stagnation, despite the fact that aggregate national product last year in the industrialized world was about 26 percent above 1972, and will probably be about the same this year. What we need to explain is a fall of 21 percent in the amount of oil used per unit of income. Total energy per unit of income has declined almost as much, with a small degree of substitution away from oil.

To take a gross simplification: under conditions existing before 1973, a 1 percent higher price meant about .75 percent lower energy consumption – eventually. But the reaction was and is very slow because it is an investment process, replacing the whole energy-using stock of capital. In a stationary economy, the half-life of this process appears to be roughly about 9 years. We can check this against the fact that the average service life of corporate capital assets is about 20 years. Were the replacement process linear, it would be one-fourth completed in 5 years, half finished in 10 years, and completed in 20 years. It seems not unreasonable that the more promising changes are made first, and approximate an exponential decline: so far as I can discern, the process is one-fourth over in 3.8 years, half over in 9.2 years, three-fourths over in 19 years, and never ceases altogether.

An allowance for economic growth shortens the half-life to about seven years. Of course, the apparent precision is misleading, but I

Table 2.1 *Approximate Non-Communist Consumption (in MMB/D)*

| | *1973* | *1980* | *January–June 1981* |
|---|---|---|---|
| 1 Non-communist production: | | | |
| a crude oil | 45.9 | 45.2 | 43.0 |
| b natural gas liquids | 2.6 | 3.4 | 3.2 |
| | 48.5 | 48.6 | 46.2 |
| 2 *plus* communist exports | 0.8 | 1.1 | 0.9 |
| 3 *less* OPEC consumption | 1.6 | 2.8 | 2.9 |
| 4 *less* stock additions | 0.4 | 0.3 | 0.4 |
| 5 *equals* non-communist consumption | 47.3 | 46.6 | 43.8 |
| Supplied by: | | | |
| 6 OPEC exports | 29.8 | 24.6 | 21.6 |
| 7 Non-OPEC sources | 17.9 | 22.3 | 22.6 |

*Sources* (by line)

1a *Oil and Gas Journal* (OPEC: 31.0, 26.8, 24.0).

b *Oil and Gas Journal*, mid-year Gas Processing Issue. Entry for 1973 for OPEC (0.252) and other non-US (.648) estimated. Entry for 1981 assumed in proportion to change in crude oil output (OPEC: 0.252, 0.591, 0.529).

2 1973, 1980: *BP Statistical Review*; and allowing 0.5 MMB/D as Soviet exports to Cuba, Vietnam, and North Korea. I am indebted to Anthony F. G. Scanlon for this information. 1981: assumed 20 percent less.

3 1973: *International Petroleum Annual*; 1980: Chase Manhattan Bank, *The Petroleum Situation*, Jan.–Feb. 1981; 1981: assumed same rate of increase as 1973–80.

4 EIA, International Energy Indicators, Oct.–Nov. 1981

6 OPEC production, see lines 1a and 1b *less* line 3.

7 Line 5 plus line 4 less line 6.

think that the change in energy consumption from 1973 to 1978 is consistent with, although it is not sufficient to prove, elasticity around 0.75 and a seven-year half-life.[18] The response for oil is somewhat greater than the response for energy in general, because there has been some small substitution of other fuels for oil. Most of the decrease in oil use, adjusted for national product, is to be explained by that original price jump in 1973–74. Indeed, in Western Europe the real price of oil in local currencies was actually lower in 1978 than it was in 1974. Yet consumption per unit of income kept creeping down year after year. The important point is that in 1981 the effects of the first price increase have been only a little more than half-way felt, and the second price increase is just beginning to be felt. Its impact will probably be greater.

Demand elasticity is not a constant but, rather, depends on the price. The higher the price of any product, the greater the reward of substituting away from it. Consider every place where one might save one, two, three, etc., barrels of oil per year by spending $100. When oil (1981 dollars) was about $2.50 a barrel, a barrel was not worth saving to earn 2.5 percent per year. When the price was $12 a barrel, a 12 percent real return before taxes was perhaps acceptable. At $36 a barrel, the rate of return is handsome and the only question is how soon the investment will be made. Now imagine an array of such opportunities in millions of homes and workshops all over the world, and we can see a strong reason for expecting elasticity of demand for energy in general, and oil in particular, to be higher now than it was in 1973. The effect will be felt from now into the next century. How drastically it will affect consumption I will not try to say.

With the energy use per unit of product declining, and that for oil declining a little faster, we need an estimate of economic growth in order to make any kind of forecast for the consumption of energy and oil. Aside from forced official optimism, I doubt that anybody looks forward to any better performance in the 1980s than the 2.5 percent per year since 1973. I would not try to guess how much of the down deflection in world economic growth is due to the direct and indirect effects of the oil price shocks. But some of it is undoubtedly due to the investment process, just mentioned, aimed at saving oil or energy. The investment is a lesser evil. It is not utilized to increase output; it is a subtraction from economic growth. With economic growth abnormally slow, and the continuing decline in energy and oil consumption per unit of product, total energy consumption will grow very slowly if at all, while oil consumption is going to drift downward.

For the first time in 120 years, oil is no longer a growth industry; it is probably a declining industry. Meanwhile, the supply of non-OPEC oil is slowly inching upward. It would be greater today if there had not been such counterproductive policies in the large consuming-producing countries, notably the United States, Canada, Australia, the UK and Norway. In every one of these countries, price controls and taxes have been overused, and the attempt to acquire all the rents has gone past the point of diminishing returns. Rising prices have aggravated the mistake. The higher the price, the greater the incentive to squeeze the goose too hard. Still, it has only diminished not reversed the normal supply response to higher prices.

The net result of stagnant consumption and non-OPEC increases in production is a decline of OPEC exports. In 1973, OPEC exports reached 30 million barrels daily. As recently as June 1978, IEA spoke the official truth: that the demand for OPEC exports would reach 45 ($\pm 3$) MMB/D in 1985. The problem was somehow to maneuver and induce and cajole and persuade them to produce 'enough for our needs'. In fact, production has been limited by consumption. The amount of OPEC oil demanded in 1981 is under 22 MMB/D - less than half of that predicted for 1985 by IEA and others.[19]

Nobody should extrapolate from short run changes, but plainly OPEC exports in the 1980s are going to be lower than in the 1970s. This does not mean that the cartel has made a mistake. Profits are far higher at the higher prices and lower sales. There is still room for further price increases, in my opinion, but anyone who takes the contrary view can muster some strong evidence.

## Future Oil Prices: a Personal View

To calculate actual elasticities of demand and of noncartel supply is worth doing, but the results seem too weak and inaccurate for direct application. The cartel will never hear the clang of a market bell: you have raised prices too high, start a retreat! The pressure upon them is rather the pressure upon their cohesion, when excess capacity becomes burdensome. Hence we must reconsider the two-model theory suggested earlier.

As the 'fringe' of OPEC producers outside the Persian Gulf run up their expenditures to equal and surpass their receipts, they will demand that the Saudis and others in the Gulf 'core' go along with them on higher prices. Their nuisance value is considerable, because their aggregate excess capacity is roughly 1 MMB/D. But the fringe can only pressure the core within limits, because if they force the core to carry all the excess capacity, then in effect the fringe will get the benefit of the higher prices, while the core will bear the burden. Or, what amounts to the same thing, they will greatly increase the elasticity of demand for oil from the core, especially Saudi Arabia. To alleviate this conflict, the report of the OPEC long-term strategy committee proposed side payments to governments reducing output: a sound strategy not easily carried out.

Both sides know that a price higher than optimal in the long run is much more profitable in the short run, because of the slow demand reaction mentioned earlier. As Appendix III shows, plausible reaction times and discount rates bring discounted elasticity to about half that of un-discounted. Finally, and perhaps most important, so long as the OPEC nations maintain the current system of production control, the system is unstable in the upward direction, and a price hike is almost guaranteed at any time unless the core nations take active roles toward preventing it. For these reasons, I would expect still higher (real) prices in the 1980s, despite weak demand.

The Saudis are rightly worried about these developments. Sheik

Yamani has been explaining the concept of demand elasticity, and Saudi actions speak louder than words. Their 1979 output cutbacks drove the price up to $32 from $12. Their output maintenance in 1980–81 has kept the price from going still higher. For the time being, at least, they have stopped telling us that they would dearly love to produce half or less of what they are now producing:[20]

> The problem now for the Kingdom is that . . . the world might simply require much less oil from Saudi Arabia by the middle of the decade than the level of oil production necessary (sic) to sustain the huge industrial enterprises the country has planned . . . The rapid fall in oil production could also spell political trouble for the Saudi government . . . 'Any sustained cutback in government expenditure and largesse could translate into political problems', said one high ranking Western diplomat.

Nobody can predict how much the Saudis would be willing to reduce their output; nobody in OPEC wants to find out. But if the current budget is around $88 billion, then there may be trouble if real prices decline below the current $32 and output drops below 7.5 MMB/D.

The great worry of the OPEC nations is a break in their solidarity. I mentioned earlier that I held little credence for the usual backward bending curve, whereby nations who prefer not to produce their oil cut back production, which raises prices, giving them even more embarrassing money, which forces them to cut production still more, etc. But I have suggested another form of the backward bending curve. The higher the price, the better the financial condition of the sellers, and the less pressure on them to cheat and undersell each other in order to pay their bills.

Whatever the reason, a backward bending supply curve is unstable, both up *and* down. Once the price begins to slip, the OPEC nations will be under great pressure to produce more in order to acquire more revenue, and the more they produce, the further the price falls. Certainly, this has been the experience with a group like CIPEC, a pitiful shadow of OPEC, which the copper producing nations have tried to operate.

If OPEC is in serious trouble trying to coordinate their aims, they would sustain great damage if the consuming countries imposed a quota auction or a sliding scale *ad valorem* import tariff.[21] A higher price would mean a higher tariff, and even lower sales. A country reducing its price gets in effect a matching grant from the US government, with which to undersell its rivals.

## Changing Role of Oil Companies

The multinational oil companies have become buyers; they are no longer sales agents of the producing countries. This process has been ongoing since 1973, and is far from complete, but was greatly speeded up in 1979–80. Most crude oil is today being sold directly by the OPEC national oil companies to a variety of multinationals, brokers, traders, independent refiners, and governments, who use some and sell some. Oil is being traded and sold around as never before. Heating oil futures are being routinely traded. We have the beginnings of a wide decentralized oil market.

Previously a few companies were tied to particular concessions, from which they lifted the oil and sold it to third parties, or used it in their own refineries. There were only a few prices to watch. Producing profits were high enough to make it cheaper to produce oil than to buy it. Today, the companies take almost nothing for sale to others. They have either been expelled from production or earn modest profits. All are now net buyers, and they actively look from supplier to supplier to obtain even a slightly better deal. During the current surplus oil companies are postponing deliveries, and inventing technical problems at the refinery in order to cancel orders or in the field to cut back production. There are reports of a 'price revolt among contract customers . . . actual bargaining is underway in a number of cases'.[22] 'Actual bargaining' over contract prices had never been reported. In June, the Kuwait Oil Minister accused Gulf Oil and BP of 'haggling'. Tradesmen, not gentlemen! – the minister was rightly shocked. Buyers free to roam the market and take advantage of better offers are destabilizers of any collusive price. They have the potential to become, what they are not yet, so many loose cannons on the deck.

US price controls are gone, and American production is now integrated into the world market, where it amounts to more than a fifth of the total. American producers have long been accustomed to respond quickly to price signals, and force a response on their rivals. There is constant comparison of prices now, and a few cents too many mean a lost sale. Sellers know not on whom to align, and find themselves reducing prices to maintain output because they cannot see their rivals, and hence cannot exchange reassurances that they will not cut prices.

The OPEC nations made a serious mistake in getting rid of the oil companies as their producing and selling agents. But the change seems irreversible. All in all, quite a spectacular situation could materialize, with the world price falling dramatically, though the chances of it happening are remote. The collapse of Iran has changed the market greatly. It is doubtful whether they can arrive at more than 3.5

MMB/D capacity, only half of what it used to be, because of their reckless behavior in neglecting the wells and driving out both Iranian and foreign skilled personnel. The Iranian disaster and the Iran–Iraq War have been a piece of great good fortune for Iran's neighbors. In future, they will contrive more such good luck. Saudi Arabia has the slight military edge to occupy neighbors, including even Kuwait if the Iraqis do not get there first. The war has shown that even a low level of air and patrol-boat power, ineffectually applied, can keep loading ports out of operation. The important point to remember is: a million barrels of your neighbor's production suppressed, which you in turn supply, is worth at current prices over $11 billion per year. It is an investment you cannot refuse. Given the Saudis, alone or with one other enforcer, the supply from cartel core should hold together.

I hope we manage to avoid such false questions as to whether 'the market will be loose', or 'the market will be tight', etc. The market will be both: loose, because of excess capacity which has existed since 1908 (the first great Persian find); tight, because when slack threatens the cartel managers haul in so quickly as to create a strain, perhaps a painful one. This happened twice in 1978–79, and might have occurred again in September 1980 had it not been for the unexpected outbreak of war, and the cancellation of the 'gentlemen's agreement'. We live in a market controlled by the cartel, and the worst thing we can do is to ignore that simple fact.

If the real price of oil goes up again, the US domestic industry will benefit. But it will make complete decontrol, that is, repeal of the so-called windfall profits tax, more difficult. On the other hand, if the price goes down, I think domestic oil and gas production will be protected by tariffs or quotas. The world in general may be heading into a great divorce between internal energy markets and world markets. There will of course be squabbles over who has access to the lower cost international crude, so circumstances may be in some respects back to where they were ten years ago.

## APPENDIX I

Note that this appendix is in effect a supplement to the model of Chapter 1. We assume a competitive industry which is in equilibrium with some expected trajectory of future prices. To assume a constant price simplifies the mathematics without changing the result. This equilibrium is to be disturbed by a change in the appropriate discount rate, for any reason.

For any given deposit's reserves, $R$ means cumulative expected output, starting at $Q_0$ and declining at a constant rate $a$:

$$R = \int_0^\infty Q_t dt = Q_0 \int_0^\infty e^{-at} dt = \frac{Q_0}{a}, \text{ or } Q_0 = Ra \qquad (I.1)$$

The present value (neglecting operating costs) of the future production, when $P$ is the constant price, and $i$ is the discount rate, is given by

$$PV = P \int_0^\infty Q_t e^{-it} dt = PQ_0 \int_0^\infty e^{-(a+i)t} dt = \frac{PQ_0}{(a+i)} \qquad (I.2)$$

$$\text{Since } Q_0 = Ra, \ \frac{PV}{PR} = \frac{a}{(a+i)} \qquad (I.3)$$

The values $R$, $i$, and $P$ are exogenous; $a$ is the decision variable. The fraction $PV/PR = a/(a+i) = F$, and cannot exceed unity.

If $i = 0$, then $F = 1$ no matter what the value of depletion rate $a$; we only have a problem because $i$ is non-zero positive. As $a$ becomes very large, $F \rightarrow 1$, so the faster the depletion the better.

The slope of $F$ is always positive, always decreasing:

$$\frac{\partial F}{\partial a} = \frac{i}{(a+i)^2} \qquad (I.4)$$

$$\frac{\partial^2 F}{\partial a^2} = \frac{-2i}{(a+i)^3} \qquad (I.5)$$

Now consider cost. $K(a)$ is the investment needed to establish the depletion rate $a$. Investment rises at least proportionately with $a$, and past some point, faster. All we know is that $\partial K/\partial a$ is everywhere positive, and $\partial^2 K/\partial a^2$ is always zero or positive.

Value will be maximized where the slope of the revenue function $F$ equals the slope of the cost function $K$, that is, $\partial K/\partial a = \partial F/\partial a$. (Moreover, $F$ must always exceed $K$.)

A change in the discount rate $i$ has no effect on the investment function $\partial K/\partial a$. It does affect the slope of $F$:

$$\frac{(\partial F/\partial a)}{\partial i} = \frac{(a-i)}{(a+i)^3} \qquad (I.6)$$

Assume now that depletion at some rate $a$ has been optimal, that is, $(\partial F/\partial a) = (\partial K/\partial a)$. But suppose the discount rate has changed. What is the effect on the depletion rate $a$?

If the initial rate $i$ is *less than* $a$, the slope $(\partial F/\partial a)$ will increase, hence it will exceed $(\partial K/\partial a)$. The operator will aim to lower it, to make it again equal to the investment slope $(\partial K/\partial a)$. He can only do this by *increasing* the depletion rate. (However, if $(\partial K/\partial a)$ is an increasing function of $a$, as it will be in some part of the range, then $a$ may be increased only slightly.)

Consider now the other case, where the initial discount rate $i$ is *greater* than the depletion rate $a$. Then an increased discount rate will *lower* the depletion rate, while a lower discount rate will raise it. A higher discount rate will lower the slope of $F$. The operator will seek a higher slope by decreasing $a$. (Again, this result is not absolutely certain because with lower depletion the cost slope $(\partial K/\partial a)$ may be lower. But with low values of $a$, the slope should be linear.)

With higher and higher values of $i$, the depletion rate will tend to be lower. If the higher discount rate brings the $(PV/PR)$ curve below the $K$ curve, then $a$ goes to zero.

In the text example, where $F = a/(a+i)$, and $K/PR = .05 + 1.9a$,

| $i$ | optimal $a$ | $i$ | optimal $a$ |
|---|---|---|---|
| .01 | .0625 | .15 | .1310 |
| .03 | .0957 | .20 | .1244 |
| .05 | .1122 | .25 | .1122 |
| .06 | .1177 | .30 | .0974 |
| .075 | .1237 | .32 | .0000 |
| .10 | .1294 | | |

At $i = .32$, optimal $a = .0868$, but $(K/PR) = .2218$, while $(PV/PR) = .2202$.

More generally, let $K/PR = \ell + ja$. For a maximum net present value,

$$\frac{\partial F}{\partial a} = \frac{i}{(a+i)^2} = \frac{\partial K}{\partial a} = j$$

Then $(a+i)^2 = i/j$, and $a = \sqrt{i/j} - i$.

Thus the discount rate works both ways, to raise and lower optimal $a$; but the higher is $j$, the lower is $a$.

## APPENDIX II

### Risk of Sudden Loss and the Risky Discount Rate

Assume a probability $p$ that the owner of a mineral deposit will, within any given year, suffer a sudden complete and irrevocable loss of his property. His chance of survival is then $(1-p)$, and chance of survival from now through the year $t$ is $(1-p)^t$, because to get through year $t$ safely one must also get through each and every previous year.

Let $i$ be the rate of discount covering normal commercial risk, but not the 'short sharp shock', or 'SSS'. Let $r$ be the risky rate covering that event in addition to normal risk. Then the present value of \$$X$ received in year $t$ is:

$$PV(\$X)_t = \$X\frac{(1-p)^t}{(1+i)^t} = \$X(1+r)^{-t} \tag{II.1}$$

$$r = \frac{i+p}{1-p}, \text{ and } p = \frac{r-i}{1+r} \tag{II.2}$$

Suppose one has a reliable estimate of the normal $i$ for a given type of operation, and also learns of the rate $r$ which is being used in such an operation which is also subject to 'SSS'. One can estimate the implied probability of 'SSS'. Also, if one defines $T$ as the number of years hence when the chances of 'SSS' are 50–50, then:

$$(1-p)^T = 0.5, \text{ and } T = -.693/1\text{n}(1-p) \tag{II.3}$$

## APPENDIX III

The usual timeless definition of price elasticity, where $Q_a$ and $P_a$ are the changed price and output, and $P_b$ and $Q_b$ are the original price and output, is:

$$Q_a/Q_b = (P_a/P_b)^E \tag{III.1}$$

Assume now that the price change is immediate, but the demand reaction takes time, and the effect declines exponentially:

$$Q_t = Q_b e^{-ct} + Q_a(1-e^{-ct}) \tag{III.2}$$

Let $i$ be the appropriate discount rate. Then the present value of production in year $t$ is:

$$PV(P_aQ_t) = P_aQ_te^{-it} = P_aQ_be^{-(c+i)t} + P_aQ_ae^{-it} - P_aQ_ae^{-(c+i)t} \tag{III.3}$$

The present value of the whole stream is:

$$\int_0^\infty PV(P_aQ_t)dt = \int_0^\infty P_aQ_te^{-it}dt = P_a\left[\frac{Q_b}{(c+i)}+\frac{Q_a}{i}-\frac{Q_a}{(c+i)}\right] \quad \text{(III.4)}$$

Had we not changed the price, the present value of the stream would have been:

$$\int_0^\infty P_bQ_be^{-it}dt = \frac{P_bQ_b}{i} \quad \text{(III.5)}$$

Now compare the present value of two options: price change or no price change. With timeless elasticity, $Q_a/Q_b = (P_a/P_b)^E$, or $(P_aQ_a/P_bQ_b) = (P_a/P_b)^{E+1}$. But with present-value-weighted elasticity, called $E'$, we have:

$$\left(\frac{P_a}{P_b}\right)^{E'+1} = P_a\left[\frac{Q_b}{c+i}+\frac{Q_a}{i}-\frac{Q_a}{c+i}\right](P_bQ_b/i)$$

$$=\frac{P_a}{P_b}\left[\frac{i}{c+i}+\frac{Q_a}{Q_b}\left(1-\frac{i}{c+i}\right)\right]$$

$$=\frac{P_a}{P_b}\left[\frac{i}{c+i}+\left(\frac{P_a}{P_b}\right)^E\left(1-\frac{i}{c+i}\right)\right]$$

Dividing both sides by $(P_a/P_b)$, we have:

$$\left(\frac{P_a}{P_b}\right)^{E'} = \frac{i}{c+i}+\left(\frac{P_a}{P_b}\right)^E\left(1-\frac{i}{c+i}\right) \quad \text{(III.6)}$$

In the special case, where we pay no attention to lags or discounting, the two sides reduce to the same $E = E'$.

Assume now that the price is raised by 50 percent, that is $(P_a/P_b) = 1.5$, timeless $E = -1.0$, $c = .095$, $i = 0.1$. Then:

$$(P_a/P_b)^{E'} = .51 + (.67)(.49) = .84, \text{ and } E' = -0.44$$

A lower discount rate, for example, .075, would raise $E'$ only to $-0.50$.

## NOTES

Research underlying this chapter has been supported by the National Science Foundation under Grant No. DAR 78-19044 and by the MIT Center for Energy Policy Research. I have benefited much from a long collaboration with Henry D. Jacoby and James L. Paddock, and from the comments of Richard L. Gordon, James M. Griffin, David Teece, and Philip K. Verleger, Jr. However, all views expressed commit only the writer, who is solely responsible for any errors.

1 Adelman (1973), p. 1256.
2 Adelman (1978).
3 Church Committee Hearings, Part VII, p. 228.
4 The following is adapted from Richard L. Gordon, who first demonstrated that the effect of interest rates on output rates is indeterminate.
5 Reasons are set forth in Chapter 1 for future price expectations.
6 This is very low cost oil in an improbably prolific deposit. More realistic assumptions would make the cost line steeper and allow much less variation among optimal depletion rates.
7 The most up-to-date and I believe most widely accepted estimates are by Ibbetson and Sinquefield (1979), esp. p. 23. It is only a minor criticism to note that their use of the Consumer Price Index overstates the inflation rate and understates the real return.
8 David Teece has pointed out that if foreign assets are in the name of the government, they are also subject to seizure. Hence it pays to keep more foreign assets in accounts which one's successors cannot claim. It does not affect the optimal revenue total.
9 This paragraph is based on *Petroleum Economist* (1978), June, p. 230; ibid., August, p. 328; and particularly December, p. 499.
10 *Petroleum Intelligence Weekly*, January 29, 1979, p. 9. A sufficient reason for not using the CIA capacity numbers is their vagueness of definition.
11 *Petroleum Economist, op. cit.*
12 *Petroleum Intelligence Weekly*, April 9 and April 16, 1979.
13 This narrative is based on several sources. The weekly prices are from a forthcoming book by Philip K. Verleger, Jr. The output changes are from *Petroleum Intelligence Weekly*, as are most of the reports of meetings and speeches; the rest from the *New York Times* and *Wall Street Journal.*
14 *New York Times*, June 22, 1979.
15 *Petroleum Intelligence Weekly*, November 24, 1980 and December 15, 1980.
16 Lovejoy and Homan (1967) and MacDonald (1971).
17 The estimate is more than usually imprecise because of our ignorance of stock changes. The second half of 1981 will probably be even more enigmatic, but consumption will be less.
18 In 1978, US energy consumption per unit of GNP was .9158 times the 1973 level. At a rough estimate, the increase in real price to final users was 40 percent. If the long run elasticity was about −.75, the ultimate reduction in energy per unit would be by 22 percent, to .7770 of the 1973 level. Substituting these values into the equation in Appendix III:

$$.9158 = e^{-5c} + .78 - .78e^{-5c}$$
$$c = .0948, \text{ half-life} = h = 7.3$$

An estimate may also be drawn from the results of the ISTUM model (Sant et al., 1980, pp. 27–37). In 1978, energy use was down 10 percent from 1973 in its sample of users, and it would pay 5 percent or more, real, to reduce it by 32 percent altogether. One can calculate:

$$.90 = e^{-5c} + .68 - .68e^{-5c}$$
$$c = .0725, \quad h = 9.56$$

But the estimated .68 as ultimate consumption seems too low because the 5 percent return seems too low. It yields an implicit long run elasticity of $-1.15$ - not impossible, of course, but on the high side.

19 In the summer of 1981, OPEC exports dropped below 20, but I believe this to be a temporary low because of massive de-stocking.

20 *New York Times*, March 23, 1981.

21 On the auction, see *Oil & Gas Journal*, January 10, 1977; on the tariff, see Adelman (1978).

22 *Petroleum Intelligence Weekly*, June 8, 1981.

# 3 OPEC Behavior: An Alternative View

DAVID J. TEECE

## I INTRODUCTION

In recent years, economists and policy analysts have exhibited considerable puzzlement over the role that OPEC as an organization plays in determining the world price of crude oil. Most Western economists refer to OPEC as a cartel while OPEC representatives and Arab scholars commonly argue that OPEC is not a cartel and that the current world price is competitive. Given that the community of professional analysts has had such a disappointing track record with respect to predicting OPEC behavior and the world price of oil,[1] it seems appropriate to question the conceptual lens through which OPEC behavior is commonly evaluated.

In this chapter I indicate that wealth-maximizing classical cartel models relying on coordinated behavior and comprehensive collusion provide an inappropriate model for analyzing OPEC behavior. Rather, I offer an alternative view which can be summarized as follows. Several important OPEC producers set oil production with reference to budgetary 'requirements'[2] and internal and external political constraints. If export receipts plus foreign earnings are such as to satisfy expenditure 'requirements', oil production policies will be determined by 'conservation' considerations, where 'conservation' involves shutting in production for future generations, even if this is not consistent with maximizing the present value of oil reserves. Conversely, if export receipts plus foreign earnings are such that expenditure requirements are not being met, production and capacity will be expanded, so long as technical conditions permit. Expenditure 'requirements' are determined by applying some percentage growth factor to last year's expenditure levels, where the growth factor is always positive, or very nearly so.

In economic parlance it appears that, at least for an important subset of OPEC producers, the relationship between current price and current output is best represented by a backward bending supply[3] curve for the short run. One implication is that once a producer is on the backward bending portion of this curve, there is no proclivity to 'cheat' on other OPEC members. Conversely, if a producer is not on the backward bending portion of the (short run) supply curve, it will display proclivities to expand output in an attempt to increase current revenues. This hypothesis has remarkable implications for OPEC behavior in that (1) it indicates that the monopoly price level is not exposed to the hazards of cheating – just so long as oil revenues (plus other foreign earnings) meet budgetary 'needs'. But once 'needs' catch up with revenues, pressures to expand production will be evident. (2) Secondly, it indicates that the stability of OPEC over the period 1974–80 need not have been the consequence of collusion. The backward bending supply curve construct implies that monopolization is possible without collusion, at least in the short run. By implication OPEC has yet to prove that it is capable of supporting the world price through coordinated action.

This view relegates wealth-maximizing considerations and portfolio theory to a secondary role. In particular, if optimizing criteria were to indicate that significantly higher current exports would maximize wealth, the revenues from which must be converted into foreign assets because they are not needed domestically in the current period, then these dictates will be ignored in large measure. The reason is that foreign assets are not viewed as a desirable investment, except for liquidity purposes. Not only are there considered to be internal and external political risks[4] associated with foreign investments, but they are perceived to yield returns less than can be obtained from keeping oil in the ground. Furthermore, the objectives of most OPEC states are not consistent with creating a nation of rentiers dependent on 'coupon clipping' for their economic survival, even if this were the wealth-maximizing strategy. The rentier concept is simply perceived to be inconsistent with national aspirations for economic development and political independence. As Turner and Bedore have noted, 'Producer governments would have political difficulties in remaining mere exporters of crude oil' (1979, p. 75).

This view of OPEC explains why the price level has not collapsed under the weight of cheating.[5] It also indicates that OPEC behavior in a tight market and in a prolonged soft market will be markedly different. With a continued soft market through to the mid-1980s, coupled with the absence of a political upheaval large enough to take say 3 MMB/D or more off the market, there is a good chance that the OPEC producers with the technical capacity to do so will expand production in order to generate higher revenues to meet internal budgetary requirements.[6] The result could well be that the real price of crude will remain in the $35 per barrel range, perhaps through to the end of this century. Conversely, a disruption in supplies could once again lift the real price above net wealth-maximizing levels, at least for several years. In short, uncertainty with respect to prices is not just simply on the upside; there is downside uncertainty as well. The theoretical and empirical underpinnings of this view are developed in more detail below.

## II PRODUCTION POLICIES IN OPEC

There is growing evidence that a number of important OPEC producers adjust output, at least in the short run, in a manner which appears to be at odds with the view that OPEC is a wealth-maximizing cartel. If discount rates, oil reserves, and demand elasticities are held constant, exhaustible resource theory indicates that current production will increase if current prices increase. Furthermore, at prices significantly above competitive levels, there are enormous incentives to increase output to obtain higher current revenues. However, OPEC production policies appear to move to a different drummer, with some producers reducing output, holding it constant, or abolishing expansion plans when prices rise. Furthermore, 'cheating' in the form of output expansion was almost completely absent in the 1970s. OPEC output fell from 31.8 MMB/D in 1973 to 26.9 MMB/D in 1980 (see Table 1.4).

This apparently anomalous behavior has a ready explanation if production decisions are made in some states with the principal objective of generating sufficient income to meet the budgetary requirements of the nations in question. Accordingly, price escalation in a given period can lead to decreased production if the additional revenues resulting from higher prices are greater than the desired expansion in government expenditures for the same period. Clearly, this explanation assumes that in some sense there are steeply diminishing returns to current revenues for some producing states. This is quite at odds with neoclassical investment and consumption theory. However, the economic and political realities of certain less developed economies render standard analysis of limited value.

Thus, consider an oil producing nation like Kuwait where oil revenues are a very large component of export receipts and government revenues. Such a nation state can allocate revenues to domestic consumption, domestic investment, or foreign investment. I now examine each of these opportunities in turn.

Opportunities for increasing domestic expenditures are severely constrained in the short to medium run by the lack of a supporting infrastructure in areas such as transportation and distribution, and by the inability of the labor force to rapidly acquire the skills needed for economic development. The concept of absorptive capacity has been developed to give content to this notion. According to Rosenstein-Rodan (1961), 'absorptive capacity relates to the ability to use capital productively . . . There are . . . narrow limits to the pace and extent at which a country's absorptive capacity can be expanded'. Absorptive capacity can be defined as the amount of investment that can be made at some acceptable threshold rate of return, with the supply of complementary factors considered as given. What is involved is a decline in the marginal productivity of capital resulting from the inability to augment the human factors of production as fast as the capital stock. The result is 'a kind of inevitable decreasing returns to the scale of investment' (Eckaus, 1972, p. 80) and a backward bending supply curve for crude oil. This is more formally portrayed in the Appendix.

Buttressing these economic factors are important political constraints in several OPEC countries where fundamentalist Islamic groups are vying for political power. Rapid economic development involves the transformation of social, cultural, and religious values. If these are cherished and provide the foundation for the existing political order, expenditure growth will be constrained on this account.

For a different set of economic and political considerations the desirability of increased foreign investment is also at issue for several OPEC producers. While some amount of investment in foreign securities and short-term obligations is considered desirable for liquidity and for diversification reasons, there appears to be a perception by certain OPEC states that these investments are risky and subject to expropriation by foreign governments or by inflation. The US freeze on Iranian assets has fueled this belief, while inflation corrected returns were very modest through the 1970s, averaging less than the rate of inflation by some estimates.[7] While myopic, these beliefs were common through the 1970s, leading in certain key OPEC countries to conclude that oil in the ground constitutes a wiser investment than does the acquisition of various foreign financial assets.[8]

These views are powerfully bolstered by the following consideration. Most OPEC producers are loath to consider the possibility that their wealth-maximizing strategy may well be to become rentiers – mere 'coupon clippers' dependent on investments in the West for their succor. Powerful evidence that this alternative has been rejected can be seen in the billions of dollars sunk into domestic projects which offer no prospect of ever becoming economic by objective efficiency standards.

Of course, there are noticeable differences among the OPEC

producers with respect to their attitudes and policies toward foreign investment. The Kuwaitis, for instance, have been quite enthusiastic about investments in the West, including equity participation. As Table 3.1 indicates, their investments abroad are much larger, relative to annual revenues, than those of any other OPEC state. Nevertheless, Kuwait has held considerable excess capacity, apparently preferring oil in the ground to money in the bank.

Of significance in this regard is the announced plans of the Saudis to build a 1.5 billion barrel oil storage facility on the Red Sea 'to insure against disruption of its vulnerable oil fields and pumping facilities along the Persion Gulf'.[9] The proposed facility will cost about $7 billion to build and is almost twice as large as the 750 million barrel planned capacity of the US strategic petroleum reserve. Such an investment cannot be explained on economic grounds alone, for if it were just a certain revenue stream which the Saudis wish to ensure, then short-term money market obligations in the United States,

Table 3.1 *Estimated Foreign Assets, Selected OPEC Members (in US$m.)*

| | *End of 1972* | *End of 1978* | *End of 1979* |
|---|---|---|---|
| Iraq | 720 | 8,619 | 17,500 |
| Iran | 884 | 11,977 | 15,900 |
| Kuwait | 2,418 | 28,000 | 40,000 |
| Libya | 2,694 | 4,105 | 6,344 |
| Qatar | 414 | 2,967 | 4,267 |
| Saudi Arabia | 2,303 | 64,000 | 75,000 |
| United Arab Emirates | 300 | 9,307 | 12,707 |
| TOTAL | 9,733 | 128,975 | 171,718 |

*Investment Income, Selected OPEC Members (in US$m.)*

| | *1972* | *1973* | *1974* | *1975* | *1976* | *1977* | *1978* | *1979* |
|---|---|---|---|---|---|---|---|---|
| Iraq | 28.4 | 65.7 | 275 | 191 | 146 | 288 | 755 | 1,750 |
| Iran | 18 | 54 | 424 | 745 | 784 | 739 | 1,078 | 1,590 |
| Kuwait | 410 | 559 | 767 | 1,361 | 1,821 | 2,111 | 2,500 | 4,000 |
| Libya | 152 | 123.7 | 312 | 228 | 202 | 266 | 370 | 634 |
| Qatar | 28 | 24.8 | 75.5 | 128 | 138 | 157 | 267 | 426 |
| Saudi Arabia | 125 | 221.7 | 1,305.7 | 1,961.8 | 3,226.6 | 4,447 | 5,750 | 7,600 |
| UAE | 20 | 49.6 | 143.8 | 268 | 470 | 731 | 838 | 1,270 |
| TOTAL | 781.4 | 1,098.5 | 3,303 | 4,882.8 | 6,787.6 | 8,739 | 11,578 | 17,270 |

*Source: Middle East Economic Survey*, April 28, 1980.

Europe, and Japan would seem to be the least-cost solution. However, the fact that the Saudis are even contemplating this project is evidence that oil in storage is perceived as more secure than financial assets held in the West.

These considerations indicate that so long as the above perceptions remain firm, OPEC producers cannot be expected to expand production for the principal purpose of acquiring foreign assets, even if by doing so they would enhance the present value of their wealth. Furthermore, if the domestic economy is already burdened with all the investment that can be supported prudently, then there is no internal reason for a producer to expand production.[10] If this is an appropriate representation of reality for a significant portion of OPEC capacity, then supply responses will be quite perverse in that large increases in the world price in one period need not occasion any increase in output in the same period. In fact the opposite is possible. Conversely falling world prices will lead to production expansion, at least in certain countries.[11]

The strength of the above considerations depends, in part, on the extent to which economic development is constrained by the economic and political considerations mentioned earlier. Absorptive capacity constraints rooted in political considerations appear to be especially important in Islamic countries; absorptive capacity constraints rooted in economic considerations will be more powerful the lower the level of economic development and the smaller the population in relation to revenues from oil. Table 3.2 categorizes the OPEC states according to these last criteria. Countries classified as Group I (low absorptive capacity) had average revenues per inhabitant of $5,799 in 1978 while the corresponding figures for Group II (moderate absorptive capacity) and Group III (high absorptive capacity) were $602 and $72, respectively. These classifications are at best highly approximate as absorptive capacity is determined in part by political factors as well as other economic considerations not captured in Table 3.2. Additional information is therefore needed if the classifications are to be refined.

What makes these categories significant, in terms of cartel theory, is that as of 1980–81 the data indicate that countries with low absorptive capacity have considerably more short run excess capacity than do producers with higher absorptive capacity (Table 3.3). Group I countries have about 3 million barrels per day or about two-thirds of OPEC's excess short run capacity. Furthermore, these countries have higher reserve to production ratios than do countries in other categories. At 1978 levels of production, remaining reserves for Group I, Group II, and Group III countries were 54, 26 and 22 years, respectively (Table 3.2). This indicates the existence of greater capacity expansion possibilities for Group I countries. In short, those

Table 3.2 *OPEC Countries*[a]*: 1978 Population, Reserves and Revenues per capita*

| | *Population (million)* | *Proven reserves (MMB)* | *Output (1000 B/D)* | *Reserves: Years (at 1978 output rate)* | *Revenue from oil exports (US$m.)* | *Revenue per inhabitant (US$)* |
|---|---|---|---|---|---|---|
| *Group I* (low absorptive capacity) | | | | | | |
| Saudi Arabia | 6.89 | 153,100 | 8,059 | 52.05 | 38,736 | 5,622.06 |
| Libya | 2.73 | 25,000 | 1,982 | 34.58 | 9,490 | 3,476.19 |
| Kuwait | 1.18 | 70,100 | 1,865 | 102.98 | 9,575 | 8,114.41 |
| Qatar | 0.23 | 5,600 | 485 | 31.63 | 2,315 | 10,065.22 |
| United Arab Emirates | 0.83 | 32,425 | 1,832 | 40.49 | 8,658 | 10,431.33 |
| Subtotal | 11.86 | 286,225 | 14,223 | 54 | 68,774 | |
| Share of total | 3.7% | 65.70% | 48.96% | | 51.5% | |
| Avg. revenue per inhabitant[b] | | | | | | $5,799 |
| *Group II* (moderate absorptive capacity) | | | | | | |
| Iran | 36.64 | 62,000 | 5,264 | 32.27 | 21,766 | 594.05 |
| Venezuela | 13.1 | 18,200 | 2,163 | 23.05 | 9,187 | 701.30 |
| Iraq | 12.65 | 34,500 | 2,629 | 35.95 | 11,008 | 870.20 |
| Algeria | 17.25 | 6,000 | 1,225 | 13.42 | 6,015 | 348.70 |
| Subtotal | 79.64 | 120,700 | 11,281 | 26 | 47,976 | |
| Share of total | 24.6% | 27.71% | 38.83% | | 35.9% | |
| Avg. revenue per inhabitant[b] | | | | | | $602 |
| *Group III* (high absorptive capacity) | | | | | | |
| Nigeria | 91.17 | 18,700 | 1,910 | 26.82 | 9,318 | 102.20 |
| Indonesia | 141.28 | 10,000 | 1,637 | 16.74 | 7,439 | 52.65 |
| Subtotal | 232.45 | 28,700 | 3,547 | 22 | 16,757 | |
| Share of total | 71.7% | 6.59% | 12.21% | | 12.6% | |
| Avg. revenue per inhabitant[b] | | | | | | $72 |
| TOTAL | 323.95 | 435,625 | 29,051 | | 133,507 | |

[a] Excludes Ecuador and Gabon.
[b] Subtotal revenue divided by subtotal population.
*Sources:* 1. *World Energy Industry*, vol. 1, no. 1, Second Quarter, 1978.
2. *Background Notes*, US Department of State, various dates.

producers with low absorptive capacities are also the countries possessing the greatest amount of short to medium run excess capacity. As such, their production behavior will be of very great importance to the world oil market, at least over the next decade. Their existing excess capacity and their ability to add to this capacity is the principle supply side threat to the monopoly prices which producers are currently obtaining.

There is mounting evidence that Group I producers behave according to the considerations specified above. The clearest evidence is the absence of widespread cheating, by which is meant the tendency to offer price discounts in order to sell more oil. While this might be explained in terms of OPEC solidarity, it will be argued below that OPEC solidarity - in the sense of individual countries adjusting their production decisions in order to meet group goals - is of minor importance. Of greater significance are the various natural characteristics of OPEC economies coupled with internal and external political factors which explain why Group I producers have not, as of 1981, engaged in competitive output expansion.

Besides the absence of cheating, there are numerous public statements by key OPEC ministers indicating that production decisions are made in reference to internal budgetary targets. Also consistent with such behavior are various endeavors to cut production or restrain output increases when prices rise. Clearly, if OPEC producers are shooting at some target level of revenue, they will tend to cut production if prices rise, and increase production if prices fall. (In economic language, target revenue producers will have a backward bending supply curve.) For instance, the Algerian Energy and Petrochemicals Minister has stated that, 'If the terms of trade improve, Algerian exports will drop'.[12] Similarly, Kuwait's Minister of Oil has stated that, 'The big increase in oil prices has given us the opportunity to review production',[13] adding that the Kuwait Council of Ministers was discussing the question of lowering production. Libya, Abu Dhabi, Qatar, and occasionally Saudi Arabia can be expected to display similar proclivities. OPEC members and other producers with modest production in relation to absorptive capacity, such as Nigeria, Ecuador, and Mexico, are less able to adjust production in this fashion, although they sometimes exhibit similar tendencies.

The increasing reluctance of OPEC countries to produce today in order to build financial assets abroad is also supportive of the view that production decisions are made with reference to domestic budgetary targets. Perhaps the one exception is Saudi Arabia. As will be pointed out in Section V below, there are complex political reasons why Saudi Arabia behaves differently, producing beyond its domestic

Table 3.3 *OPEC[a] Countries: 1981 Production and Short Run Excess Capacity (1000 B/D)*

| | *Capacity* | | *Production* | | | |
|---|---|---|---|---|---|---|
| | *Installed*[b] | *Maximum sustainable*[c] | *Available*[d] | *Latest post-embargo peak* | *Current*[e] *(JFMA 81)* | *Short run excess capacity*[f] |
| *Group I* (low absorptive capacity) | | | | | | |
| Saudi Arabia[i] | 12,500 | 9,500 | 9,500 | 10,200 (Jan.81) | 10,209 | 0 |
| Libya | 2,500 | 2,100 | 1,750 | 2,210 (Mar.77) | 1,612 | 598 |
| Kuwait[i] | 2,900 | 2,500 | 1,500 | 2,990 (Dec.76) | 1,471 | 1,519 |
| Qatar | 650 | 600 | 600 | 610 (Dec.75) | 501 | 109 |
| United Arab Emirates | 2,570 | 2,415 | 1,630 | 2,260[g] | 1,601 | 659 |
| Subtotal | 21,120 | 17,115 | 14,980 | 18,070 | 15,394 | 2,885 |
| Share of total | 52.5% | 51.1% | 51.6% | 49.5% | 62.9% | 63.4% |
| *Group II* (moderate absorptive capacity) | | | | | | |
| Iran | 7,000 | 5,500[h] | 3,500[i] | 6,680 (Nov.76) | 1,650 | – |
| Venezuela | 2,600 | 2,400 | 2,200 | 2,950 (Jne.74) | 2,214 | 736 |
| Iraq | 4,000 | 3,500 | 3,500 | 3,500 (Jne.79) | 825 | – |
| Algeria | 1,200 | 1,100 | 1,000 | 1,160 (Dec.78) | 938 | 222 |
| Subtotal | 14,800 | 12,500 | 10,200 | 14,290 | 5,627 | 958 |
| Share of total | 36.8% | 37.4% | 35.1% | 39.1% | 23.0% | 21.0% |
| *Group III* (high absorptive capacity) | | | | | | |
| Nigeria | 2,500 | 2,200 | 2,200 | 2,440 (Jan.79) | 1,840 | 600 |
| Indonesia | 1,800 | 1,650 | 1,650 | 1,740 (Mar.77) | 1,629 | 111 |
| Subtotal | 4,300 | 3,850 | 3,850 | 4,180 | 3,469 | 711 |
| Share of total | 10.7% | 11.5% | 13.3% | 11.4% | 14.1% | 15.6% |
| TOTAL | 40,220 | 33,465 | 29,030 | 36,740 | 24,490 | 4,554 |

[a] Excluding Ecuador and Gabon.

[b] Installed capacity, also called nameplate or design capacity, includes all aspects of crude oil production, processing, transportation, and storage. Installed capacity is generally the highest capacity estimate.

[c] Maximum sustainable or operational capacity is the maximum production rate that can be sustained for several months; it considers the experience of operating the total system and is generally some 90–95 percent of installed capacity. This capacity concept does not necessarily reflect the maximum production rate sustainable without damage to the fields.

[d] Available or allowable capacity reflects production ceilings applied by Abu Dhabi, Kuwait, Iran, and Saudi Arabia. These ceilings usually represent a constraint only on annual average output, and thus production may exceed the ceilings in a given month. These ceilings are frequently altered and not always enforced.

[e] Production estimates are the average for January, February, March, and April 1981 as reported in *Monthly Energy Review*, US Department of Energy, Energy Information Administration, August 1981.

[f] Except in the case of Iran and Iraq this is calculated by subtracting current production from the latest post embargo peak. In the case of Iran and Iraq it is assumed that there is no excess capacity because of the dysfunctional effects of revolution and war.

[g] This figure is composed of the following: Abu Dhabi 1,930 (Jul.'75), Dubai 370 (Jul.'79), Sharjah 60 (Dec.'74).

[h] The precise loss in sustainable capacity remains uncertain.

[i] This figure represents the upper end of the range of available capacity, according to government statements.

*Sources: International Energy Statistical Review*, CIA, April 28, 1981 and *Monthly Energy Review*, US Department of Energy, August 81.

budgetary needs and investing the surpluses in financial assets. Yet even in the case of Saudi Arabia, there is increasing reluctance to do so. An objective assessment based on economic analysis might indicate an incentive to build financial assets but this is of little importance for predicting OPEC behavior if production decisions are made based on a different set of criteria.

An important implication of this analysis is that in a tight crude market, collusion among producers is not necessary for the price to remain at levels generating large monopoly rents.[14] This explains why the price during the 1970s did not collapse under the pressures of competitive output expansion. It also indicates that OPEC as an organization has been essentially irrelevant to price determination in the 1970s. With only modest exaggeration OPEC can be considered a price stamping organization, attempting to ratify marketplace prices resulting from the actions of individual producers. In short, OPEC does not appear to be a cartel. The trappings of a cartel are absent, other than the frequent price conferences. There are no prorationing and policing mechanisms in effect; nor is there agreement about how they should be accomplished if they were needed.

This view of OPEC has important implications for the behavior one can expect in the future. It means that OPEC has yet to demonstrate that it has the ability to obtain the coordination necessary to support the monopoly price should pressures arise which would threaten to unravel the benefits acquired in the 1970s. Accordingly, there are conditions under which expanded production from OPEC is to be expected.

This possibility becomes apparent when OPEC behavior is considered under conditions in which crude prices fail to rise for a prolonged period. If production and prices are constant, export revenues are constant. However, as explained earlier, revenue 'requirements' in the next period depend on a markup over the previous period's 'requirements' in order to accommodate rising expectations and increased absorptive capacity. Depending on the rapidity with which expenditures expand, it might take only a few years for expenditures to catch up with receipts. As this point, pressures arise to draw down liquid foreign assets, and then to increase revenues via increased crude oil production. If OPEC is unable to construct and police a prorationing agreement - and there is no tangible evidence that it can do so - competitive output expansion would commence creating downward pressures on prices. As discussed in Section V below, there are reasons to believe that this scenario might arrive by the early 1980s, provided there is no major disruption which takes a significant amount of production off the market.

In Sections III and IV which follow, OPEC behavior since 1970 is reviewed against this conceptual background. There appears to be evidence in support of the model presented. Section V evaluates implications for the future.

## III OPEC BEHAVIOR, 1970–74

At a minimum, a theory of OPEC behavior must be able to explain why the price of oil quadrupled in 1973–74. This is a particularly challenging task for those who assert that the world oil market is competitive. Proponents of the competitive view (Johany, 1978; Mead 1979) argue that this turbulent period witnessed a fundamental reassignment of ownership rights and control of production policy from the multinational oil companies to the producer states. As the rapacious policies of the multinationals were abandoned in favor of policies that paid proper attention to conservation goals and the welfare of future generations, the constriction of output which followed led to the restoration of the price to a much higher but nevertheless competitive level.[15] If this argument is correct, then one need search no further for an explanation of OPEC stability, since there are no monopoly profits to be competed away, and hence nothing to challenge the level of prices. However, this explanation must confront many economic studies which indicate that the world price since 1973–74 contains a large element of monopoly profit.[16]

The alternative explanation offered here recognizes that in the early 1970s there occurred a transfer of control from the companies to the countries. The attendant modification to property rights can explain part of the price increase. But of far greater importance is the fact that in the period 1970–74, a series of events unraveled in an unplanned, uncoordinated fashion which elevated the price considerably above competitive levels. Once established, this price yielded such an enormous increment to revenues in relation to the ability of the producers to absorb them domestically that the proclivities of individual producers to capture a greater share of the monopoly rents through output expansion were severely attenuated in several important cases. This explains why the price structure did not collapse to previous levels.

Indeed, what is remarkable about the 1970–74 transformation is that few of the key changes were achieved by OPEC countries acting together. Generally, one or a few governments drove the bargains and OPEC subsequently ratified the results. Of enormous significance was Libya's successful attempt to negotiate higher prices with the companies. Libyan pressures were severe and included threats of nationalization and enforced reduction in output.[17] Ghaddafi received some encouragement but no tangible help from Algeria and Iraq, but because of the peculiar market conditions prevailing at the time, Ghaddafi prevailed. His success can be attributed to a combination of factors. First of all, the 1967 Arab-Israeli War caused the closure of the Suez Canal and the interruption of the 'Tapline' (the oil pipeline that carries oil from Saudi Arabia to the Mediterranean). Both events served to raise freight rates from the Gulf substantially. Secondly, the Biafra War stopped oil production in Nigeria. Thirdly, new environmental regulations in Europe made the low sulphur Libyan crudes especially desirable. As a result of these factors there was a strong demand for the shorthaul low sulphur Mediterranean oil. Fourthly, a large quantity of Libyan oil was produced by 'independents' who had no alternative sources of supply to honor their previous contracts and to keep their refineries in operation. Competition among the majors and independents prevented the companies from presenting a unified front.

The terms negotiated by Libya were generalized to other OPEC countries in the Tehran and Tripoli agreements of 1971. These agreements were designed to raise the revenues per barrel and also to stabilize them in real terms. However, the devaluation of the US dollar reduced the real price of oil to the producers, thereby challenging the sanctity of the agreements, since posted price escalators had been specified in US dollars. An additional threat to the agreement came from enhanced market demand, especially in the United States, as domestic consumption began to outstrip production at a quickening rate. In addition, the integrated multinationals became increasingly concerned about the extent to which the participation of host governments in their major concessions would affect the availability of crude for their downstream operations. As a consequence, they began reducing their outside sales of crude oil, which increased the competitive pressures on less integrated refiners.

Spurred by these considerations, Iraq led a move at the OPEC Vienna Conference in June 1973 to scrap the Tehran and Tripoli agreements, but the effort failed. By September 1973 all OPEC countries were prepared formally to request a revision of the price agreements and new negotiations with the companies to revise the Tehran agreement opened on October 8 in Vienna. On October 6 Egypt and Israel went to war. On October 16 the ministerial committee representing the six Gulf States of OPEC, including Iran, decided to negotiate no further. The governments henceforth posted their own prices, thus completing the transfer of control over pricing policy, taxes, and production to the producer states. New posted prices were announced which embodied a 70 percent increase for Gulf crudes (from \$3.01 to \$5.12 for 34° API Arabian Light).

The output and destination restrictions imposed by the Arabs on October 27, 1973 further tightened the market for oil and, in particular, for oil free of destination restrictions. Spot prices soared, which led some OPEC countries, especially Iran, to demand that the posted price match the spot price. The Saudis resisted the increase, on the grounds that the high prices reflected the embargo situation. A compromise was reached on a posted price of \$11.65 a barrel for 34° API Arabian Light. Thus, the posted price was quadrupled from where it existed before the outbreak of the Arab-Israeli War.

The transfer of oil policy from the companies to the host countries would explain at least a portion of this price increase since some concessionaries had been producing as if there was no tomorrow; but while this conflicted with underlying conservation aspirations of several producer states, it was encouraged by others such as Iran, which had ambitious development plans. In short, fear of nationalization may have led some companies to produce at higher rates in the 1960s, thereby contributing to the downward drift of prices in that period. Accordingly, the ownership changes brought about in 1970–74 may account for some part of the price increase. More important, however, is the fact that with demand very insensitive to price changes in the short run, the embargo sent prices rocketing. Once flooded with additional revenues it became both possible and convenient for the producers to cut back production while sanctimoniously proclaiming conservation objectives. There was no proclivity to cheat because internal budgetary needs were being satisfied.[18] In short, the nature of the market and the goals of the key producers were such that a quadrupling of the world oil price could be engineered and sustained with the minimum of collusion. More explicit treatment of this phenomenon as well as competing views are offered for the post-embargo period in Section IV below.

## IV OPEC BEHAVIOR, 1974–80

The classical cartel of the economics textbooks raises price by restricting output. The restriction of output is a result of a concerted and coordinated action on the part of cartel members. Price generally does not act as the rationing mechanism which allocates sales among the cartel members. Rather, sales are allocated among cartel members on the basis of a quota or prorationing system which is agreed upon by cartel members. The quota system may be specified in terms of percentage market share, physical units of output, assignment of particular customers or regional markets, or some combination of all of these arrangements. The basis for the quota system is typically the historical market share or the producing capacity of the individual cartel members. In the classical cartel there is a strong incentive for members to cheat on the cartel price. Cheating by one of the cartel members initially increases that cartel member's market share at the expense of the other members of the cartel. The cheating may take the form of secret price concessions, enhancement of product quality, special credit terms, etc. But as cheating, particularly price cheating, is detected, other cartel members first attempt to attenuate such behavior but the lack of effective policing and disciplinary measures typically leads producers to retaliate in kind to protect their monopoly profits. The result is a violation of the quota system, a scramble for market shares, and the collapse of the cartel. In the classical formulation, this is supposed to be the fate of all successful cartels. Why has it not happened to OPEC?

A satisfactory theory of OPEC behavior must be able to explain why cheating has not driven the price down to competitive levels in the post-embargo period. One explanation is that the monopoly profits are just so huge that every member recognizes the importance of solidarity and tacitly refrains from cheating. But the opposing argument seems just as plausible. If monopoly profits are huge, the incremental profits and therefore the incentives to cheat are also huge for an individual producer. Another explanation is that the multinational oil companies prorate output for the OPEC states, thereby minimizing the amount of coordination needed at the national level. Others have postulated that by agreeing to agree on just one price - the price of the marker crude - the process of collusion is greatly simplified and cartel stability is thereby secured. A close examination of OPEC, however, would seem to indicate that it has few if any of the hallmarks of a classical cartel. OPEC has no prorationing mechanisms or agreements, a chaotic pattern of pricing, and unstable market shares.

Consider pricing. OPEC attempts to administer prices rather than output. As discussed below, it does not limit total production or control the market share of the member states. Attempts at price administration are focused on a single type of crude, the marker crude, which is currently Saudi Arabian Light, 34° API. Efforts to administer the entire price structure to take account of crude oil quality and location differentials have never been successful. Rather, the OPEC meetings attempt to determine the price of just *one* particular kind of crude, the marker. Each producer is then free to set differentials for their own crudes at whatever level seems appropriate. In essence, this means that each and every producer - OPEC member or otherwise - has complete liberty over its pricing decisions, subject of course to market acceptance. There is no mechanism to solicit and police agreements over 'appropriate' differentials – a near impossibility to determine objectively.

Not surprisingly, OPEC's pricing structure has become increasingly chaotic. Whatever pricing uniformity existed in earlier years has evaporated. By February 1980 four distinct tiers of prices could be recognized (Table 3.4). The chasm between Saudi Arabia and the rest of OPEC had widened in 1980 to the point where some Middle East crudes were $7.00 per barrel more than the benchmark Arabian Light, and African crudes were $10 a barrel more.[19] The dividing line between the various pricing policies pursued by individual producer nations cut across any geographical or commercial considerations, and appears to reflect political decisions.

One of the most intriguing aspects of the pricing regime which has emerged is that Saudi Arabia has consistently attempted to moderate any increase in the world price of oil, and has underpriced its oil on the market. Saudi Arabia has stated that it will cut back output if and when the 'radicals' exercise pricing restraint. Furthermore, on several occasions the Saudis have increased crude oil production in order to moderate increases in the world price. A very important question in terms of understanding the behavior of OPEC is the motivation for this behavior. One interpretation, and the one favored by most economists, is that the Saudis, being net wealth maximizers, recognize

Table 3.4 *The Widening OPEC Crude Oil Price Split in 1979–80*

| | *Selling Prices* | | |
|---|---|---|---|
| | *Feb. 1980* | *Dec. 1978* | *Total Rise* |
| The 'benchmark' | | | |
| Arabian Light-34 | 26.00 | 12.70 | 13.30 |
| The 'moderates' | | | |
| Venezuela Medium-24 | 25.93 | 12.39 | 13.54 |
| Venezuela Light-31 | 28.90 | 13.54 | 15.36 |
| Kuwait-31 | 27.50 | 12.22 | 15.28 |
| Iraq Basrah Light-35 | 27.96 | 12.66 | 15.30 |
| The 'intermediates' | | | |
| Indonesia Sumatran-34 | 29.50 | 13.55 | 15.95 |
| Abu Dhabi Murban-39 | 29.56 | 13.17 | 16.29 |
| Qatar Marine-36 | 29.23 | 13.00 | 16.23 |
| The 'radicals' | | | |
| Iranian Light-34 | 32.87 | 12.81 | 20.06 |
| Nigerian Bonny-37 | 34.20 | 14.12 | 20.08 |
| Libyan Zueitina-41 | 34.72 | 13.90 | 20.82 |
| Algerian Saharan-44 | 37.21 | 14.10 | 23.11 |

that higher prices today will provide incentives for conservation and the development of substitutes in consuming nations, all of which will serve to shrink the market for crude, especially in the long run. Saudi Arabia, having the largest reserves and the highest reserves to production ratio, has the most to lose from such a policy.

An alternative interpretation advanced in this chapter is that the Saudis do not have a very accurate estimate of the price at which substitutes will become a threat because the large scale development of substitutes depends on political decisions to be made in the importing countries, and especially in the United States. Furthermore, whatever threat from substitutes exists lies in the distant future, given the long gestation period for the development of most synthetic fuels. In any case, so long as their oil can realize the cost of production for substitutes, the economic welfare of the Saudi people is guaranteed for the foreseeable future.[20] Rather, the more immediate concern of the Saudis is that higher oil prices will create greater instability in the West and especially in the Gulf since the additional revenues occasioned by higher prices can be used to fuel the military machines of various 'radical' producers. Furthermore, by appearing as the moderating element in the market, the Saudis are able to cement their alliance with the West and particularly the USA, an alliance which the Saudis consider essential for their survival. With the Gulf exposed to external and internal threats, this view posits that the oil policy of the conservative Saudis is driven primarily by political considerations, at least in the short run.

Now consider output. Does OPEC orchestrate production restraints? OPEC has not attempted production prorationing since the abortive attempts of the 1960s. Indeed, having failed to observe OPEC exercising any form of prorationing mechanism, some observers have imputed the function to the multinational oil companies. Professor Adelman's view (Adelman, 1977) is that:

> The oil cartel nations do not face the difficult, divisive and probably impossible task of setting production shares. They need not meet together to quarrel over the gain of one being the loss of another. The governments need only agree that they will sell the bulk of their output through the oil companies, whose margins are too narrow to allow any but trifling price cuts . . . so long as nearly every government refrains from independent offers, the total offered in the market by the companies adds up to the total demanded by consumers at the going price. (p. 5)

This statement seems to suggest that formal prorationing is being conducted for OPEC by the companies. Blair is more explicit on this point, claiming that 'if the OPEC members have neither agreed on standards of allocation nor set up the necessary allocating machinery, the responsibility for curtailment necessarily rests with the companies'. In particular (Blair, 1976):

> The initiative for the 1975 production cutbacks came from the oil companies. Had it not been for the cutbacks, the market would have been flooded with 'distressed' oil, OPEC would have broken down, and oil prices would have fallen sharply. That none of this occurred stems from the nature of the relationship between the companies and the countries. (p. 293)

It is indeed the case that OPEC has never been able to devise and enforce a formal program for allocating production. Although there have been assertions that the companies perform this function, evidence has yet to be produced to support this claim. The analysis here indicates that unless a prolonged soft market occurs, production prorationing is not necessary to sustain the world price since the proclivities to cheat by the key producers are attenuated by limited absorptive capacity.

A form of voluntary prorationing does, however, occur. For instance, in the first half of 1980 supply cuts of 200,000 B/D, 350,000 B/D, and 500,000 B/D, were announced by Venezuela, Libya, and Kuwait, respectively. Algeria announced a 15 percent reduction in contract volumes in March 1980 citing 'conservation' as reason. Of course, there is a delicate line between output restriction based on 'conservation' considerations and output restrictions based on the desire to contrive a scarcity and drive up the world price. The difference is that whereas output restrictions for monopoly purposes will require explicit or tacit collusion, output restrictions for conservation reasons need not. Conservation among OPEC producers appears to be motivated by political and absorptive capacity considerations. Further, oil production policy is considered a matter of national sovereignty, and not a matter which can be determined by OPEC.

The nation with the largest oil reserves and the largest export volume is Saudi Arabia. One interpretation of OPEC stability in the 1974–80 period is that Saudi Arabia is the dominant producer adjusting world supply so as to maintain the cartel price. This 'dominant producer' monopoly model bears some similarities to reality, but there are very important differences. In particular, Saudi Arabia has in no sense fine-tuned the world market to the degree that, say, the Texas Railroad Commission fine-tuned the US domestic market before the removal of import controls. Indeed, Sheik Yamani has announced on several occasions that Saudi Arabia will bear no more than its fair share of production cuts should prorationing appear necessary. Furthermore, Saudi Arabia is severely constrained in its ability to administer the world price: it could not sustain the OPEC price on the face of large scale discounting by other members, and it cannot restrain price increases once it is producing at full capacity, as it was through much of the 1980–81 period. While Saudi Arabia undoubtedly has more influence on the pricing structure than any other producer, it does not appear to have used this influence with the sole objective of maximizing the net present value of its oil reserves. It has given considerable weight to important political objectives, and the pricing policy prevailing at any point very much reflects the political and economic context of the time.[21] Thus to the extent that it is able to restrain the excess of the radicals, Saudi Arabia is able to capture political benefits from the oil importing nations. By helping to moderate price increases, it not only denies revenues to other oil producers, but receives credit for the savings across the total volume of OPEC exports, not just those exports emanating from Saudi Arabia. Clearly, Saudi Arabia has enough leverage over price to make other producers share the costs of the political favors it wins abroad.

In this regard, consider some of the reasons advanced by Saudi Arabia for pursuing a policy of moderate price increases. Sheik Yamani has stated that Saudi Arabia's reasons for advocating a moderate price posture during the two-tier pricing episode following the Doha meeting were related to Saudi fears of renewed economic recession in the West, Communist gains in Italy and France, and concern over the shaky situations in Britain, Spain, and Portugal. 'The Kingdom is very anxious to prevent any deterioration of the world economy because that would hurt us financially in view of the large investments we have in the Western countries. To increase oil prices now would also expose us to certain political repercussions because we are bound to the West by clearly defined political interests.'[22] Yamani has also expressed fears about Soviet designs on Mideast oil, making it clear that he considered the economic prosperity and goodwill of the West and particularly the United States to be important to countering Soviet ambitions. These worries have been sharpened by the invasion of Afghanistan, and help explain why the Saudis and several other Gulf producers have from time to time adapted policies which involve economic costs in the form of forgone profits. For instance, following the Iranian revolution, Saudi Arabia, Kuwait, and the UAE increased their production by 3 MMB/D to compensate for the Iranian shortfall 'earning in the process unwanted revenues'. The Saudis took this initiative 'in order to avoid disaster in the West'. With the outbreak of hostilities and loss of production as a result of the Iran–Iraq War, the Saudis again increased output in order to relieve pressure on the price. Such behavior is not consistent with the pursuit of economic self-interest narrowly defined.

In short, the limited absorptive capacity cum target revenue view of OPEC provides a viable explanation of the underlying production policies of OPEC. However, additional political factors intervene as well, at least in the case of Saudi Arabia. The Saudis have a large enough market position that their production policies are under close scrutiny from the West. Given the precarious military and security conditions which prevail in the Gulf, Saudi production decisions are exposed to an additional set of political influences stemming from its delicate relation with the United States. These pressures will remain so long as tensions in the Gulf are high, which appears to be the case for the foreseeable future.

## V OPEC BEHAVIOR, 1981–2000

OPEC behavior in the future will depend on economic and political considerations, as it has in the past. The analysis to follow focuses principally on the economic factors.

One distinct possibility is that the conventional wisdom - that OPEC production will remain about where it is today - will prevail. According to one leading expert, there is 'growing recognition that the Saudis and other Persian Gulf producers will not expand their production to meet the demand growth that would be generated at today's energy prices' (Manne, 1979, p.2). There is in fact a possibility that because of political disruption or because of rapidly increasing demand, prices might tend to move upward rapidly, moderated only by the possibility of Saudi attempts to restrain them.

However, the above is by no means a foregone conclusion. As the demand for crude oil, and especially OPEC oil, begins to moderate in the early 1980s a window of opportunity for consumers will open, should demand for OPEC oil remain stationary for several years, or at least long enough to enable OPEC expenditure growth to encounter a revenue constraint. There are several powerful reasons suggesting that this may occur. One is the fast clip with which OPEC expenditures have grown in the past; another is the perception that financial assets invested abroad now yield attractive real returns; a third is the impact on consumption of the previous crude price increases. Each will be briefly examined.

Table 3.5 summarizes rates of growth of oil income and government expenditures within OPEC. It is quite apparent that expenditures have grown almost as fast as oil revenues, a situation also reflected in Table

3.6, which shows that the foreign assets of selected OPEC members are modest relative to annual oil revenues.

Clearly, if oil revenues remain constant for several years, past rates of expansion of government revenues cannot be sustained. The data in Table 3.6 indicate that foreign assets, relative to annual expenditures, are not enormous, amounting at the end of 1979 to about 2 years for Saudi Arabia, 4 years for Kuwait, 2 years for Qatar, 18 months for Iran and Iraq, and less than a year for Libya. By 1981, Iraq and Iran had largely exhausted their liquid assets. To the extent that some foreign assets are illiquid, as with Kuwait, the period would be shorter. This is not to imply that the OPEC producers would necessarily deplete their liquid assets before adjusting production upward. The point is merely that the foreign assets of the OPEC producers are not enormous relative to the levels of government expenditure and their annual increments.

Confronted with zero increase in oil revenues, OPEC governments could undoubtedly slow the rate of increase of government expenditure, without creating economic hardship. However, it is generally easier to win friends and placate enemies at home and abroad when prosperity is increasing rather than decreasing. Obviously, the degree to which this is true will vary accordingly to society's value structure and the desire for consumption of imported

Table 3.5 *Rates of Growth of Oil Income, Government Expenditures (annual averages, in percent)*

| *Country* | *Oil income*[a] | *Government expenditure*[b] | *Time period* |
|---|---|---|---|
| Kuwait | 31.2 | 38.2 | 1972–79 |
| Libya | 29.8 | 20.0 | 1972–78 |
| Qatar | 116.0 | 50.0 | 1972–77 |
| Saudi Arabia | 46.5 | 42.7 | 1972–79 |
| UAE | 43.7 | 39.0 | 1972–79 |
| Algeria | 41.5 | 22.3 | 1972–79 |
| Ecuador | 49.6 | 20.0 | 1972–79 |
| Indonesia | 57.7 | 38.9 | 1972–78 |
| Iran | 43.1 | 40.5 | 1972–78 |
| Iraq | 65.0 | 35.7 | 1972–79 |
| Nigeria | 36.9 | 33.6 | 1972–78 |
| Venezuela | 20.0 | 24.3 | 1972–78 |
| Simple average | 48.41 | 33.76 | 1972–79 |

[a] *OPEC Bulletin*, January 1981.
[b] *OPEC Statistical Bulletin*, 1979.

commodities. Islamic fundamentalists might be heartened by a slacking of economic development, but professional and commercial groups are likely to see it in a different light. In short, if the world

Table 3.6 *Selected OPEC Producers Foreign Assets, Oil Revenues, and Total Foreign Assets as a Percentage of Annual Revenues, 1979 (in US$m.)*

| | *Foreign assets*[a] | *Revenues from oil 1979* | *Foreign assets divided by annual revenues 1979* |
|---|---|---|---|
| Iraq | 17,500 | 11,008 | 1.589 |
| Iran | 15,900 | 21,766 | .730 |
| Kuwait | 40,000 | 9,575 | 4.177 |
| Libya | 6,344 | 9,490 | .668 |
| Qatar | 4,267 | 2,315 | 1.843 |
| Saudi Arabia | 75,000 | 38,736 | 1.936 |
| UAE | 12,707 | 8,658 | 1.467 |
| TOTAL | 171,718 | 101,548 | 1.691 |

[a] *Middle East Economic Survey*, April 18, 1980.

price of crude were to stay constant for several years, pressures for increased revenues, and hence production, would mount in various OPEC countries. This might be fueled by changing expectations with respect to the attractiveness of foreign investments. As mentioned earlier, foreign investment has never been embraced enthusiastically by any OPEC producer because the notion of a rentier nation is not compatible with national pride. However, the evident failures and inefficiencies of many domestic development programs may ameliorate the stigma attached to 'coupon clipping'. Couple this with the generous real returns on financial assets experienced during the early 1980s and widely held perceptions that oil in the ground is better than money in the bank will start to crumble. This is especially likely if the price of crude oil stays flat into the mid-1980s.

There are demand secondary reasons to expect such an outcome. In Chapter 2 Professor Adelman indicates that the change in energy consumption from 1973 to 1978 is consistent with a long run elasticity for total energy of around −.75 and a nine-year half-life, and Griffin *et al.* employ −.73 in Chapter 6. Furthermore, the reduction in oil consumption evident by 1981 can be explained by the original price jump of 1973–74, the point being that the effects of the first price increases have been only about halfway felt, and the 1979 impact is only just beginning to register. If economic growth at the abnormally slow rate of 2.5 percent per year experienced since 1973 is coupled with the continued decline of energy and oil demand per unit output, total energy consumption will grow only very slowly. This means that oil consumption throughout the period will be flat, and may drift downward very slightly. If similar trends are experienced elsewhere in the world, then 'for the first time in 120 years, oil is no longer a growth industry and is probably a declining industry'.[23] Meanwhile, the supply of non-OPEC oil is inching upward, which means that OPEC exports must decline, or the price must fall. In 1980 they were about 26 MMB/D, below the 1973 peak of 31 MMB/D. If OPEC exports fall to around 20 MMB/D annually, the pressures for output expansion will be considerable. Considering that OPEC has yet to demonstrate that it has the wherewithal to delimit competitive output expansion, two decades of constant real prices is a strong possibility – in the absence of a supply disruption of significance. This is all the more likely if Iran and Iraq restore production to pre-1978 levels.

## VI CONCLUSION

This chapter has advanced the somewhat novel position that the world price was elevated above competitive levels by good luck and special circumstances. Individual OPEC nations forged gains which might not have been obtained had collective action been necessary. Furthermore, competitive output expansion has been absent not out of recognition of mutual interdependence among producers, but simply because internal economic and political circumstances have so far displaced desires for higher current revenues. A backward bending supply curve for OPEC oil is thereby postulated, at least for the short run. This indicates that the world price is subject to considerable instability, with modest increases (decreases) in demand translating into sizable price increases (decreases) in the absence of Saudi ability and willingness to stabilize the market.

Whereas the possibility of upward instability is commonly recognized, the possibility that OPEC production may expand significantly is usually dismissed by most OPEC analysts. The conceptual view advanced here indicates that competitive output expansion is possible if real prices can remain constant long enough to permit expenditures to press up against revenue constraints in countries that have excess capacity or the ability to add to it at low cost. Modest output expansion by OPEC will suffice to keep real prices constant through the 1980s and perhaps to the year 2000, in the absence of a serious oil supply disruption.

A number of policy implications follow from these observations.

The most conspicuous is the need for policies to further reduce demand for imported oil. Sustained demand reduction can be expected to foster competitive output expansion by producers, and hence lower prices. Since OPEC constitutes the world's residual supply for energy, energy conservation and production enhancement anywhere in the world is likely to reduce the demand for OPEC oil.

The need to reduce imports is all the more apparent whenever the market is tight, such as in periods of disruption or rapid economic growth. Because of the inelastic and perhaps even backward bending nature of the aggregate supply curve when exporters are attaining their expenditure targets, demand reduction policies are essential to curb price hikes and the associated wealth transfers from consumers to producers. A tariff on imported oil ought be implemented in all consuming nations to reduce oil consumption and to switch demand toward domestic crudes and alternate fuels. The tariff should be permanent and ought not be reviewed until the world price has dropped to competitive levels. Supplementary tariffs coupled with redistributive mechanisms (such as reduced withholding taxes in the United States) ought be imposed immediately in the event of a supply disruption.

Another implication is that sovereign states should avoid the temptation to restrict investments abroad by OPEC states since factors which encourage the false notion that oil in the ground is a good investment tend to discourage production expansion in producing countries. It might even be worthwhile to provide instruments designed to meet OPEC objectives for a guaranteed return. However, as discussed earlier, the principal reasons why certain Arab states are cautious about investing abroad are political, and these concerns cannot be relieved by the verbal guarantees of host countries. Thus, foreign investment policies should be liberalized worldwide to facilitate diversified long-term investment by oil exporting nations. European and Japanese capital markets needs to be receptive to investments of all nationalities.[24] The implementation of policies along these lines should hasten the dissipation of OPEC's monopoly profits, and the restoration of a more equitable international economic order.

## APPENDIX

### A Backward Bending Supply Curve for OPEC Oil

The backward bending supply curve is more than a theoretical curiosity; it has found useful application in labor economics. It may also have applicability to the export of exhaustible natural resources by developing countries where the natural resource in question is the dominant export industry. With respect to oil, there is growing evidence that a number of important OPEC producers first determine their domestic investment requirements and then set production goals that will reach this target. This notion can be formulated in terms of investment theory as follows. A marginal efficiency of investment schedule exists which displays the investment opportunities open to an economy. There are a few projects which yield high returns, but as the rate of return requirement is lowered, more and more projects become viable. If planners pick a threshold rate of return level $\bar{r}$ below which investment projects will be rejected, then the level of desired domestic investment requirements $I^*$ can be readily determined (see Figure A3.1). Once investment needs are determined, an isorevenue curve showing different combinations of prices and quantities for the

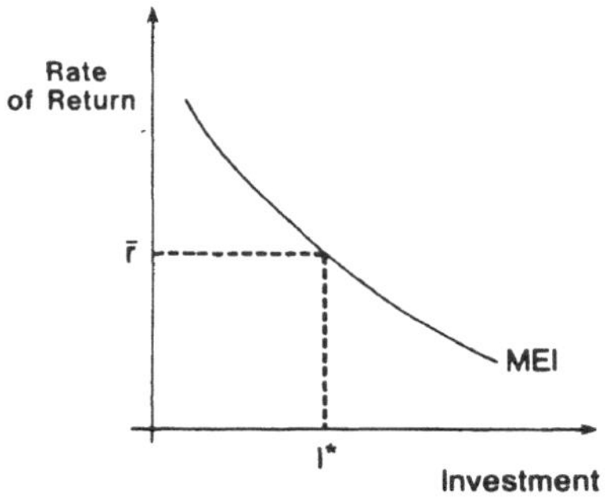


Figure A3.1 *Marginal efficiency of investment function (MEI).*

natural resource can be constructed. This is drawn to show export earnings equal to $I^*$ (it is assumed that the natural resource in question is the only export commodity and that export earnings constitute the only source of investment funds). In Figure A3.2 this is represented by the hyperbola $P=I^*/Q$. The isorevenue curve also represents the individual producer's supply curve for production levels involving less than full capacity production.

If the demand curve facing the individual producer is $d_X^0$, the country's desired production is $q^*$ (Figure A3.3). $d_X^0$ has some slope because of quality and location differences among producers of the natural resource. However, because this producer is small relative to the market, $d_X^0$ is shown to be highly elastic.

If the producer has a very high target income, as represented by $I^{**}$ (Figure A3.4) then production is adjusted to the technical maximum $\bar{q}$, but revenues fall short of the target in the amount of the cross-

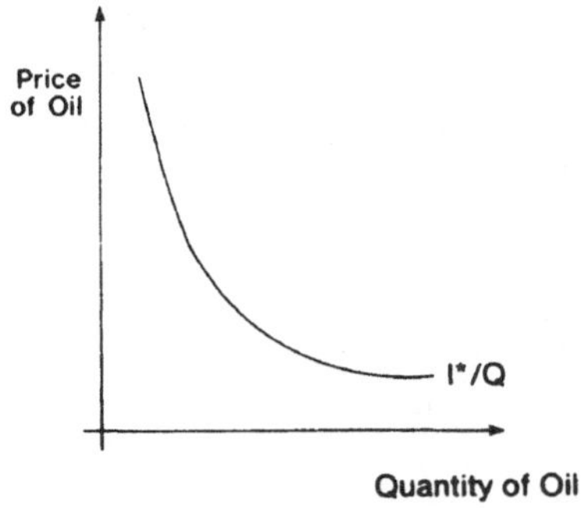


Figure A3.2 *Isorevenue graph/supply curve.*

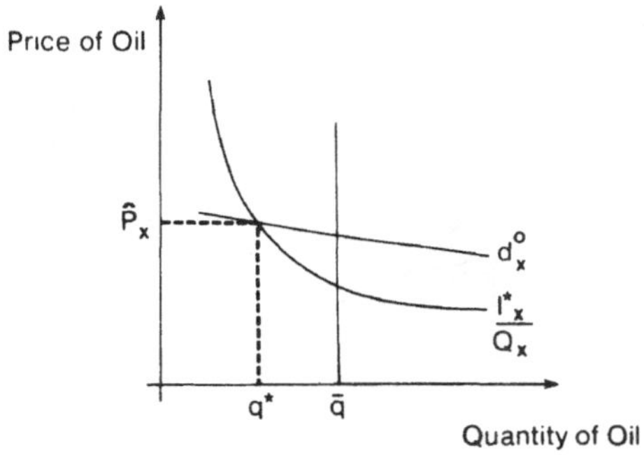


Figure A3.3 *Individual demand curve for small producer (country* x*). Desired revenue* I* *results in production* q* *less than technical maximum* q̄.

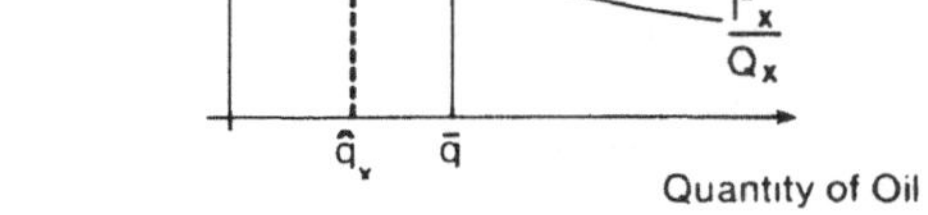


Figure A3.4 *Individual demand curve for small producer (country* x*). Desired revenue* I** *results in production equal to technical maximum* q̄.

hatched area. If revenues always fall short of the target then production will remain at capacity $\overline{q}$, irrespective of the price. The supply curve will be vertical at $\overline{q}$, at least in the short run. The producer's only hope of reaching his revenue target is if world supply and demand intersect in a fashion which raises the world price, and hence $d^0_X$.

It is some importance to observe that the target revenue approach implies a backward supply curve for prices above those needed to support the target revenue. If the world price increases, and the isorevenue curve is stationary (Figure A3.5a), then production falls. Output can increase in the absence of a price decline if the marginal efficiency of investment and hence the isorevenue curve moves to the right (Figure A3.5b). If there are a sufficient number of countries with backward bending supply curves, then the market supply curve will

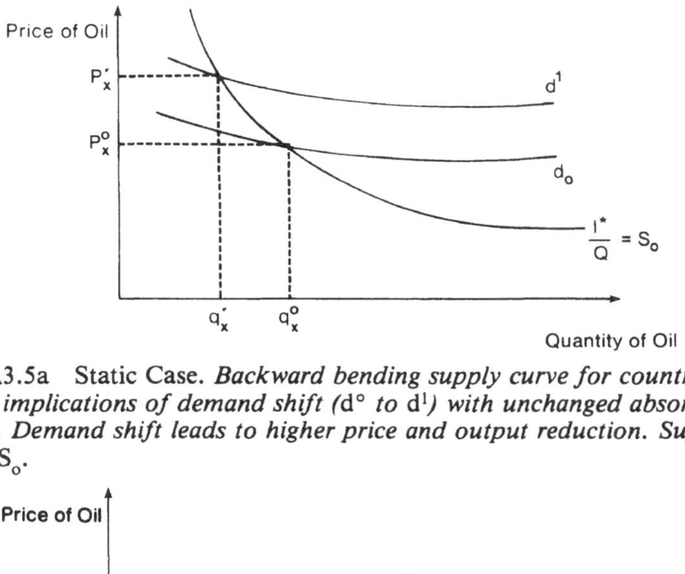


Figure A3.5a Static Case. *Backward bending supply curve for country* x *showing implications of demand shift (*d° *to* d¹*) with unchanged absorptive capacity. Demand shift leads to higher price and output reduction. Supply curve is* $S_o$.

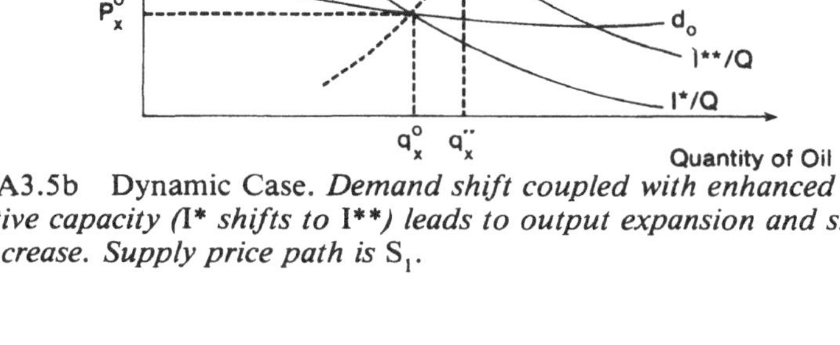


Figure A3.5b Dynamic Case. *Demand shift coupled with enhanced absorptive capacity (*I* *shifts to* I***) leads to output expansion and smaller price increase. Supply price path is* $S_1$.

take the same shape. This is represented in Figures A3.6a and A3.6b. If world demand is inelastic (as in Figure A3.6b) the price is unstable in the range over which the supply curve is backward bending. An initial price at $P_a$ will collapse to the lower equilibrium $P_b$ or may spiral up above $P_a$. The more realistic case, where demand is elastic (as in Figure A3.6a), results in a stable equilibrium. However, the near parallelism of the supply and demand curve means that an increase in demand will generate a large price increase. Conversely, a decrease in demand will generate a large price decrease.[25]

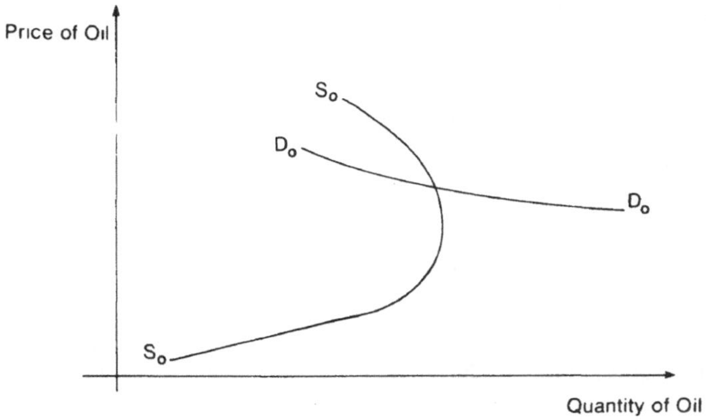


Figure A3.6a *World supply and demand (elastic demand).*

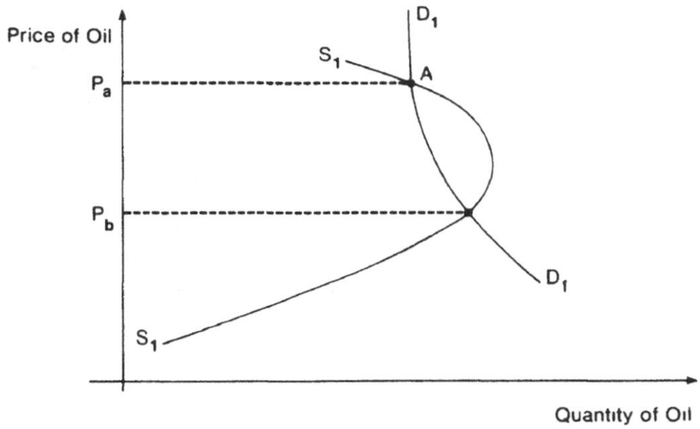


Figure A3.6b *World supply and demand (inelastic demand).*

## NOTES

1 Nobel Laureate Milton Friedman reflected the views of many in the economics profession when in 1974 he predicted the collapse of OPEC and world crude prices.

2 Further definition of what is meant by 'needs', 'requirements', and cheating is provided below.

3 A backward bending supply curve implies a negative relationship between current price and current production. This construct is developed more fully in Section II and in the Appendix.

4 The political risks are not just the expropriation risk but the internal political risk stemming from the negative reaction of Islamic fundamentalists to a perception that conservation is being abandoned in favor of profligate policies which serve the interests of the consuming nations.

5 Quite simply, export receipts at existing levels of production have been more than adequate to meet current budgetary requirements. The loss of Iranian production in 1978–79 is partly responsible for this outcome.

6 As explained below, this will be assisted by the new investment environment of the 1980s which promises to yield real returns to producing country investments.

7 As one Kuwaiti observed, 'Kuwait was losing a large amount of money in its portfolio investments as a result of rising inflation and currency depreciation. Oil in the ground is better than continuously depreciating cash' (Al-Sabah, 1980, p. 35).

8 It is not uncommon for OPEC ministers to appeal for lower production on grounds that (1) development is a slow process and (2) that the real price of oil will 'increase'. Sheik Ali of Kuwait, for instance, has advocated that OPEC countries adopt a 100:1 reserve to production ratio, arguing as follows (*MEES*, October 29, 1979):

> The attitude of the OPEC countries, amongst them Kuwait, on production should be to adopt a reserves to production ratio of 100:1, for two important economic reasons. The first is that economic development is a very long process. It is not a five- or ten-year plan, but takes hundreds of years. Change does not come overnight or from one year to another. It is a question of social development and of changing certain concepts. The second reason is that we will always be in need of oil supplies, and the real price of oil will increase over the next 20 years and, for that matter, in the first part of the next century. (p. 4)

9 *Wall Street Journal*, October 13, 1981.

10 As discussed below, placating foreign consumers and political allies in the West may provide a reason.

11 As discussed below, oil producing nations with small oil revenues (as a percentage of GNP) or large economies, such as Mexico and Nigeria, are unlikely to have a backward bending supply curve in the relevant range of prices. The opposite can be expected for several OPEC nations, including Libya, Kuwait, Abu Dhabi, and Qatar, which have low or moderate absorptive capacities. In the Saudi case, I argue that there proclivities are attenuated by political considerations.

12 *Petroleum Intelligence Weekly*, May 12, 1980, p. 4.

13 *Middle East Economic Survey*, October 29, 1979.

14 This might appear to be a contradiction in that monopoly rents are attached to a market structure which is 'competitive' in the sense that each producer is independently pursuing its own 'best' interests. However, the result is the same as would be obtained under monopoly, namely, the existence of substantial economic rents, where per barrel rents are the difference between price and the sum of

marginal costs and user costs determined on reasonable discount rate, elasticity, and reserve assumptions.

15 See Chapter 1 for a discussion of the property rights perspective.

16 See Chapter 1 for a discussion of monopoly profits in a Hotelling framework.

17 Ghaddafi ordered a cutback in output for the companies operating in Libya. Occidental Petroleum was forced to cut back by more than 50 percent at which point it capitulated by agreeing to pay 30¢ more per barrel by raising posted prices from $2.23 to $2.55 per barrel for 40° API Arabian Light.

18 This is notwithstanding that if wealth maximizing were the goal, each producer will have powerful incentives to cheat.

19 The chasm had narrowed by October 1981 as OPEC appeared somewhat closer to an agreement on a unified price of $34 a barrel.

20 Unless, of course, synthetics turn out to be a decreasing cost industry, which appears highly unlikely.

21 This view is quite at odds with Professor Adelman, who has argued as follows (Adelman, 1977):

> Nor shall we be distracted by the alleged political objectives of the oil producing nations, which are served perfectly by economic gain. There is no sacrifice or trade off of one or the other. The more money one has, the better position one is to make friends and put down enemies. (p.28)

22 *Middle East Economic Survey*, June 19, 1978.

23 See Adelman, Chapter 2 of this volume.

24 Consuming countries should also recognize that the removal of developmental bottlenecks (such as skills and transportation facilities) in key OPEC states will also serve to increase production to the extent to which it enhances domestic absorptive capacity.

25 Consider the effect of a shift in the demand curve. Let $p(\lambda)$ be a solution of $kD(p) = S(p)$. We have $\hat{p} = \hat{p}(1)$. The elasticity of $\hat{p}$ with respect to $\lambda$, for $\lambda = 1$, is equal to $1/(E_s - E_d)$ where $E_s$ and $E_d$ are the elasticities of supply and demand. On the backward bending part of the supply curve, $E_s > 1$; on the downward part, $E_s < 1$. Hence, assuming a constant elasticity of demand, the elasticity of $p$ with respect to $\lambda$ is higher in the downward sloping part of the supply curve.

# 4 Modeling OPEC Behavior: Economic and Political Alternatives

THEODORE MORAN

From a knowledge of the economics of the oil market, is it possible to predict how OPEC, in general, or its largest and most important members, in particular, will act in formulating price and production policy? Can one construct a model of rational behavior, the constraints on behavior, and counterproductive behavior on the part of the petroleum exporting nations? What decision rules do the principal players follow? What patterns or consistencies are likely to emerge over time?

This chapter critically reviews attempts to construct a framework for modeling OPEC behavior based on the calculation of maximizing economic benefits, and suggests an alternative political decision rule to account for the conduct of energy policy by OPEC's largest member, Saudi Arabia. From an examination of the key points in the determination of OPEC prices between 1973 and 1981, it will be demonstrated that not only does the political decision rule explain Saudi actions better than an economic optimizing approach but also that no economic formula alone, such as tightness of energy markets or concern for the health of the Western economies, is consistent with Saudi behavior. Finally, this chapter traces the implications of this mode of Saudi policy formation for the course of future OPEC prices, and suggests why the US government is systemically constrained in influencing Saudi oil policy in the direction of greater 'moderation' in periods of weak as well as tight energy markets.

## I THE ECONOMIC MODELING OF RATIONAL MONOPOLY

The distinguishing characteristic of most attempts to model OPEC behavior is the contention that economic self-interest provides the best predictor of the cartel's price and production decisions over time.

Political decisions, to be sure, may produce short-term deviations from the economic path. And destructive events, such as wars or revolutions in the Middle East, may like hurricanes remove capacity from production, and generate unexpected jumps in the price of petroleum. But in general the most likely price for OPEC oil will be the best price for OPEC oil, that is, the price that maximizes the economic benefits received by the cartel. Clearly, a price that is too low deprives the members of revenue; but so does too high a price, by inducing conservation, stimulating substitution, and damaging the economic health of the consuming countries. A price policy that is too timid will prove self-denying; a price policy that is too aggressive will prove counterproductive. When OPEC governments do set the wrong price, from ignorance or intent, the feedback from world oil and financial markets will demonstrate the cost they incur from their own actions. Over time, this argument concludes, economic self-interest will pull them toward the optimal price path.

Such a contention, eminently plausible and easily accepted, provides a powerful tool for the analysis of OPEC behavior. In its simplest form, it reduces the forecasting problem to the task of tracing the price path that would be chosen by a rational monopolist.[1] On the one hand, the revenue stream must be adjusted to reflect the impact of the price chosen at each moment on the structure of subsequent supply and demand. On the other hand, the revenue stream must be discounted at a rate that reflects income lost by postponing earnings rather than taking and investing them in the present. By estimating elasticities of supply and demand, however, and assigning an appropriate discount rate, the monopoly pricing problem is readily solved.

The situation is slightly more complex, however, in the case of an exhaustible resource like oil. The existence of a fixed stock of a commodity has an important independent impact on the structure of the monopoly pricing decision. Any resource derives its value from the prospect of being extracted and sold. If left in the ground, however, a nonrenewable resource can also generate an implicit return for its owner by appreciating in value. Thus, to the analysis of elasticities of supply and demand, and the determination of a suitable discount rate, the rational monopolist in the oil industry must add considerations about the rate of exploitation that balance oil in the ground and money in the bank.

## Modeling OPEC Behavior

For this, OPEC modelers go back to the classic work explicating the economics of exhaustible resources published by Harold Hotelling in

1931.[2] Hotelling views resources as assets just like any other asset. They can yield a return to the owner either as current dividend or as capital appreciation. To achieve equilibrium in asset markets, total returns must be equal.[3] As a consequence, the value of a resource in the ground must be growing fast enough to equal the value of future sales for a producer to be willing to leave it there. Hence, the choice between exploiting or conserving the resource will depend on whether he expects its net price to increase exponentially at a rate equal to his discount rate on future earnings.[4] If he forecasts a higher rate, he should delay production and enjoy the capital appreciation of the assets in the ground. On this calculation will be based his decisions about building more, or less, capacity.[5]

Ultimately, increasing scarcity will price even the most vital resource out of the market until the last barrel or ton produced is the last barrel or ton in the ground. More realistically, resource exhaustion resembles the squeezing of juice from an orange, with the total amount extracted dependent upon the effort expended and always a little left behind.[6] To simplify the exhaustion problem for modeling purposes, most energy modelers now use the idea of 'backstop technology,' which places a ceiling, albeit a high ceiling, on the price of the original commodity via photovoltaics, breeder reactors, synfuels, and controlled nuclear fusion.[7] The specification of a supply function based on backstop technology takes the place of speculation about geological exhaustion.

This backstop technology supply function, added to the behavior of energy markets along the way to reaching the backstop, bounds the price path for both competitive and monopolistic producers. The gain to producers from the successful cartelization of a nonrenewable resource comes from the manipulation of the rate of exploitation, and the consequent shape of the price trajectory, over the life of the resource. As Sweeney, Stiglitz, and Pindyck demonstrate, the price

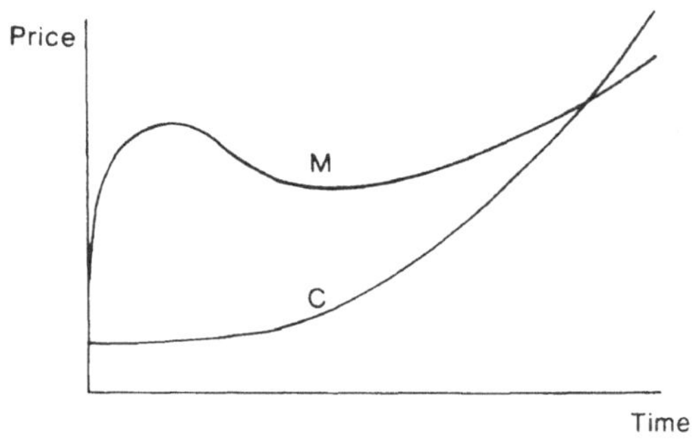


Figure 4.1 *Monopoly and competitive pricing. M = monopoly price trajectory; C = competitive price trajectory.*

path of the monopolist will be initially higher and subsequently lower than the price path in the competitive case (see Figure 4.1).[8] The monopolist produces his rent by holding output off the market in such a way as to maximize the present value from the combination of the flow of resources produced and the stock of resources left in the ground for later production.

The contention of this mode of analysis is that the exogenous variables of supply and demand for energy (on the demand side, elasticities of price, income and substitution, and on the supply side, elasticity of energy outputs not under OPEC control), the cost of backstop technology, the extent of nonrenewable reserves possessed by OPEC, and OPEC's discount rate determine both the opportunities and the constraints on the cartel and offer the best predictor of price trends over time.

## Cartel Behavior

While useful in sketching a general path of aggregate self-interest, the rational monopolist approach suffers from representing the OPEC cartel as if the members are motivated to behave over time as a single unified actor.[9] In reality, the individual governments of OPEC have differing 'rational' economic interests depending upon domestic social pressures, revenue needs, alternative sources of export earnings and fiscal income, hard currency, financial assets, and geological reserves. Hence, they have different discount rates for present versus future earnings and different strains or pains associated with holding spare capacity or not developing additional capacity. Ultimately the members of OPEC have different preferred price and production paths for the exploitation of their petroleum reserves.

The principal simplifying technique to cope with this diversity of economic preferences has been to divide OPEC into subgroups according to time preference for oil revenues and resource endowment. The most ambitious attempt to model OPEC interaction is the work of Hnyilicza and Pindyck.[10] They divide OPEC into two groups: saver countries (Saudi Arabia, Libya, Iraq, UAE, Bahrain [sic], Kuwait, and Qatar) and spender countries (Iran, Venezuela, Indonesia, Algeria, Nigeria and Ecuador). The groups differ according to two variables: high or low immediate cash needs and large or small proven reserves, with a reserve: production ratio of 5.7 for the savers and 2.8 for the spenders. The extent of immediate cash needs is reflected in the discount rate used to compute the sum of discounted profits (2 percent per year for savers, 10 percent per year for spenders).

Hnyilicza and Pindyck use the theory of cooperative games

developed by Nash to simulate the interaction between the two groups.[11] This approach develops a bargaining frontier bounded by the outcomes that would result if negotiations were to break down and competitive (noncooperative) behavior were to ensue. Nash's solution along this frontier is based on the premise that the 'relative power' between the two groups is given by the utility of a solution at the point of no agreement. That is, a formula for cooperation may be found in the willingness of each side to accept a division of the net incremental gains from cooperation in proportion to the losses they would incur by not making an agreement.

The mere existence of such a game-theoric 'solution' is of potentially enormous significance. It is clear, rational, even intuitively 'just'.[12] It can provide not only a guide to accommodation but also a focal point for reestablishing stability within the cartel if cooperation breaks down.[13] Like other principles of coordination in mixed-motive games (e.g. the mini-max solution to the prisoner's dilemma) it is not expected to determine behavior in every instance but may be a good predictor of outcomes over a long series of interactions.

But the resolution of divergent OPEC interests according to the Nash formula is not ultimately plausible in the real world, as Hnyilicza and Pindyck discover. Using the Nash framework, they find that in all cases the optimal outcome involves a 'bang-bang' solution that assigns zero production to saver countries for an initial period of time and zero output to spender countries for the rest of the time. This follows directly from the different discount rates. With saver-country oil losing its value less rapidly, it should be kept in the ground while spender-country oil is produced first.

Admitting that this 'may be a politically infeasible solution', Hnyilicza and Pindyck are left to require the analyst who uses their framework to assign the division of output among the cartel members purely arbitrarily; for example, they themselves hold market shares constant at their average historical value. When market shares are fixed *a priori* and only price can be chosen optimally, the resulting solution is close to the monopoly solution. When the market shares are allowed to fluctuate, however, the optimal price path varies widely (e.g. 10 percent to 1000 percent) with considerable welfare losses to one or the other group of countries – as much as $600 billion over forty years to the spender countries alone in 1975 dollars.

Thus, after a promising sortie into game theory, no plausible formula emerges for resolving the internal conflicts of self-interest within OPEC. In the course of the attempt, however, the analysis underscores two important facts: first, that within the optimization framework the actual price path for OPEC depends heavily upon the relative balance in cartel policy formation among the individual

OPEC governments; and second, that the stakes for these individual actors in approximating their optimal price and production policy are extremely large.

Hnyilicza and Pindyck conclude that 'when output shares are open for policy dicussion, OPEC members will have a lot to argue about, and any resulting optimal policy will depend considerably on the relative bargaining power of the two groups of countries'.[14]

A second attempt to examine internal OPEC behavior using an economically optimal approach is that of Eckbo.[15] He divides the cartel into three different member categories. The first could expand output substantially but only at a lower price. This is the 'hard core' of the cartel (Saudi Arabia, Kuwait, UAE, Qatar, and Libya). The second produces close to potential and has a strong need for current income. These are the 'price pushers' (Iran, Venezuela, Algeria, and Gabon). The third category has smaller reserves than the core, has a strong need for current income, but produces at a slower rate of depletion than the 'price pushers'. This is the 'expansionist fringe', which would like other members to accommodate it with a higher market share (Indonesia, Nigeria, Iraq, and Ecuador).

Eckbo begins, like Hnyilicza and Pindyck, by constructing an optimal price path for OPEC acting as a rational monopolist. To penetrate beneath the unified actor framework, Eckbo 'subtracts' first the price pushers and then the expansionist fringe from the cartel, leaving an optimal price path for the 'hard core' of the cartel. This illuminates, in disaggregated form, the contrasting route along which economic self-interest should drive the member governments (see Figure 4.2).

Once again, given a low discount rate and a large resource base, a country like Saudi Arabia should be motivated to choose a lower price

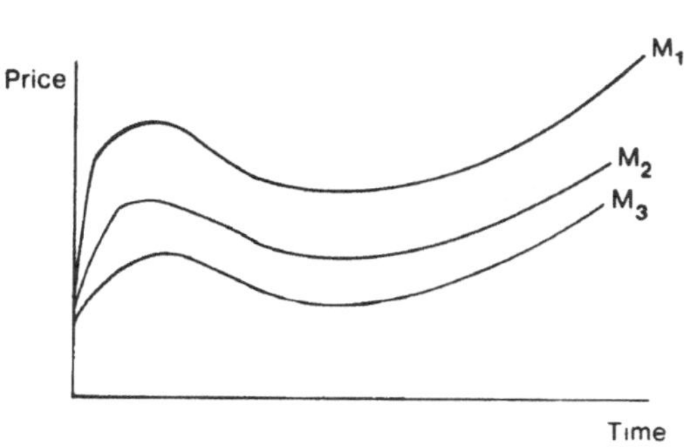


Figure 4.2 *Alternative optimal cartel prices.* $M_1$ *= monopoly price trajectory (OPEC aggregate);* $M_2$ *= monopoly price trajectory minus 'price pushers';* $M_3$ *= price trajectory of 'core' led by Saudi Arabia.*

trajectory because it is less attracted to quick profits than the 'pushers' and more concerned about the robust state of future demand. In addition, the country's huge reserve endowment should stimulate a greater concern about the outcome; to the extent others push the OPEC price from what would be optimal from the Saudis' point of view, the losses to the Saudis are proportionately greater.[16]

These calculations confirm that there is a substantial divergence between preferred prices for the Saudi-led core and the hawkish pushers (e.g. a price level 60 percent higher for the latter in 1983 than for the former), with great stakes for each group riding on the outcome of the bargaining among them. Rather than trying to discover a game-theoretic formula to model the interaction of the groups, however, Eckbo merely constructs scenarios with varying balance among the groups (e.g. 'price-pusher dominance', 'cartel core dominance'). Like Hnyilicza and Pindyck, he leaves the choice of scenarios and the specification of the outcome to arbitrary selection by the reader.

Other authors who focus on the dynamics within OPEC follow roughly the same methodology as Eckbo, contrasting the optimal price paths for the cartel as a whole (or for the more 'militant' members) with the preferred course of the 'conservatives', especially Saudi Arabia.[17] To the observation that the Saudis have an economic interest in oil prices much lower (30 to 60 percent lower) than that which would be optimal for the militants, Willett and Singer, for example, add two further points: first, that higher prices will require the Saudis to bear a disproportionate share of the required production cutbacks for the cartel as a whole; second, that the large stake of the Saudis in the success of the cartel will make it risk-averse against the threat of chiseling and possible collapse that higher prices would produce.

Thus, the economic optimization approach consistently emphasizes that self-interest should propel the Saudis to pull the price path for OPEC substantially lower than that which the more hawkish members desire. But it also points out that the penalty the hawks will have to pay if hypothesized Saudi preferences prevail will be large; that the contention among the divergent economic interests is consequently bound to be intense; and that there is no intuitively logical or rational formula based on economic self-interest for adjusting the conflicting interests of the cartel members.

## Uncertainty in Energy Forecasts

That the outcome of intracartel bargaining makes a great difference as to what the preferred price path should be and that there is no game-theoretic formula available that might lead to a 'rational' outcome, deal a strong blow to the idea of economic optimization as a satisfactory framework. But there is a more fundamental critique of the economic optimization approach. The approach's applicability to the real world depends upon the ability of self-interested actors to identify the price and production paths that will render their activities counterproductive. This ability, as the preceding analysis of intra-OPEC bargaining has shown, is by no means a sufficient condition to determine OPEC prices, but it is a necessary condition for cartel actors to determine where self-interests lie. Moreover, a well-defined picture of the impact of any given OPEC action on energy markets and on the economic vitality of the consuming states might allow the producers with the largest stake in the outcome to turn back the persistent push of others to take advantage of short-term inelasticities by an appeal to the longer-term common good of the cartel.

How precise a guide has the analysis of energy markets provided for the calculation of optimal price and production strategies? How broad a range of actions does the analysis of supply and demand for petroleum permit?

In fact, of course, the forecasts for energy markets have varied widely since the fourfold price rise of 1973–74, from Milton Friedman's or Thomas Enders's predicting that the initial oil price jump would bring forth huge supplies of alternative energy sources, to the Central Intelligence Agency's projecting large and enduring 'gaps' between supply and demand.[18] Three years after the embargo six major estimates of demand for OPEC oil in 1980, then five years hence, still diverged by 33 percent, and estimates of price diverged by 50 percent.[19] As will be seen below, the range in calculating the impact of a particular OPEC action has persisted, with eleven major energy models forecasting a spread of 29 percent in demand for OPEC oil and 47 percent in price of OPEC oil for 1984 as the consequence of the 1979–80 price jump.[20]

The discrepancies in estimating how energy markets might behave in response to any particular OPEC decision might not matter so much if there were prompt and effective feedback mechanisms that could bring OPEC back on course toward behavior as a rational monopolist when the price path strayed too far from optimal. But the feedback loop is in fact weak and obscure. The major industrial countries, especially the United States, have been (and may again be) likely to react to higher oil prices in a perverse way, that is, through price controls that mask the impact of OPEC decisions or through an entitlements program that subsidizes the importation of foreign oil to keep 'undeserved' profits out of the hands of domestic producers. By the time data are available to show the impact of an OPEC oil price decision it is very hard, economically, to demonstrate authoritatively how much of a loss in Gross National Product (GNP) growth, increase in unemployment, fall in the value of the dollar, or rise in inflation, has been due directly to the oil price effect.

Moreover, improvements in estimating capabilities have proceeded slowly. On the supply side, some of the forecasting difficulties have sprung from disagreements over the resource base for hydrocarbons.[21] Others have come from the uncertainty surrounding the size and development rate for new fields, such as those in Mexico or China (Yamani, at one point, identified China as one supplier whose output might swamp OPEC). There have been swings of optimism and pessimism about overcoming the environmental and technological obstacles to the production of alternatives such as coal, nuclear power, and solar energy. Finally, there have been problems in estimating the response of producers to the incentive of higher prices. Hendrick Houthakker predicted in 1976, for example, that the United States would become a net oil exporter if prices stayed above $14, largely because his model extrapolated historical patterns of natural gas development into the future.[22] Subsequent forecasts were more bearish on natural gas. In 1980, however, Herman Kahn and William Brown again pointed to natural gas supplies as the key to lowering demand for OPEC oil.[23]

On the demand side, forecasters have been bedeviled by similar difficulties in modeling the response of industrial economies to price rises when the econometric deviations of the central relationships, such as elasticities, come from historical data far removed from contemporary figures (e.g. the demand response being the same when oil moves from $20 to $25 per barrel as when it moved from $5 to $10); or when calculated on the base of reverse interactions (e.g. response of demand to reduced oil prices being an accurate predictor of response to demand to increased oil prices).[24] Thus, a survey of six of the most sophisticated energy models in 1977 produced a variation in the key demand variable, elasticity for primary energy, ranging from 0.2 to 0.9.[25] A broader survey of twenty-four modelers in 1980 produced estimates from 0.3 to 0.9.[26]

As a result of the great uncertainties about how the major oil importing countries may respond to any given OPEC policy, even when many of the relationships are specified arbitrarily, there has been a broad divergence among outputs.[27] A comparison of eleven of the most widely regarded energy models in 1980 revealed that even for the reference case in which oil prices ($27 in 1980) and demand elasticities (0.4 for primary energy and 0.6 for crude oil), as well as economic growth rates and energy supply elasticities, were given endogenously, the predictions for 1984 ranged from $25 to $37 per barrel for crude prices, 24 MMB/D to 31 MMB/D for OPEC exports, and $200 to $500 billion for OPEC revenues.[28] When two of the central variables, demand elasticities for primary energy and for crude oil, were arbitrarily allowed to drop to five-eighths of the reference case - 0.25 for primary energy and 0.38 for crude oil - the crude price prediction for 1984 ranged from $26 to $67 per barrel, OPEC exports from 22 to 31 MMB/D, and OPEC revenues from $275 to $769 billion. Thus, the variations both *among* the models and *between* the cases have continued to be very great.

It is not surprising, therefore, to find that OPEC leaders show the same skepticism about economic analysis at key moments in their decision-making as the rest of the world. Before an important OPEC meeting in 1976, examined below, the Shah referred to a prestigious, detailed study by the Petroleum Industry Research Foundation that did not support his position as 'laughable . . . We have our own statistics'.[29] Or Yamani, when asked about an analysis by OPEC's own Economic Commission, commented to newsmen, 'Do you want me to confuse you, as I was confused. There are all kinds of figures - you know when the economists get together they have that remarkable ability to produce figures and play with them . . . And in the economic report you always find Saudi Arabia having a different view, or a different methodology, or whatever it is'.[30]

In short, the idea of economic rationality and the pursuit of economic self-interest have not been able to play the role of precise guide to, or constraint on, the determination of OPEC oil policy. Rather, there has been considerable leeway for the OPEC states, or a particular OPEC government, or individual ministers at the subnational level, to suggest alternative courses of action without being met by a decisive demonstration that the damage to national economic interests would be overwhelming.

## II THE POLITICAL MODELING OF SAUDI OIL DECISIONS

The OPEC countries are thus faced with a broad spectrum of oil policies that can be defended as rational, or criticized as counter-productive, from the point of view of their medium- to long-term economic interests. How do their policymakers choose among them? On what basis do the key OPEC governments act within the broad latitude given by energy economics?

This section looks at the crucial moments in the determination of OPEC policy with a focus on the actions of the cartel's largest member, Saudi Arabia. It argues that an operational code of advancing Saudi political priorities, while minimizing hostile external and internal pressures upon the kingdom, explains Saudi behavior better than the economic optimizing model does. No economic calculation alone, such as strength or weakness of oil markets or the state of the world economy, can account for Saudi Arabia's use of its petroleum base to shape the course of OPEC's price path. Insofar as Saudi Arabia has exercised price leadership within the cartel, the decision to do so has required a deeper dimension of policy-making which sprang from Saudi political priorities, especially concern about the structure of an Arab-Israeli peace agreement and the status of East Jerusalem, and from the constellation of domestic and international political forces upon the kingdom.

What is price leadership? In the literature on oligopoly behavior in natural resources, price leadership refers to the explicit enunciation of future offering prices by the self-appointed 'leader' backed by a production policy that supports the announced offering prices, and accompanied by the maintenance of enough spare capacity to discipline cheaters or dissenters within the oligopoly and to protect against unforseen output crises.[31] It is this leadership role that energy modelers understood when they hypothesized that the economic self-interest of the kingdom would lead it to pull the OPEC price path in the direction of 'modernization'.

In the Saudi context, there may be some latitude for a national style that prefers to build consensus discreetly behind the scenes rather than appearing to impose one's will in public. But the history of intra-OPEC bargaining since 1973 shows that price leadership means the same to the Saudis as it does to oligopolies of private firms, namely, the willingness to insist on a given price path and fashion production policy so as to take markets away from other producers who do not agree with them. Whether to exercise such leadership constitutes the 'high politics' of Saudi energy policy. There have been six occasions since the end of the 1973–74 embargo when the issue of Saudi leadership has come to a head.

## Events since 1973

### *1 Phantom oil auction of 1974*

In the second half of 1974 the world economy was falling into the worst recession of the postwar period. At the annual meetings of the World Bank and the International Monetary Fund, Britain, France, and West Germany warned that the world might be facing 'an economic crisis paralleling that of the 1930s'.[32] Inflation was running at 15 percent worldwide. Spare capacity within OPEC was nearly 8 MMB/D. The key question was whether the cartel had overshot the mark with the fourfold jump in oil prices in 1973–74. Yamani argued that it had, and publicly proposed that Iran join in a 20 to 25 percent reduction in the posted price, from $11.65 to $9.00 per barrel, to enable the world to recover and 'avoid a depression'.[33]

*Modeling OPEC behavior.* The United States was using both carrots and sticks in its relations with the Saudis. On the one hand, Secretary Kissinger was trying to lead the West on what Europeans and Japanese feared was a 'confrontational course' with OPEC. He told the UN General Assembly that 'the delicate structure of international cooperation, so laboriously constructed over the last quarter century, can hardly survive . . . What has gone up by political decision can be reduced by political decision'.[34]

On the other hand, the United States negotiated a broad cooperative agreement with the Saudis as the beginning of a special relationship with the kingdom. The economic and military agreement, according to a US spokesman, should give Saudi Arabia a reason for expanding production.[35] In July, Secretary Simon inaugurated the US-Saudi Joint Commission in Riyadh with a further sweetener, special issues of US Treasury securities to absorb oil earnings without driving down the interest rate. Putting his arguments for letting the market carry oil prices lower to financial and planning authorities as well as Sheik Yamani, the Oil Minister, and Dr Abdul Hady Taher, the Governor of Petromin, Simon got the leadership of Saudi Arabia to announce publicly an auction of approximately 1.5 MMB/D in the open market, and accept whatever price the conditions of surplus would produce.[36] This would amount to a unilateral lowering of the OPEC marker.

The reaction of the other OPEC members was immediate and intense. Even the low-population states, Kuwait and the UAE, spoke out against lowering oil prices in a way that 'would destroy the current system of oil prices'.[37] Faced with 'considerable pressure' from its neighbors, there was, according to the *Petroleum Intelligence Weekly*, 'clearly a considerable division of opinion' within the Saudi circles.[38] Just as abruptly as they had announced the auction, the Saudis canceled it and transferred the price debate back into the OPEC arena. Here the Shah led the counterattack against Saudi Arabia, insisting that the cartel's principle be that producer revenues should not be allowed to decline (i.e. prices or taxes should rise if volumes dropped).[39]

As the December OPEC meeting approached, the Saudis sought a compromise between the demands of consumer governments for price relief and the demands of its OPEC neighbors for revenue maintenance. This included 'as a gesture to the West' a formal reduction in posted prices of 40¢ per barrel. But the price cut was more than offset by royalty and tax increases of approximately $1.05

added to the cost of crude. Thus, the kingdom endorsed a net price 65¢ per barrel higher than before and absorbed the largest share of the shrinkage of total OPEC exports. Saudi production fell to 6.5 MMB/D by February, 24 percent lower than the level of 1974. This Saudi reduction averaged 1.4 MMB/D compared to 1974, whereas the Iranian drop was only 0.6 MMB/D.

The *Oil and Gas Journal* editorialized, 'As for the Saudis, their actions . . . destroyed any illusions the world may have had about them as seekers of lower crude prices'.[40] Yamani later insisted that if the USA wanted the kingdom to use its production capacity on behalf of moderation, even during the most adverse economic conditions, the US government would have to play a more active role in relieving pressure from Iran.

*2 'Standoff' increase of 1975*

For the first three quarters of 1975 OPEC production ran at fewer than 27 MMB/D, down 17 percent from the similar period in 1974. Saudi production averaged 7.1 MMB/D, or 1.4 MMB/D below the nominal 8.5 MMB/D ceiling and 4.7 MMB/D below capacity. There was widespread price discounting by Abu Dhabi, Libya, Nigeria, Iraq, Algeria, and Ecuador, and market squabbling (the Iraqi market share was up 17 percent).[41] The world economy was at the bottom of the recession with industrial activity at minus 3 percent in comparison to 1974. Inflation averaged 14 percent worldwide. The US position, enunciated by Secretary Simon at the IMF and Secretary Kissinger at the UN, was that a price increase 'would seriously jeopardize the balance upon which global economic recovery now depends'.

As the September OPEC meeting approached, the Saudis favored a freeze or 'small increase' to help 'assist the emerging signs of recovery' - a small increase would mean a price decline in real terms. The OPEC majority, however, favored a price rise if only to make their own crudes, discounted by extending credit or absorbing difficulties, more competitive *vis-à-vis* the Saudis. The Shah, as usual, was among the more hawkish, claiming that a 35 percent increase would be justified. His regime faced a $4 billion trade deficit and was obliged to seek foreign loans.[42] The question for the September meeting in Vienna was whether the Saudis would allow prices to rise, despite the risks that that would pose for reigniting the recession and the subsequent impact that would have on the kingdom's market share.[43]

The Vienna meeting produced, according to the *Middle East Economic Survey*, 'what was possibly the worst bout of internal tension' the organization had experienced since 1964.[44] The sides deadlocked, with Yamani offering a 5 percent increase and Jamshid Amouzegar of Iran insisting on 15 percent. At that point Yamani dramatically left the conference, flew to London for better communications with his country's leadership at Taif, and returned with the assertion that if the majority backed the Iranian plan, Saudi Arabia would freeze prices and let production rise to the limits of its capacity. Iran called the kingdom's bluff with the suggestion that it would be quite happy if Saudi Arabia went its own way with the others free to determine pricing policy and reduce output as they wished.

The result was a compromise at 10 percent. Amouzegar announced that he 'was very satisfied'.[45] Yamani said the settlement 'was the best I could get', an assertion that was accurate only so long as the Saudis were unwilling actually to use their 4 MMB/D in spare capacity to enforce either the preservation of their own market share or the maintenance of a cartel price more attuned to the weakened global economy.

*3 Doha price split of 1976–77*

In the fall of 1976 there was a broad expectation that the December OPEC meeting in Doha would result in a sizable price rise.[46] Industrial activity was up 8 percent over 1975 in the market economies. Inflation was down slightly to 11 percent. Demand for OPEC oil was 4 MMB/D higher, at 30.5 MMB/D, than at the time of the Vienna meeting. On the moderate side, the Petroleum Minister of UAE, Mana Saeed al'Otaiba, had specified 10 percent as what his government would propose. Among the hawks, Iraq, Qatar, and Venezuela called for 25 percent; the Shah, a 'very reasonable' 15 percent. The Saudis were unusually ambiguous, even by Saudi standards, about their position.

During the US presidential campaign, Jimmy Carter had made an issue of tougher bargaining with OPEC on oil prices, raising the possibility of withholding arms to gain leverage with the producers, and specifying that he would consider a future embargo 'an economic declaration of war'.[47] On the other hand, Carter was a candidate not deeply beholden to traditional Democratic Party structures, contributors, and foreign policy positions. By December the Saudis decided to fashion an oil policy 'that will serve political purposes similar to those for which the kingdom led the oil battle in October 1973'.[48]

Yamani proposed a zero increase, Iraq 26 percent, Iran 15 percent. Again, Yamani left in the midst of a session, flew to Jiddah for consultations with Crown Prince Fahd (King Khalid, considered less pro-American than Fahd, was absent in Geneva), and returned with a 5 percent compromise, representing a small price decline in real terms on an annual basis. When the others, led by Iran, balked, Yamani refused to negotiate further, lifted the 8.5 MMB/D production ceiling, announced that production could expand up to maximum installed capacity of 11.8 MMB/D, and indicated that the kingdom would take another look at expansion plans then scheduled to go to 14.2 MMB/D by January 1981 and 16.2 MMB/D by December 1982. In justifying the kingdom's dramatic action, the Saudi Oil Minister noted particularly the 'great panic' in Israel over the Saudi decision, and made it clear that 'we expect the West to appreciate what we did, especially the U.S.'.[49]

Iran's exports dropped 32 percent from 6.6 MMB/D to below 4.5 MMB/D immediately. Iraq predicted its exports to be down by an equal percentage, from 2.4 MMB/D to 1.7 MMB/D. Both counterattacked fiercely. Iraq accused Saudi Arabia of acting in the service of imperialism and predicted that its plans would not succeed 'under the pressure of the liberation forces in Saudi Arabia'.[50] The Shah called 'overproduction' by Saudi Arabia 'an act of aggression against us', said the Saudi actions were 'not in accord with King Khalid's views', and dispatched his Minister of War to discuss oil policy with the king.[51]

Saudi oil production never reached the 10 MMD/B average Yamani targeted for the first quarter. In the latter part of January 1977, bad weather reduced loadings at Ras Tanura. Iran's Kharg Island seemed to offer better protection against the adverse winds, however, raising the Shah's exports from 4.5 MMB/D to 5.1 MMB/D.[52] The bad weather stretched into February, giving Iran 6.2 MMB/D while holding the Saudi exports to 8.9 MMB/D. By June, the Saudis agreed to raise their price another 5 percent to reunify OPEC.[53]

Later in 1977, the Saudis did in fact 'take another look' at their capacity expansion plans. Seeing how large amounts of capacity exposed them both to pressure from consumers to use it and resentment from neighbors that they might actually do so, and taking 'no more Dohas' as their motto, they decided to revise their capacity program downward, not upward![54]

### *4 Aborted price confrontation of 1977–78*

The first meeting in May 1977 between President Carter and Crown Prince Fahd paved the way for the Saudis to reunify OPEC prices but it elicited the 'hope', expressed by both leaders, that prices would remain frozen 'through 1978 at least'. There was considerable uncertainty throughout the second half of 1977 about whether this hope would be realized.[55] Eleven of the thirteen OPEC members were calling for a sizable increase. Yamani and Otaiba, the UAE Oil Minister, stressed that OPEC unity – to avoid 'another Doha' – was the 'primary concern' of the two countries.[56] The Saudi Foreign Minister, Prince Saud, announced publicly that some increase was justified.[57] Industrial activity in the market economies was 5 percent higher than in 1976. Inflation was holding steady at 11 percent. Demand for OPEC oil was running between 30 and 31 MMB/D.

In a move potentially strengthening the US position, the White House was preparing to present Saudi Arabia's request for F-15 fighters before the US Congress. But powerful members of both House and Senate were strongly opposed. It was clear that the Carter Administration would have to work hard from the fall of 1977 through the spring of 1978, argue persuasively about the tangible value of the friendship of Saudi Arabia, and call in a lot of debts in Congress to gain approval for the sale. The Saudis were scrupulous in denying linkage between the oil price freeze and the F-15s; the US Ambassador to Saudi Arabia, John West, made the point on the Hill for them.[58] The key question was how the Saudis would react in the December OPEC meeting in Caracas if they were caught in a squeeze between the United States and their powerful neighbor, the Shah.[59]

The choice never had to be made. Facing his first meeting with Jimmy Carter in November, and knowing that a review of his military needs and his human rights record would be high on the agenda, the Shah unilaterally announced one week before coming to Washington that he would be just a spectator at the December OPEC Conference. After a sympathetic reception of his arms requests, he went further and stated his support for the freeze.[60] A repeat of Doha became a nonevent. President Carlos Andres Perez of Venezuela led a personal campaign to turn the US oil freeze campaign around, including trying to postpone the meeting in his own capital, but to no avail.[61]

### 5 *Production crisis of 1979*

The loss of Iranian exports preceding and following the fall of the Shah provided the setting for the 'second oil crisis' of 1979–80. But the precipitating event and the actions that sustained the panic buying came, in fact, from the opposite side of the Gulf. A precise date for the onset of the crisis, insofar as one can be fixed, would have to be January 20, 1979, four days after the departure of the Shah. Throughout the fall of 1978, the shortfall in production due to strikes and disorders in Iran had largely (depending upon how one measures the comparison) been made up for by expanded production by other OPEC members. Saudi production had risen from 8.4 MMB/D in September, Iran's last 'normal' month for oil exports, to 10.4 MMB/D in December, a level roughly maintained through the first nineteen days of January. Then, on the twentieth, Saudi authorities suddenly reimposed a 9.5 MMB/D ceiling on Aramco for the first quarter, measured month by month, which meant a precipitous cutback to approximately 8 MMB/D to meet the ceiling for January.[62] Spot prices soared in a process reinforced when the Aramco parents announced *force majeure* reductions in shipments to third parties and affiliates. Saudi production remained at 9.5 MMB/D in February and March. Following an OPEC meeting at the end of March, at which members promised the representative of the new Iranian regime 'to go back to their earlier production levels', the Saudis cut output to 8.5 MMB/D.[63] This ceiling was not raised until July, when Prince Fahd denounced the Camp David treaty, called publicly on the United States to enter into a direct dialogue with the PLO, and pledged a production level of 9.5 MMB/D in a letter to President Carter, using Ambassador Robert Strauss, the Arab–Israeli negotiator, as the messenger to underscore the political nature of the oil production decision.[64] By then the effective price level for crude had almost doubled.

It is clear that during this period the Saudi leadership was experiencing severe internal stresses. They disliked the Camp David framework and felt President Carter's personal trip to negotiate the Egypt-Israeli peace treaty in March was 'deplorable'.[65] They were under great pressure from other Arab states to distance themselves from the US peace efforts, a pressure backed by threats of Palestinian sabotage against Saudi oil facilities.[66] They told Defense Secretary Harold Brown that without a solution to the Palestinian problem there was no hope of restoring stability to the region.[67] With the shock of the Shah's departure, Soviet encroachments in South Yemen, and uncertainty about US dependability, Saudi leaders showed extreme reluctance to offend either the new regime in Iran or the newly preeminent Iraq.

To help reassure the Saudis, President Carter extended an invitation to Prince Fahd to come to Washington, which Fahd accepted. This was fiercely opposed within the Royal Family with Prince Abdullah (Commander of the National Guard), Foreign Minister Saud, and King Khalid forcing an abrupt cancellation of the trip.[68] While there is no certain explanation for Saudi behavior from January to July, it seems apparent that the Saudi leadership could not or would not build the consensus necessary for an oil policy that would deny higher spot market premiums to its neighbors (the new Iranian regime proved to be the most aggressive price hawk in OPEC) or deprive them of markets, except for the highest political stakes. Even Finance Minister Aba al-Khail, customarily the Saudi leader most concerned about maintaining international economic stability, argued after the second Baghdad conference in March 1979 had condemned Egypt for accepting a separate peace, 'You're asking too much. You're asking us to produce more oil, and to accept your inflation. Yet you don't help us with our political problem in the region. It's not a balanced relationship . . . The question of a comprehensive peace that recognizes Palestinian rights and returns Moslem holy places in East Jerusalem is so important to us, so emotionally felt by us, that it is the core of the problem. Solve that and all other problems disappear. Obviously we would give you more oil'.[69]

The Saudi action of holding the country's price below that of other producers without expanding production only exacerbated the conflicts in the government over oil policy. Production decisions closely tailored to Iranian output kept the market tight; the month-by-month, quarter-by-quarter export determinations fed the uncertainty of buyers, stimulated extraordinary stock-building, drove up spot prices, and made other OPEC members hypersensitive to Saudi moves to relieve the pressure. Moreover, many Saudis complained that the policy of restraint on prices was doing no more than padding the pockets of the oil companies rather than benefiting consumers.[70] Hence, even independent of the Arab-Israeli controversy, there were strong political pressures on the kingdom both to hold back production and to raise prices to the level that the self-induced shortage had created.

Fahd broke through this vicious cycle to the extent of adding 1 MMB/D of supply above the 8.5 MMB/D ceiling, to send to Washington the message that Saudi interests in a comprehensive Arab-Israeli settlement and in the ultimate status of Jerusalem could neither be ignored nor taken for granted.

### 6 *The oil glut of 1981*

The predominant feature of world energy markets in 1981 was the glut of oil, with OPEC exports running at approximately 24 MMB/D (in comparison to 27 MMB/D at the depth of 1974–75 demand). Even so, production was estimated to be 2–3 MMB/D above actual consumption, with the possibility that the capacity lost due to the Iran–Iraq War might gradually come back on-line. The International Energy Agency forecasted a continuing decline in demand to the year 2000.[71] Spokesmen as disparate as Sheik Yamani of Saudi Arabia and Fadhil al-Chalaki, the Iraqi Deputy Secretary General of OPEC, voiced fears that the producers might have pushed oil prices too far too fast.[72]

The global economic picture showed the United States and Japan relatively strong, inflation declining, and the dollar up, with the European countries in weaker straits. As in 1976, there was a new and untried administration in the United States, weighing not only Middle East options but a large arms request from the Saudis for AWACs and enhanced equipment for F-15s.

One month prior to the key OPEC meeting in May, Sheik Yamani visited Washington, disavowing linkage between security and energy issues but dwelling so forcefully on the importance of the Reagan Administration sticking to its arms sale pledge in the face of opposition from Congress that most commentators drew the opposite conclusion.[73]

At the meeting in Geneva, Saudi Arabia was adamant in refusing either to raise prices above $32 per barrel or to cut production from levels above 10 MMB/D unless the others lowered their quotations to a unified OPEC price of $34 per barrel. Both sides held firm. As one of the leaders of the hawks explained, 'we would rather cut our throats than reduce our prices'.[74] And threats were made: the *Middle East Economic Survey* depicted Iran's Deputy Oil Minister Hassan Sadat as 'hinting darkly of the likelihood of "other measures" if the Saudis did not "readjust themselves" in the near future'.[75] But the Saudis would not budge on either price or production. In an attempt to compensate, the rest of the OPEC members took the 'historic decision' to agree to jointly imposed production cuts. But, with the exception of UAE and Venezuela, the newly established ceilings were above actual production levels.

## Price Leadership and Saudi Decisions

The examination of these six key historical episodes, which have determined the direction of OPEC prices since 1973–74, suggests that the Saudis fully understand what price leadership within the cartel means in terms of the hostile reaction from other cartel members and Arab allies. For this reason, they approach such leadership very cautiously, acting most forcefully when there is either political opportunity or political pressure in their relations with the consumer governments, and are easily frightened off.[76] Twice they braved the rancor of their neighbors to use price and production policy to send signals about Middle East and defense issues (1976 and 1977). Twice they backed off from a position of price leadership under pressure from their neighbors and local allies (1974 and 1975). When they exercised price leadership in the 1977 case, they stuck to a personal pledge to the President of the United States, but only after he had neutralized the force of a possible hostile reaction from Iran. When they exercised price leadership in 1981, political and security issues in the Saudi relationship to Washington, as well as economic concerns, hung in the balance.

The evidence not only suggests a behavioral code that can be described as advancing national political priorities while deflecting adverse pressures on the kingdom; it also demonstrates that such a decision rule better explains Saudi decision-making than other proposed rules. The calculation of economic self-interest as determined by resource base and discount rate is not consistent with the array of Saudi actions from raising prices and accepting a smaller market share (1974, 1975), to freezing prices and taking a larger market share (1976, 1977, 1981), to engineering a large price jump but offering a discount to shift the market losses onto others (1979). Nor can Saudi behavior be accounted for by a primary focus on how tight oil markets are prior to the pricing decision.[77] As measured by the ratio of demand for OPEC oil to existing OPEC capacity, prices were raised twice when the market was relatively weak (75 percent capacity utilization preceding the 1974 decision; 72 percent capacity utilization preceding the 1975 decision). Prices were restrained twice when the market was relatively stronger (84 percent capacity utilization preceding the 1976 decision; 78 percent preceding the 1977 decision). Only once, in 1979–80 was there a definite, although not inevitable, market push involved in a price rise; that is, success of the market push was not inevitable had the Saudis willed it otherwise. Only once, in 1981, was there a clear concern for market weakness reflected in a price freeze.

Does the 1981 decision at Geneva represent a fundamental turning point in the Saudi approach to oil decisions?

On the one hand, there was evident preoccupation within the Saudi leadership about allowing the price of petroleum to rise too high at least from the point of view of a larger-resource-base, lower-discount-rate producer. As Yamani explained the strategy to Saudi audiences: 'We do not want to shorten the life-span of oil as a source of energy before we complete the elements of our industrial and economic development, and before we build our country to be able to depend on sources of income other than oil. In this respect, the Kingdom's interests might differ from those of its OPEC colleagues. In OPEC, there are countries that will stop exporting oil before the end of the eighties; for such countries the life-span of oil should not extend beyond that time. But if the life-span as a source of energy ends at the close of the present decade, this will spell disaster for Saudi Arabia'.[78] As he explained it in Washington, 'We think [the rise in oil prices] went too far'.[79]

On the other hand, there was a concern, like the 1975 Doha decision, to get off on the right foot with a new Administration, especially when the American President would have to point to the tangible benefit of the US-Saudi relationship in fighting for a major arms sales package for the kingdom on the Hill.

There is no definite way to separate out the economic and political-security components of the Saudi decision for the 1981 Geneva meeting. They reinforced each other. But the historical record suggests caution in concluding that there was a decisive reorientation toward economic criteria. In 1976 and 1977, in a similar posture toward the Carter Administration on political and security issues, the Saudis stood firm for moderation on oil prices. In 1974 and 1975, in a similar posture toward the question of whether the cartel had overshot the mark, the Saudis acquiesced in the demands of the OPEC hawks. (For an analysis of future Saudi behavior if weak energy markets persist, in the light of conflicting pressures on the kingdom's leadership, see the concluding section of this chapter.)

If the calculation of economic self-interest on the basis of resource base and discount rate is unreliable as a predictor of Saudi willingness to exercise forceful cartel leadership, still less dependable is the state of the world economy. Of the six cases, the Saudis pushed three times for lower oil prices when the global economy was relatively strong and inflation comparatively low: the two-tier split at Doha in 1976–77; the price freeze of 1977–78; the refusal to bow to the hawks in 1981. They backed off from a firm stand on behalf of moderation three times when the global economy was weak and inflation comparatively high: the 1974 phantom auction with the world heading into recession; the 1975 'stand off' increase with the world in a deep trough; the second oil crisis of 1979 with the international economy again weak. This perverse behavior deals a blow to even the most generous formulation of the economic optimization idea, which holds that the extent of Saudi hydrocarbon reserves is so large and the period of managing them and the financial assets they generate so protracted that the Saudis should identify rational management of their resources with the long-term health of the world economy and the strength of its financial institutions. It is equally damaging to the hypothesis of 'interdependence' as a determinant of Saudi policy, namely, that a growing web of financial, commercial, and investor relations leads to a mutually reinforcing perception of the common good on the part of energy importing and energy exporting states.

The operational code proposed here in place of the economic optimization framework – that the Saudis try to advance their political priorities while minimizing hostile pressures on the kingdom – does not suggest that economic factors can be ignored. The long-term evolution of world oil markets, of course, defines the limits within which the Saudis can exercise their considerable discretion. The health of the world economy meshes at some point with Saudi political and security concerns such as the viability of democratic institutions in the West, or the prospects for the electoral victory of leftist coalitions in Italy, France, or Japan. Ultimately, political, security, and economic considerations become identical: on all three grounds the Saudis must fear, in Henry Kissinger's phrase, the 'strangulation' of the West. But political and security concerns wag the economic tail, not vice versa; where they have conflicted, the former have prevailed.

Finally, the evidence supports a decision rule that constrains the pursuit of national goals with the desire to minimize menacing pressures from inside or outside the kingdom. This differs from the maximization of political power. Maximizing Saudi power is not consistent with the kingdom's dramatic cutback and stretchout of capacity expansion plans, from a target of 16 MMB/D in 1983 to a target of 12 MMB/D or less in 1986. If the Saudis were driven by the desire to enhance their political clout with the West, with OPEC, and within Arab councils, they could be expected to expand capacity substantially and allow production swings to be decisively large as punishment or repayment, threat or deterrent. But their sense of vulnerability to internal and external forces appears to preclude this.

The vulnerability of the kingdom also conditions what it can realistically promise as the reward for success in advancing national political goals. Thus, Prince Fahd has promised 'good things' in oil policy if the Arab-Israeli controversy is settled on terms acceptable to the Saudis. Yamani has referred to 'a new era' in the same context. But the impact on other OPEC members of a large production jump and the hostile security threats in the region that would be inevitable if prices declined precipitously effectively foreclose the option and deprive the promise of credibility. As a consequence, the linkage between Saudi oil policy and the Arab-Israeli controversy is asymmetrical: lack of progress toward a long-term solution (including East Jerusalem) that the Saudis consider acceptable or are able to live with can have costly negative consequences for oil policy; success in achieving a long-term solution is likely to offer, at best, only small and short-lived benefits.[80]

## III THE FUTURE OF OPEC PRICES

The characterization of Saudi decision-making developed in the preceding section – that fundamental decisions about cartel leadership are made to advance national political goals subject to security concerns about alleviating adverse pressures on the regime – differs fundamentally from the economic optimizing model. It does not picture OPEC as a single monopolist carefully maximizing over the long term the discounted present value of its earnings, guided by its aggregate discount rate and resource base. Still less does it suggest a cartel dominated by a price leader made moderate by his own large resource base and low discount rate. Rather, within an environment lacking agreement about an optimal price path, the long term for

OPEC becomes a succession of short terms in which Saudi behavior, in turn, is a function of its internal priorities and the external pressures upon it.

Economic factors provide the context for political decisions. Conditions in world oil markets determine how much of an effort the Saudis do or do not have to make to keep them in equilibrium, and how much pressure they will face from their neighbors. The economic health of the West overlaps to a certain extent with the political and security concerns of the Saudis. But the Saudis can weaken tight oil markets, tighten weak oil markets, and have shown that they will use their discretion to send political signals or dampen the potential hostility of their neighbors even when the blow to global economic welfare is great.[81]

The failure of the economic optimization approach underscores the unpredictability of outcomes for OPEC price behavior. Beyond this, however, the analysis of Saudi decision-making presented here suggests a more pessimistic view of oil prices (pessimistic from the point of view of energy consumers) than the economic optimization approach for any given set of assumptions about supply and demand for energy.

In the long run, the desire of the Saudis to avoid the vulnerability that the mere existence of huge export capability brings - vulnerability to consumer government pressures to use it, vulnerability to producer government pressures to let it lie idle - exercises a great dampening effect on capacity plans for the kingdom, irrespective of what huge reserves and low discount rate might indicate. This pushes OPEC in the direction of behaving like a cartel with a much smaller resource base and much higher need for revenues than estimates based on either Saudi price leadership or aggregate weightings of exhaustible resources and discount rate would suggest. It pushes OPEC to take risks more willingly in order to exploit inelasticities of supply and demand and increase current earnings.

In the short run, the balance of forces that help shape Saudi energy policy appears to be biased over time toward the more hawkish end of the spectrum. In the external realm, two groups push for higher prices and lower production. Among other OPEC members, nine of Saudi Arabia's twelve fellow members (Indonesia, Nigeria, Iran, Algeria, Libya, Iraq, Venezuela, Ecuador, and Gabon) have some combination of large populations, rapid social mobilization, rising expectations, large revenue needs, low petroleum reserves, and more costly production. Even in the wake of large price jumps in 1974 and 1980 they have remained militant on oil prices. The new regime in Iran has emerged as a relentless advocate of higher prices, in part to make up for its own production difficulties. For Libya and Iraq, which have higher petroleum reserves and less costly production, a hard-line position on Middle East issues reinforces their position on oil prices. The same may be becoming true of Kuwait.[82] All are worried about depleting their petroleum reserves too quickly. All find the price of even maintaining current export capacity painful because it requires them to be friendly and generous to the foreign oil companies.

Secondly, the principal Arab allies and rivals of the Saudis that are not members of OPEC press for a hawkish position on oil as part of their militancy on Arab–Israeli issues. This group includes Syria, Jordan, Lebanese groups, and Palestinians. Iraq and Libya join them.

Within these two groups lie the principal potential sources of external and internal threats to the security of the kingdom.

Those external forces pushing for lower oil prices, higher exports and larger capacity include, first, oil importing countries other than the United States. Of the oil importing countries, the British and the French are inconstant on the issue of Saudi oil policy, the former because of interest in higher prices for North Sea exports, the latter because of a propensity to search for mercantilistic special deals (petroleum and commercial) with producer governments rather than joining in a united front of consumers. The Third World has become more outspoken in protesting against the burden of higher oil prices rather than submerging itself in New International Economic Order rhetoric. But the Third World is still split by the desire to negotiate special aid agreements with oil exporting patrons rather than provoking the antagonism of OPEC.[83]

Finally, the United States, is in a special position among all importing countries. There are cogent reasons for arguing that the United States should be able to exercise preponderant influence over Saudi oil policy because of its special relationship with the kingdom. Potentially, leverage should come from the following factors: (1) only the United States can provide a meaningful security guarantee to the kingdom; (2) the United States is the principal military supplier to Saudi Arabia, undertaken within a training and tutorial context that cannot easily be duplicated by other sellers of equipment and the presence of US military personnel serves as a tripwire; (3) the United States is a major source of assistance and intelligence to the Saudis on domestic matters; (4) the United States holds a key to Arab-Israeli issues; (5) the United States constitutes the ultimate bulwark against communism and Soviet expansionism in the world.

But there are structural reasons why it is extraordinarily difficult to translate the strength of the US position into effective influence on Saudi oil policy.

## Moderation in Prices: US Tactics

Most of what the United States does for Saudi Arabia - provide a quasi-security umbrella over the kingdom against external threats, provide assistance and intelligence in ensuring domestic tranquility, provide a counter to Soviet moves - the United States has to do anyway, out of self-interest. Thus, in the security area, the United States cannot credibly threaten to withdraw what it 'gives' to the Saudis. Indeed, given Saudi sensitivity to internal and external threats, both real and imagined, of what the United States undertakes is interpreted by the Saudis as too little too late. Thus, rather than being a source of leverage, American actions on security and intelligence issues tend to become a source of complaint.[84]

*Using Access to the US Economy to Reinforce Moderation on Energy.* The fundamentally open nature of the US economy makes it extraordinarily difficult to attempt to use access to financial and technological assets as a source of reward or punishment. To do so would require a review and licensing structure at least twice as burdensome (inward and outward) as COCOM control over transactions with the Soviet Union. Furthermore, with a hypothetical focus on OPEC or Saudi Arabia, America's industrial allies would be much less likely to concur than in the case of COCOM. For some products such as grain, the agreement to manipulate the economic relationship would have to involve many more suppliers. The result, therefore, is likely to be both ineffectual and greatly self-damaging.

*Direct Presidential Appeals.* On oil issues specifically, a strong US *démarche* at the highest level, such as the request for the Saudis to raise their production ceiling from 8.5 MMB/D to 9.5 MMB/D in the spring of 1979, is hard to present and sustain for two reasons. First, a direct, explicit presidential appeal, to be effective, must be a rare event. Second, the President needs to save what political, military, economic, intelligence, and security chips he has for use on other issues besides oil policy. These involve a broad spectrum, ranging from support for the dollar, aid for Turkey, or military funding for Pakistan, to enlisting Saudi support for periodic initiatives in Arab-Israeli relations.

*Special Long-Term Agreements.* Since direct presidential appeals must be rare and rationed, medium- or long-term agreements might seem a better alternative. But Congressional strictures and domestic pressures hinder the President in searching for long-term bargains with the Saudis. A multi-year agreement on military sales for oil output, for example, is not compatible with continual Congressional review and possible veto. (One must stress the argument that the United States is not likely to find it in its own economic or security interests to abandon the development of Saudi military capabilities to other suppliers irrespective of what oil policies the Saudis adopt.) Similarly, the coaxing of higher levels of Saudi production with specially indexed and protected bonds impervious to inflation, the decline of the dollar, or the freezing of assets, would require the creation of a financial instrument insulated with an extraordinary degree of self-denial on the part of Congress and US courts. Even an agreement on the part of the Saudis to build a specified amount of 'surge capacity' (e.g. to 18 MMB/D) in return for a pledge by the United States that it could be called upon only in certain circumstances, such as a major industrial accident or sabotage whose effects both the United States and the Saudis have an interest in softening, but not in an Arab-Israeli war, would be very difficult for the United States to negotiate credibly.

*Bureaucratic Standard Operating Procedures.* The principal US agencies that deal with the Saudis at the middle levels of government tend in their standard operating procedures to weaken rather than strengthen the US-Saudi relationship. With regard to the State Department, representatives from the level of Ambassador and regional Assistant Secretary down, whether consciously or unconsciously clientelistic, are prone in the absence of explicit instructions to the contrary to compose or pick up and use in Ridyah those talking points that put the best face on what the Saudis are doing. With regard to the Defense Department, military officers train Saudis, promote US weapons, and carefully eschew any hint of linkage between their efforts and Saudi behavior on larger political and economic issues; civilian officials at the Assistant Secretary level and below begin every consultation with a spontaneous apology that the United States is not doing more to pursue security interests in the Gulf area. From the Treasury and Energy Departments, middle-level officials similarly lament in meetings abroad what they lament at home, namely, that the American government is not taking stronger measures on inflation, conservation, synthetic fuels, and the defense of the dollar. In sum, on a day-to-day basis, American officials at middle levels tend to transmit the thesis that US efforts on issues the Saudis care about are deficient and the American government lags behind in the ratio of favors rendered to favors received.

*Conflicting Signals.* The principal US government energy forecasting agencies, the CIA and the Department of Energy, traditionally have published extremely pessimistic forecasts for energy supply and demand, which imply that the short-term moderation on the part of the Saudis desired by American leaders is illogical. Indeed, they convey a message, sometimes literally, that the Saudis are doing the United States a favor by cutting back on capacity and production, and raising prices, which will bring America to its senses on conservation before it is too late.[85] To this may be added suggestions that the Saudis might adopt a tough posture on oil issues to aid in the US domestic struggle over energy legislation.[86]

As a result of these factors, the structure of the US-Saudi relationship is such that American leaders find it difficult to translate American military, economic, and technological strength into pressure for expanded capacity, increased production, and lower prices on the part of Saudi Arabia. And without continuous high-level instruction and supervision, US government agencies at the middle levels tend to dilute or neutralize the pressure for moderation in Saudi oil policy.

## Saudi Politics

Within Saudi Arabia, there are roughly six groupings of individuals and agencies whose views and bureaucratic interests have an impact on the determination of oil policy.

*Traditional figures* such as Prince Mohammed, the older full brother of King Khalid, and Prince Nayef, Minister of the Interior, criticize the rapid exploitation of petroleum resources because the consequent high level of government spending brings the corruption of historical Saudi values and culture.[87] There is a certain disingenuousness in this position, however. A lower export level often raises the intake of revenues and stimulates, or at least does not dampen, the pace of government spending.

*The foreign policy establishment* of Prince Saud, the Foreign Minister, and other older members of the Royal Family such as Prince Abdullah (head of the National Guard) argue that solidarity with fellow Arabs plus Iran, who tend to be militants on oil prices, is a more important guide for policy than responding to the day-to-day energy needs of the United States. Significant concessions to the US government should, according to this group, be hoarded for use in reinforcing or underscoring the Saudi position on major foreign policy issues.

*Developmentalists and technocrats* form a grouping that combines individuals who want to push ahead with costly programs in heavy industrial development, education, domestic regional modernization, and social welfare with critics of the waste and profligacy that massive spending entails.[88] The balance tends to be tilted in the direction of higher spending, however, by the fact that many princes and technocrats rely for their personal income and the expansion of their circle of retainers on the steady awarding of new contracts.[89] The needs of this group can be met through either lower volumes of oil at higher prices or higher volumes of oil at lower prices, with the tendency since 1978 being toward the former.

*The petroleum bureaucracy*, headed by Sheik Yamani and Dr Abdul Hady Taher, Governor of Petromin, has shown both conservationist and expansionist tendencies.[90] Yamani, for example, has periodically alternated between lamenting the criticism to which Saudi efforts at price leadership have exposed him, and lamenting the loss of clout within OPEC that large capacity gave the kingdom. The conservationist impulse is strengthened by Petromin geologists, who have an extremely cautious approach to oilfield management.[91]

*Security officials*, headed by Prince Sultan, Minister of Defense, and intelligence officers, such as Prince Faisel al-Turki, Director of Intelligence, identify their interests with a strong United States and a robust world economy. Insofar as they play a role in oil matters, they appear to favor lower prices, higher production, greater capacity (to absorb shocks), and depoliticization of petroleum policy.[92]

*Financial agencies*, specifically the leading officers of the Finance Ministry and the Saudi Arabian Monetary Authority, have predominant interests in a strong dollar, lower inflation, and a strong international economy. They are thus sensitive to the shock of higher oil prices and the burden of recycling. Their bureaucratic position translates most naturally into a preference for moderation on energy issues.

## Implications for the 1980s

Within this milieu, Saudi oil policy can be determined by a variety of coalitions of policymakers responding to both internal and external criteria. At one end of the spectrum a possible coalition of moderates might consist of financial, security, and developmental officials, plus Royal Family members headed by Prince Fahd, who urge greater capacity, greater production, and a lower price path. At the other end, a coalition of more hard-liners on oil policy might include foreign policy officials, conservationists in the petroleum bureacracy, traditionalists in the religious hierarchy, plus Royal Family members headed by Prince Abdullah or Prince Saud whose impulses run in the opposite direction except when political or defense considerations are overriding.

At the end of the 1970s, the latter appeared to be dominant. The first test of the 1980s was inconclusive as to whether there was a basic shift to the other side taking place.

Even at the extremes, few members of the coalitions would represent themselves as extremists, either in terms of oil policy or in terms of US-Saudi relations. But they have been willing to run large risks, as 1973–74 and 1979–80 reaffirmed, on behalf of Middle East or national security objectives.

What will happen to the process of coalition-building in Saudi Arabia in a period of market weakness (if it persists)? It is possible that in a setting of market weakness long-term economic concerns will be more compelling for the Saudis (especially if consumer stockpiling, import tariffs, excise taxes, decontrol of energy prices, and stimulation of alternative energy sources reinforce the anticipation of long-term market weakness). After all, the Saudis have the most to gain from modulating the price path of the cartel carefully and the most to lose from being reckless. The lesson of the 'second oil crisis' of 1979, leading to market glut, could impel them to take the cartel leadership role more seriously; the upheavels on the other side of the Gulf could impel them to expand, harden, and make redundant their own production facilities if only as an insurance policy against disaster. One might plausibly hypothesize that the mid-1980s could see the Saudis pursuing a downward sloping price path maintained by continuous pumping of 8–10 MMB/D even when the market is in excess, with the sustainable production capacity built up beyond 14 MMB/D. Such behavior is clearly in the US national interest, but should come, according to some analysts, spontaneously. A few go so far as to argue that Saudi actions can be taken for granted since economic self-interest will condition all the kingdom's options. As Eliyahu Kanovsky states, 'why make political concessions to persuade the Saudis to do what their economic interests dictate?'.[93]

But the analysis of Saudi decision-making since 1973 casts doubt on such a complacent assessment. Declining demand for OPEC oil will intensify the pressure on Saudi Arabia from its colleagues and neighbors to reduce production, pick up a disproportionate share of the common export cutback, slow or reverse capacity expansion, adopt budgetary restraint (including restraint toward multilateral financial institutions and bilateral aid programs), and pay for the basic fiscal needs that remain through low exports at high prices rather than high exports at low prices. Any refusal of the Saudis to cooperate as the other OPEC members try to deal with their own more pressing fiscal demands and larger populations (populations growing restive in the face of austerity provoked by low exports) will magnify the enmity, and the threats, from the latter. In such circumstances, one could predict a growing divergence for the Saudi leadership between the perception of economic self-interest and the perception of political (or security) self-interest, with the contention that high prices and reduced production are in the long-term Saudi national interest more than offset, for many officials, by the nearer term appeal of solidarity with neighbors and protection against their hostility. This could be reinforced by domestic complaints that the kingdom is not getting enough of a response on Arab-Israeli issues in return for high production. Even the more economically sophisticated among the Saudi hierarchy may conclude that the discounted present value (to them and their descendants) of the barrels produced the day *après* a possible *déluge* is zero. A forecast for the mid-1980s based on this scenario could envision Saudi exports continuously modulated to accommodate the demands of the hawks for a tight market, with maximum sustainable capacity actually shrinking to 8.5 MMB/D, and periodic oil shocks permitted to keep the West from concluding that it can ignore Saudi views on the Middle East.

In this scenario, OPEC would continue to be an oligopoly with a predominantly short-term, high discount rate, high price orientation; a group of producers willing to take risks of benefiting from short-term inelasticities at the expense of longer-term elasticities without much downward pull from the member who has the largest resources and the largest ostensible stake in the future; a loose cartel that is less than the sum of its parts. It would continue to be an organization of oil exporting countries in which Saudi Arabia opts to ride the path of the price hawks on the low side, despite a general availability of oil.

Where between these two scenarios Saudi behavior will fall in the 1980s is uncertain. But past behavior suggests that, curiously, the complex US-Saudi relationship could be at least as difficult for Washington to manage in a period of relative market weakness as in a period of recurrent shortage.

Clearly, it should be possible for Washington to weave together the threads of the US-Saudi relationship at the level of the principals in the Departments of State, Defense, Energy, and Treasury, so as to strengthen the hand of those in the Saudi hierarchy who favor more determined price leadership on the part of the kingdom.

But to accomplish this, the United States, far from ignoring Saudi concerns or taking Saudi behavior for granted, will have to stay constructively engaged with Saudi Arabia on the political and security issues in the Middle East that the kingdom has demonstrated it considers of overriding importance.[94]

## NOTES

1 The most widely found elements in modeling OPEC behavior are (1) rational monopoly pricing, (2) with an exhaustible resource, (3) with a multi-part cartel. There are modeling efforts, however, that incorporate the idea of economic self-interest on the part of OPEC without proceeding explicitly through this sequence of formal steps. Some of these approaches, as embodied in simulation and 'interdependence' models, will be dealt with later in the text.

2 See Hotelling (1931); also Solow (1974), Peterson and Fisher (1977), and Pindyck (1978a).

3 Strictly speaking, total returns must be equalized after adjusting for different categories of risk. Thus, 'money in the bank' may be more secure than 'oil in the ground' if the owner with a choice fears revolution in his country, or vice versa if he fears that his financial assets might be frozen by a foreign government. As the later analysis of Saudi behavior will show, Saudi officials do refer frequently to their stewardship responsibilities to ensure a heritage of wealth for future generations. In addition to the Hotelling problem of weighing the appreciation or depreciation of the value of their petroleum assets in the ground versus the appreciation or depreciation of the value of those assets if converted into financial instruments, they have other considerations as well: (1) whether the assets, if converted to financial instruments, can be seized abroad; (2) whether the assets, if left in the ground, will pass into the hands of a hypothetical post-coup political regime hostile to them and their children; and (3) whether a balanced portfolio of financial assets subject to foreign seizure is more or less risky than an undiversified portfolio of below-ground assets subject to domestic seizure. In the late 1970s, the predominant method of covering all contingencies was to limit production (saving oil for future generations), accept higher prices (making up for depreciating financial assets by adding to those assets), and keep domestic spending up (allowing for the creation of diversified private fortunes for the provision of one's own children).

4 Under competition, net price stands for market price less marginal cost. With monopoly, it is the rent (marginal revenue minus marginal cost) that must be expected to rise at the discount rate.

5 The dynamics of oligopoly behavior suggests that a major producer like Saudi Arabia will build more capacity than a Hotelling analysis would suggest, even if the capacity is left idle, for use in disciplining other oligopoly members, insuring against natural supply disasters, and discouraging the development of higher priced substitutes. See Section II below.

6 Peterson and Fisher (1977), Herfindahl and Kneese (1974).

7 Nordhaus (1973).

8 Sweeney (1977), Stiglitz (1976), and Pindyck (1978a). This conclusion assumes that extraction costs are positive and/or the elasticity of demand is rising. Stiglitz gives an interesting (but implausible) demonstration that if extraction costs are zero and demand elasticity is constant the monopoly and competitive price trajectories will be equal.

9 A number of economic optimizing modelers leave the treatment of OPEC at the level of a single actor, 'dominant firm', or 'unified enterprise'. Cf. Gilbert (1978), Salant (1976) (for an unpublished attempt by Salant to examine intra-OPEC behavior, see Salant (1979)), Cremer and Weitzman (1976). For the unified monopoly approach to be helpful in modeling the real world, one would have to postulate a trusted system of side-payments among the OPEC members over time.

10 Hnyilicza and Pindyck (1976). See also Pindyck (1977, 1978b).

11 This differs from Nash's better known noncooperative theory of bargaining. In the latter, each player ignores the effect of his actions on the strategies of the other. Salant (1980), for example, uses the Nash noncooperative framework for a 'unified actor OPEC' that maximizes its own discounted profits in the aggregate while taking as given the sales path of the competitive fringe outside the cartel. When Salant tries to apply the Nash cooperative approach to internal OPEC dynamics (Salant, 1979), however, the requirement that a 'large extractor' optimize his profit accumulation while assuming others are doing the same appears to put a country like Saudi Arabia into the role of passive residual supplier. This results from the requirement that no player be able to influence or manipulate the reactions of others.

12 Hnyilicza and Pindyck argue that Nash's cooperative solution to the bargaining problem is in fact the only outcome that satisfies axioms of rationality, feasibility, Pareto optimality, independence of irrelevant alternatives, symmetry, and independence with respect to linear transformation of the set of payoffs. For an extended proof, see Hnyilicza and Pindyck (1976), p. 146.

13 On the importance of 'focal points' and 'rules of thumb' under conditions of conflict and uncertainty, see Schelling (1960), Baumol and Quandt (1964).

14 Hnyilicza and Pindyck (1976), pp. 152–3.

15 Eckbo (1976).

16 Some analysts, for example, those who stress 'interdependence', adduce further reasons why the Saudis should pull the OPEC price in a much more moderate direction than the hawkish members of the cartel: namely, the desire to ensure the stability of international financial institutions, the health of the countries in which they have investments, and the strength of the currencies in which their non-petroleum assets are denominated. In the 'interdependence' perspective, the growing number and size of commercial, financial, and investment relationships between the largest energy producers and the largest energy consumers will act as a constraint on oil price policy. Like the rational monopolist approach, the interdependence argument is also built on the idea of economic self-interest as the motivating force behind OPEC behavior. Modelers who confine themselves to monopoly pricing in international energy markets capture only a portion of the hypothetical constraint produced by 'interdependence', namely, the drag on aggregate economic activity in the consuming countries caused by high energy prices. For the interdependence argument, see Choucri with Ferraro (1976) and Bohi and Russell (1978).

17 Willett (1979), Singer (1978), Ben-Shahar (1976), and Kalymon (1975). For modelers who leave OPEC at the level of a unified actor, the impact of Saudi Arabia is felt pulling the cartel toward a moderate price path, not through the kingdom's hypothetical role in intra-OPEC bargaining but through the addition of the weight of Saudi reserves and discount rate in constructing aggregate estimates for the cartel as a whole.

18 Friedman (1974), Enders (1975), Central Intelligence Agency (1977, 1979).

19 For a summary of early post-embargo estimates, see Riefman (1975).

20 Energy Modeling Forum VI (1981). The models are Gately/Kyle IEES (Kilgore), Choucri, Salant/ICF, ETA-MACRO (Manne), WOIL (Naill, Stanley-Miller), Kennedy/Nehring. Ervik, MIT-World Oil Project, British Petroleum, and OILMAR (Potter).

21 For an optimistic view of the geological prospects for oil, see Grossling (1978). Grossling develops comparative statistics on intensity of drilling activity and suggests that petroleum resources might be more than two or three times larger than conventional industry views if exploration activity elsewhere were to equal efforts in the United States (77 percent of all drilling for petroleum in the world has been done in the United States). His estimate of recoverable conventional oil is 2.5 to 6.0 billion barrels. For a more pessimistic view, see Nehring (1978). Nehring argues that additions to world oil resources have been primarily a function of the rate of discovery of giant oil fields (only 10 percent of known crude oil resources comes from the 20,000 plus fields smaller than 100 million barrels each). Since the early 1960s, the rate of discovery of giants and supergiants has dropped, and, Nehring suggests, will continue to do so as the easiest and most promising areas are explored. His estimate of ultimately recoverable conventional crude oil is 1.7 to 2.3 billion barrels.

22 Houthakker (1976).

23 Brown and Kahn (1980).

24 Cf. Koreisha and Stobaugh (1979).

25 Energy Modeling Forum I (1977). The models are Hudson–Jorgenson, Kennedy–Niemeyer, Pilot, Wharton, DRI–Brookhaven, and Hnyilicza.

26 Manne (1980). In this survey, twenty-four modelers responded that there was less than a 20 percent probability that the elasticity for primary energy demand exceeded these figures. For a similar finding of wide disparities in elasticity estimates, see Bohi (1980).

27 For an excellent analysis of the problems in modeling energy markets on the demand side, especially the construction of the price elasticity of demand (the amount by which a given price will reduce demand with aggregate economic activity held constant), the income elasticity of demand (the amount by which a given price will reduce aggregate economic activity, and hence demand), interfuel substitution (e.g. coal for fuel oil), and interfactor substitution (capital and labor for energy), see Energy Modeling Forum IV (1980). This study points out that modeling difficulties are aggravated by extensive data limitations, measurement problems, and divergencies in classification schemes, even including rigorous definitions of the concepts of primary energy, aggregate elasticity, and constancy of aggregate economic activity. A further analysis of the difficulties in reconciling elasticity estimates (including those derived from 'virtually identical' data) is given in Bohi (1980).

Beyond forecasts of supply and demand for energy per se, there is the problem of predicting the rate of OECD economic growth (or its major components such as US economic activity) all other things being equal. The difficulties in perfecting the latter technique are extensive, yet the impact of small variations on the weakness or tightness of the market for OPEC oil is quite large. In comparing the results of eleven energy forecasts made between 1977 and 1979, Susan Misner finds that aggregate economic growth assumptions are the largest factor in explaining the differences among the predictions. Misner uncovers an anomaly in these forecasts, however; the higher the GNP estimate, the lower the demand for oil! See Misner (1979).

28 Energy Modeling Forum VI (1981).

29 *Middle East Economic Survey* (hereafter *MEES*), November 29, 1976. For the Shah's use of statistics to portray himself a leader of the 'moderates', see Pahlavi (1980).

30 *MEES*, December 25, 1978.

31 For the oil industry, see Adelman (1972). For the copper industry, see Moran (1974).

32 'Documentary rundown on world reactions to U.S. campaign for lower prices', *MEES*, October 4, 1974, p. 2. In the analysis that follows, inflation figures come from *International Financial Statistics* (IMF), measures of growth and industrial activity come from *Yearbook of National Accounts Statistics* (United Nations), and estimates of OPEC capacity come from *Intelligence Weekly*.

33 'Yamani proposes cutting posted price of Arabian Light to $9/barrel and invites Iran to cooperate with Saudi Arabia in this endeavor', *MEES*, May 31, 1974, p. 1, supplement; 'Yamani says OPEC's posted crude prices $2/bbl too high', *Oil and Gas Journal*, September 30, 1974, p. 17.

34 'Documentary rundown on world reactions to U.S. campaign for lower oil prices', *MEES*, October 4, 1974.

35 'U.S.-Saudi agreement should help oil climate', *Oil and Gas Journal*, June 17, 1974, p. 38.

36 'Saudi Arabia plans major oil auction for early August', *MEES*, July 26, 1974. Simon met with the Finance and Planning Ministers, as well as the Governor of the Saudi Arabian Monetary Agency, before he talked with Prince Fahd. They were the officials most likely to be receptive to an oil position buttressing the international financial system as well as being sensitive to the counterproductive

nature of an OPEC price drop at that time, since Saudi funds were being sought to expand the IMF's petrodollar recycling facility. *Petroleum Intelligence Weekly* called the auction 'the long awaited sale that may set the direction in crude oil prices' (29 July 1974). According to the *Middle East Economic Survey*, the lower market price would be used for the crude sold to the Aramco owners as well.

37 'Gulf States react to price reduction moves', *MEES*, August 2, 1974, p. 1; 'Otaiba emphasizes resolve to maintain oil prices', *MEES*, August 9, 1974.

38 *MEES*, August 12, 1974.

39 *Oil and Gas Journal*, November 18, 1974, p. 47. At the time of the auction, the Iranian position was summed up by Finance Minister Hushang Ansari: 'If Mr. Yamani wishes to make a gift to the rich industrialized countries, he can do so from his own treasury.' *Oil and Gas Journal*, August 12, 1974.

40 *Oil and Gas Journal*, November 18, 1974. The Saudis orchestrated the tax jump/price fall arrangement with Qatar and Abu Dhabi prior to its acceptance at the December OPEC meeting. For Yamani's subsequent appeal to Secretary Simon to help relieve the pressure from Iran, see note 43.

41 *Oil and Gas Journal*, August 4, 1975, p. 39.

42 'Shah says Iran faces $4 billion deficit in 1975', *MEES*, August 1, 1975.

43 On September 3 Yamani wrote a 'strictly personal' letter to Treasury Secretary Simon saying that Saudi Arabia could not hold to an independent position on oil prices unless the United States used its influence with the Shah. See Jack Anderson's column, *Washington Post*, September 21, 1976, and Oppenheim (1976–77). For an account of the attempt to link oil and other issues (or the lack of such linkage) in the 1974–77 period, see Nau (1980).

44 'OPEC: a battle of wills', *MEES*, September 19 and 26, 1975, p. 1.

45 *Oil and Gas Journal*, October 6, 1975. The ability to characterize oil prices in either real or nominal terms is used by the Saudis to try to take the edge off criticism on the part of fellow producers, or consumers.

46 'Pressure mounts for oil price increase in January', *MEES*, October 11, 1976; 'Some OPEC views on the impending oil price increase', *MEES*, November 29, 1976.

47 On Carter's position see *MEES*, October 18 and November 15, 1976.

48 Yamani's explanation of the Saudi decision on television in Jiddah, December 22, 1976, reproduced in *MEES*, January 10, 1977.

49 *MEES*, December 20, 1976, January 3 and 10, 1977. For the Aramco expansion program, see *MEES*, September 19, 1977.

50 *MEES*, January 10, 1977.

51 The Shah made his 'act of aggression' statement on French television; see *MEES*, January 24, 1977. For the visit of the Iranian Minister of War to see King Khalid, see *MEES*, February 7, 1977.

52 Iran had predicated its 1976–77 budget on exports of 5.4 MMB/D. The preceding year it had run a deficit of $2.4 billion.

53 Yamani consistently claimed that bad weather rather than bad nerves was the softener of Saudi policy. Saudi production in March was 9.5 MMB/D, in April 9.5 MMB/D, and in May 8.1 MMB/D (in May there was a fire at the Abqaiq oil facilities). In June, the rest of OPEC concurrently agreed to forgo an additional 5 percent jump in July.

54 There was also a debate about the technical condition of their major oil fields. For details, see US Senate (1979). While the report catalogs Saudi oilfield limitations, the evidence present, combined with the extreme assumptions needed to construct a pessimistic outlook for Saudi production possibilities (such as no new oil discoveries and no addition to reserves in existing Saudi fields despite a history of recalculating existing fields upward), in fact supports the contention of the Aramco partners that a very protracted production plateau above 12 MMB/D is quite feasible from a technical point of view.

Senior Saudi officials consistently disputed the idea of technical limitations on their oilfields; see *MEES*, March 12, 1979. Yamani commented on the Senate study: 'I read that report, I had to smile. For a layman – not even for someone who knows about the oil business – the US reserve is about 38 billion barrels and they are producing almost what we are producing in Saudi Arabia, though our reserves are several times bigger than those of America and our oilfields are not exhausted as the US ones are. So the man in the street might even question that statement.' *MEES*, April 12, 1979.

Aramco estimated proved crude oil reserves of 113.4 billion barrels and probable reserves at 177.9 billion barrels at the end of 1979, both up from a year earlier despite record output: *Wall Street Journal*, May 20, 1980. For the Saudi view, 'Shaikh Yamani pointed out that Saudi reserves were continuing to increase from year to year, with annual production more than offset by discoveries and additions to reserves'. *MEES*, May 5, 1980.

55 'U.S. plea for oil price freeze unlikely to cut much ice with OPEC', *MEES*, November 7, 1977. Iranian opinion was being expressed, however, at a level below the Shah.

56 'Pre-Caracas price consultations gather momentum', *MEES*, November 14, 1977.

57 *Petroleum Intelligence Weekly*, October 31, 1977.

58 *MEES*, March 20, 1978, p. 2. The campaign to win approval of the F-15 sale to the Saudis began in the fall of 1977.

59 Throughout the fall of 1977, the Saudis canceled water injection and separation equipment associated with their previous expansion program (requiring the payment of large penalty costs). If technical worries about pressure maintenance were predominant in the capacity cutback decision (as the Senate Foreign Relations Committee Study argues) rather than the desire to be less exposed in the battle between producers and consumers over the course of oil prices, they would hardly have cut back on the water injection program.

60 *MEES*, November 21, 1977.

61 'Venezuela turns down U.S. proposal for an oil price freeze', *MEES*, November 29, 1977; *MEES*, December 19, 1977.

62 *MEES*, February 12, 1979.

63 Interview with National Iranian Oil Company Chairman Hassan Nazih, *MEES*, April 2, 1979. For Arab criticism of Saudi Arabia for filling in the gap left by Iranian production declines, cf. 'Algerian news agency criticizes OPEC states which have raised output', *MEES*, February 26, 1979.

64 'Prince Fahd says no decision taken on production increase: calls for immediate dialogue between U.S. and P.L.O.', *MEES*, July 2, 1979; 'Yamani links oil and Palestine issue', *MEES*, July 9, 1979; 'Carter receives "personal commitment" from Prince Fahd on increased Saudi production', *MEES*, July 16, 1979.

65 Prince Fahd, interview with Arnaud de Borchgrave, *Newsweek*, March 26, 1979.

66 Samore (1980a), p. 14.

67 Prince Saud: 'Without a solution to the Palestinian problem there is no hope of restoring stability not only in Lebanon but in the region as a whole. This is what we told Harold Brown and what we have continually stressed to our American friends.' *MEES*, March 12, 1979. See also, 'Fahd fears regional convulsions', *MEES*, March 26, 1979.

68 'Prince Fahd to visit Washington in March', *MEES*, February 12, 1979; 'Fahd postpones Washington visit', *MEES*, March 5, 1979; 'Vance sees decline in U.S.-Saudi links', *New York Times*, May 9, 1979.

69 In Samore (1980), p. 15.

70 *MEES*, April 2, 1979.

71 *Wall Street Journal*, March 9, 1981.

72 'OPEC members expressing doubt about wisdom of raising oil prices', *Wall Street Journal*, March 13, 1981.

73 'Saudi official vows high output of oil until prices drop: timing of Yamani's remarks stirs conjecture about a link with proposed U.S. arms sale', *New York Times*, April 20, 1981; 'Saudis move to cut OPEC price on oil', *Washington Post*, April 20, 1981.

74 Dikko (1981), the OPEC representative from Nigeria.

75 *MEES*, June 1, 1981.

76 As Sheik Yamani has characterized the Saudi strategy, 'I have never said that oil will not be used as a political weapon. I have said repeatedly that oil is a political weapon which can be used in different ways. In fact, we have never stopped using this weapon. For example, in 1973 we used it for a specific purpose, namely to draw the attention of the Western nations to their dependence on the Arabs. Again in 1977 and earlier, when we adopted a particular stance *vis-à-vis* the oil price issue we used oil not only to remind the Western nations that they are dependent on the Arabs but also that they can rely on the Arabs in the sense that the friendly attitude of the Arab states should be taken into account by the West in their political calculations', *MEES*, June 2, 1980.

77 Some simulation models hypothesize that OPEC prices will vary as a function of OPEC capacity utilization, but include no method of determining how close to capacity the largest cartel member will be willing to produce nor how much capacity it will decide to build. Cf. Gately et al. (1977) and Gately (1980).

78 Yamani (1981).

79 *New York Times*, April 20, 1981.

80 Two factors make the Saudi position on Arab-Israeli issues particularly difficult for US officials to deal with. First, the Saudis tend to have a less critical view of Palestinian groups, especially the Fatah, than others who have had more direct dealings with them (Syrians, Jordanians, Iraqis, Egyptians). Second, because of the desire not to arouse opposition, the Saudis are more easy going about being able to accept 'whatever solution the Palestinians determine for themselves', from full autonomous armed nation, to semi-demilitarized state, to entity associated with Jordan, than the Front-Line Arab governments. Cf. 'Arab reactions to Camp David peace agreement: Saudi Arabia', *MEES*, September 25, 1978; 'Interview with Prince Fahd on the Egyptian-Israeli Treaty', Arnaud de Borchgrave, *Newsweek*, March 26, 1979; and 'Interviews with Crown Prince Fahd and Prince Abdullah', *Washington Post*, May 25, 1980. Within the PLO, the Saudis have tended to support the Fatah at the expense of the leftist groups (Quandt, 1980).

81 Saudi behavior parallels, with exaggerated impact, what Stephen Krasner has discovered about the decision-making of large corporations; it is precisely in the strongest oligopolies that corporate managers can engage in very broad satisficing strategies with regard to economic achievement and use (or be pressured by outsiders into using) their discretionary power on behalf of political goals whether or not those goals are congruent with profit maximization. In the Saudi case, there is simultaneously more discretion (because of the uncertainty about what constitutes long-term profit maximization) and more vulnerability to outside pressures (because the kingdom does not enjoy the equal protection of the laws against those who dislike its actions) than in the case of corporate behavior. See Krasner (1973).

82 'Kuwait's tougher oil stance', *New York Times*, April 17, 1980.

83 Cf. 'Poor nations drop oil-price proposal: group of 77 instead accepts vow by OPEC of cash assistance to help their economics', *New York Times*, November 18, 1979.

84 For the Saudi reaction to US attempts to bolster its security presence in the Gulf after the fall of the Shah, see 'Frustration marks Saudi ties to U.S.', *Washington Post*, May 6, 1979. For Saudi complaints that Secretary Haig's attempts to build a 'strategic concensus' focuses too much on the Soviet Union and not enough on Israel, see *New York Times*, April 9, 1981.

85 For a rare public glimpse of this point of view, see 'Oil price rises by OPEC next year aren't likely to be fought by Carter', *Wall Street Journal*, June 23, 1978.

86 J. P. Smith of the *Washington Post* suggests that this may have been the motivation behind Secretary Schlesinger's suggestion to Prince Fahd that the Saudis adopt 12 MMB/D for technical reasons as their ultimate capacity plateau. Smith's is the most charitable interpretation for a bizarrely perverse episode, which aggravated Saudi suspicions that the Aramco partners were grossly mishandling the management of Saudi oil reservoirs, strengthened the hand of those conservationists in the Saudi hierarchy who wanted to lower the capacity target from 16 MMB/D to 12 MMB/D, and rendered much more costly any future American effort to persuade the Saudis to enlarge their capacity (whether or not such capacity is used). See Smith (1978a, b). For Schlesinger's position upon returning from Saudi Arabia, see Schlesinger (1978); see also Hersh (1978). Oil industry and senior Saudi petroleum officials dismissed the idea of technical limitations on capacity expansion above 12 MMB/D, but other Saudi government authorities acknowledged that the assertion left them 'disturbed'. 'New chief of Aramco says Saudi Arabia is capable of producing much more oil', *New York Times*, January 6, 1978; *MEES*, March 12, 1979; *MEES*, July 9, 1979.

87 For an insightful discussion of the positions of individual members of the Saudi hierarchy, see the essay by Samore (1980b).

88 For defense as well as a criticism of large expenditures on behalf of programs of modernization, see 'Saudi Industry Minister Qusaibi reiterates determination to go ahead with oil-based industrial projects', *MEES*, January 1, 1979; 'Saudi Arabia pursues development on a vast scale', *New York Times*, March 3, 1980; 'Oil pressure: Saudi Arabian citizens urge slash in output but leadership resists', *Wall Street Journal*, April 7, 1980. Dr Faisal Bachir, Deputy Minister of Planning, asserted that the takeover of the Grand Mosque in Mecca and the uprising of Shiites in the Eastern Province in late 1979 reinforced, rather than retarded, spending on welfare and modernization (*New York Times*, March 7, 1980). Hisham Nazer, the Minister of Planning, however, has argued on behalf of lower oil production and a slower pace of development spending.

89 For an account of this phenomenon, see 'U.S. aides say corporation is threat to Saudi stability' and 'Saudi Prince is said to have made a fortune in business', *New York Times*, April 16, 1980.

90 *MEES*, October 2, 1978; *MEES*, July 9, 1979; *MEES*, May 5, 1980.

91 The conservativeness of Petromin's geologists leads to pressure maintenance practices that may in fact lower the ultimate recovery of Saudi oilfields (e.g. water injection from the periphery of the field as opposed to pattern injection throughout the field). Cf. US Senate (1979).

92 Cf. 'Prince Sultan says Saudi Arabia does not bargain on oil prices', *MEES*, March 20, 1978; 'Saudi Defense Minister opposes use of oil weapon for political ends', *MEES*, October 29, 1979.

93 Kanovsky (1980); also, 'An economic analysis of Middle East oil: a look backward and a look ahead', *Middle East Contemporary Survey*, 1979–80. Cf. Feith (1981): 'Whether [Saudi] rulers are "pro-Western", "friendly" or pleased with any or all of the elements of U.S. foreign policy is an issue "linked" to Saudi oil policy only in diplomatic rhetoric and in the minds of those who do not actually bear responsibility for turning Saudi oil into money.' For a similar point of view, see Singer (1978) and Rowen (1981a, b).

94 For an attempt to dissect critically what 'linkages' do, and do not, exist between US policy toward the Arab-Israeli controversy, the security of the Gulf, and the Saudi oil behavior, see Moran (1982).

# 5 The Limitation to OPEC's Pricing Policy

JOHN H. LICHTBLAU

The world oil developments of the last eight years sometimes seem like a series of random events without any underlying logical pattern. We saw crude prices quadruple almost overnight in 1973, then decline again in real terms over the next four and a half years, and then rise by over 70 percent in less than one year. We experienced real physical shortages, which caused chaotic market conditions, followed by substantial world oil surpluses. We had permanent price increases brought on by short-term interruptions and we have had price declines during a lengthy large scale interruption.

Yet the erratic, and therefore largely unpredictable, nature of these developments has not been due to the absence of any identifiable logic underlying and connecting them, but rather to the fact that they were often triggered by extraneous events, such as a war or a revolution, which are inherently difficult to predict, particularly within a specific time frame. In retrospect, we can clearly see a compelling logic relating all of these developments in the world oil market.

Consider the quadrupling of world oil prices between mid-1973 and January 1974. Until that price increase, non-communist world oil demand had risen at an average annual growth rate of 7.5 percent. The rate was approximately the same whether measured over the ten-year period or the five-year period ending in 1973. Thus, it must be assumed to reflect the long-term growth rate at the average world oil price prevailing in the 1960–73 period.

Had growth continued at that rate since 1973, or even at a somewhat reduced rate (assuming a move toward market saturation during the 1970s), the amount of oil required by 1978 would demonstrably have been substantially more than the world's physical and technical petroleum resource base would have been able to provide. At a growth rate of just 5 percent annually, non-communist world (NCW) oil demand by 1978 would have been 61 MMB/D instead of the actual 51 MMB/D. If all OPEC members had been willing and able to maintain output in 1978 at their hypothetical maximum sustainable capacity of 34.5–35.0 MMB/D, instead of their actual production of 30.3 MMB/D, they could only have supplied slightly less than half the 10 MMB/D additional requirements. By 1980 the 5 percent growth rate would have resulted in a consumption of 67 MMB/D, or 18 MMB/D more than the actual consumption. Furthermore, at the oil price assumed for the 5 percent demand growth rate (which would be over four times the actual growth rate registered during this period), non-OPEC oil supplies would have increased by far less than the 2.0 MMB/D realized between 1973 and 1978 or the 3.5 MMB/D realized by 1980. This would have raised the hypothetical supply/demand gap still further.

Thus, it is obvious that a sharp increase in the real price of oil was required by the mid-1970s at the latest to avoid a major resource shortage by the end of the decade. The international oil companies' individual ability to bring about such an increase was limited by their need to remain competitive with each other. Had they tried to act collectively, or even given the impression of doing so, they would have run into major political and legal trouble in their home and other consuming countries. In retrospect it is clear that the pre-1974 production strategy of the private companies was essentially consumer oriented in that it was based on sales maximization rather than price maximization.

Thus, for the world price increase to take place when it did, it had to come from an oil producer body with considerable collective enforcement power beyond the reach of consumer country legal and political control, a strong self-interest in substantial price increases, and the motivation to produce less oil in the short run in order to have more available for the long run. OPEC was such a body and that is why it succeeded so spectacularly in 1973–74 in bringing about the increase in the world oil price.

However, OPEC apparently overshot the mark at the time, that is, the price increase was too fast and went too far. This helped to set the stage for the world oil surplus of the next five years. There were two reasons for this development: (1) non-communist world oil demand from 1973 through 1978 rose at an annual rate of only 1.2 percent, which must be considered a quantum reduction from the previous growth rate (and in the industrial nations the growth rate was half that much); and (2) the higher prices stimulated additional production in areas outside OPEC, such as Alaska, the North Sea, and Mexico. As a result, the small increase in world demand during this period was met entirely from non-OPEC sources while OPEC exports actually declined (see Table 5.1).

The surplus caused world oil prices to fall fairly significantly in real

Table 5.1 *OPEC Exports and Non-Communist World Oil Demand, 1973–80 (in MMB/D)*

| | *Demand* | *OPEC exports* | *OPEC export share of demand (%)* |
|---|---|---|---|
| 1980 | 49.0 | 24.7 | 50.3 |
| 1979 | 51.6 | 28.8 | 55.9 |
| 1978 | 50.9 | 27.9 | 54.8 |
| 1977 | 49.5 | 29.6 | 59.8 |
| 1976 | 48.0 | 29.3 | 61.0 |
| 1975 | 45.2 | 25.6 | 56.7 |
| 1974 | 46.3 | 29.1 | 62.8 |
| 1973 | 47.9 | 29.5 | 61.6 |

terms from 1974 through 1978, particularly in countries like Germany, Switzerland, and Japan, whose currency rose *vis-à-vis* the dollar. But even in the United States the decline, in real prices, of the OPEC marker crude amounted to about 12.5 percent in the four and one-half year period between the second quarter of 1974 and the fourth quarter of 1978.

This is not to say that in the 1974–78 period world oil prices were shaped primarily by market forces. Far from it. Throughout these five years the OPEC 'cartel' effectively determined the level of world oil floor prices, which were invariably higher than they would have been under free market conditions. However, some OPEC members, led by Saudi Arabia, the group's largest producer, were concerned about the apparent negative economic effects of the 1973 price increases on the industrial and, even more, the developing countries of the world, and the potential political ramifications of these effects. Thus, in 1977 Saudi Arabia, supported by Abu Dhabi, forced the other OPEC members to accept a price increase substantially below what they had voted for and also below the world inflation rate. In December 1977 Saudi Arabia and Iran joined forces to freeze OPEC prices for all of 1978 at the mid-1977 level.

Market forces did play a significant, if indirect, role in these decisions, for without the market-induced surplus producing capacity of most OPEC members throughout this period, Saudi Arabia would probably not have succeeded in imposing its relatively moderate pricing policy on the rest of OPEC. Nor would there have been any sense in trying to, if oil supplies had been tight despite the quantum price increases.

Before discussing the second OPEC price explosion and its consequences and speculating on the price trends to 1990, it might be useful to consider briefly the question of whether, and for how long, the OPEC price in existence on the eve of the Iranian revolution could have been maintained in the absence of that revolution and the ensuing Iran–Iraq War. The answer might tell us whether the OPEC-imposed price rises of 1979–80 accelerated or reversed an underlying longer-term trend in the world oil market.

Oil demand, after falling sharply in 1974 and 1975, recovered sharply in 1976 and then rose at an annual rate of about 3 percent in both 1977 and 1978. A similar growth rate had generally been forecast for 1979 in the absence of significant real price changes. This could be taken as a very tentative indication that at the price level and the state of technology of energy conservation and oil substitution prevailing in 1978, the long-term annual growth rate in NCW oil demand would have been around 3 percent. However, we know that even before the Iranian revolution OPEC members had agreed to reverse the real decline in their oil prices by raising the OPEC marker crude faster than world inflation. The price increase for 1979 agreed at the OPEC ministerial meeting in Abu Dhabi in December 1978 would have raised the organization's official marker crude by year-end 1979 to $14.80/bbl, or by 14.5 percent over the year-end 1978 price. When that decision was made, consumer price inflation in the OECD area was running at an annual rate of just under 8 percent. There is little doubt that OPEC could and would have maintained its price level in 1979 under normal supply conditions.

A 14.5 percent increase would of course have lowered the demand growth rate from what it would have been under the 1978 price. Let us assume, somewhat arbitrarily, that the longer run effect of this price increase would have been to reduce demand growth from our previously expected 3 percent annual rate to 2.5 percent. Growing at that rate from 1979 on, NCW demand in 1985 would have been 60.6 MMB/D, or 9.6 MMB/D above the 1978 level. Could this additional volume have been supplied at the assumed end-1979 price of $14.80/bbl, adjusted for inflation, if there had been no Iranian revolution? The estimates in Table 5.2 attempt to answer this question.

The 37.1 MMB/D volume for total OPEC production in 1985 would not have represented the organization's physical resource limitation at our assumed price. Rather, it would have been a combination of resource limitations, technical limitations at a point in time, and political constraints on allowable output. Thus, on the basis of resource limitations alone, OPEC's collective output in 1985 could have been significantly higher under our price and political scenario than the figure shown in the table. But it would be highly unrealistic to consider only the physical resource base in forecasting actual output.

The single most important figure in the table is the 12 MMB/D

Table 5.2 *Hypothetical Non-Communist World Crude Oil and Natural Gas Liquids Supply, 1985*[a] *(in MMB/D)*

| | *1978 (Actual)* | *1985* |
|---|---|---|
| Saudi Arabia | 8.3 | 12.0 |
| Iran, Iraq, Kuwait | 9.9 | 11.6 |
| Other OPEC | 11.6 | 11.8 |
| OPEC natural gas liquids | 0.7 | 1.7 |
| TOTAL OPEC | 30.5 | 37.1 |
| Non-OPEC crude | 16.6 | 19.3 |
| Non-OPEC natural gas liquids | 2.2 | 2.4 |
| Net Sino-Soviet exports | 1.5 | 0.4 |
| TOTAL non-communist | 50.8 | 59.2 |

[a] Assuming a $14.80/bbl OPEC marker crude price (in real terms) from 1979 to 1985 and no Iranian interruption.

volume forecast for Saudi Arabia, since the Saudi increment accounts for almost 60 percent of the total OPEC crude oil output increase between 1978 and 1985. It was known in 1978 that Saudi Arabia was actively planning to raise its sustainable crude oil producing capacity to at least that level by 1985, but whether the Saudi government would have permitted actual production to rise to that level is not at all certain. However, given an oil price which, under our assumption, would have been less than half the current (August 1981) price for Saudi crude, budget considerations might have motivated the Saudis to maximize the utilization of their sustainable capacity, particularly if market conditions had warranted it. The probability of a sustained Saudi production level significantly *above* 12 MMB/D by 1985 would have been very low, in our view.

As we have seen, under our 2.5 percent annual growth rate assumption NCW demand would have reached 60.6 MMB/D by 1985. Our supply forecast shows that this growth rate could only have continued to 1984 before running into constraints. Thus, the oil price in existence just prior to the Iranian revolution plus the increase initially intended by OPEC for 1979 would have been adequate (in real terms) at the most for five years, more likely less, even under our very low growth rate projection - one-third of that of the pre-1974 period.

Higher real oil prices in the early 1980s would therefore have been inevitable even if Iranian oil supplies had continued to be available at their pre-revolutionary producing capacity. In fact, many forecasts made in the 1975–78 period assumed a 3–5 percent annual increase in real oil prices from the late 1970s onward in order to close the hypothetical 'gap' between world oil supply and demand.

Thus, the OPEC price increase since the end of 1978 was indeed a galloping acceleration of an underlying trend. Had the price increase intended by OPEC for 1978 continued at that rate in subsequent years (which might be about 5 percent above the world inflation rate), it would have taken until 1985 to reach the average price level of nearly $35 actually attained by January 1981. The difference in international income transfer is of course enormous if we consider that each one dollar increase in the world oil price raises the collective annual receipts of oil exporters by some $12.5 billion.

However, in appraising the 1979–80 OPEC price increases we must also consider the fact that the post-revolutionary Iranian oil 'policy' has resulted in the indefinite, perhaps permanent, elimination of about 3 MMB/D of previously available Iranian oil producing capacity. This is equivalent to 9 percent of OPEC's total pre-revolutionary producing capacity, and would eventually have had to be reflected in a higher price level. In addition, the Iran–Iraq War has reduced available supplies by at least another 2.5 MMB/D since October 1980. Had it not been for that war, the underlying world oil surplus which became obvious to everyone by February/March 1981 would have been obvious by October 1980. Hence, the $5/bbl price increase announced by the African producers at the OPEC meeting in Bali in December 1980 would very probably not have taken place.

Hence, once again, market forces would have raised real oil prices significantly from 1980 onward to reflect the new reality of supply and demand. And, once again, OPEC raised prices probably earlier and certainly higher than the market would have done. But directionally its actions were clearly supported by the underlying market conditions.

This brings us to the present. It differs from the past, as I have just described it, in one essential aspect: market forces do not support any significant[1] further real price increases. In fact, there is now strong evidence that recent prices have been too high in relation to the underlying market structure. The indications of this are seen most clearly in the industrial countries, that is, the OECD area. Demand peaked at 41.1 MMB/D in 1979. This year it will probably be below 37 MMB/D. Some of that decline is undoubtedly due to general economic recessions in several OECD countries and to the aftereffect of the 1979 price shock. But the bulk of the decline appears to be structural and irreversible: Japan, which had a healthy economic growth rate last year, nevertheless registered a 9 percent decline in oil demand; Germany, which had a modest economic growth rate, registered a 11 percent decline in oil demand; and the United States, whose economy was stagnant last year, had a 9 percent decline in oil demand. The same has been true so far in 1981. Decline in oil demand was on the order of 6 percent in the United States in the first six months in the face of a significant increase in the GNP. A similar development has occurred in Japan during the same period.

Another significant indication is that the decline in OECD oil demand since 1979 has not been part of a decline in total energy requirements but has almost everywhere been limited to oil. Thus, in 1979 when oil demand declined by about 0.5 percent, nonoil energy demand rose by 4.0 percent. The same divergent movements occurred in 1980 when NCW oil consumption dropped by 5.2 percent while total energy consumption rose by 1.5 percent. They reflect the fact that conservation and substitution have increasingly forced oil into the role of the marginal energy supply source.

There is good reason to assume this trend will continue for quite some time. Certainly, the potential for oil conservation and substitution is far from exhausteα. It apparently took the economic stimulation of the second oil price shock to really trigger it, although the groundwork for it was laid by the first shock.

To be sure, this trend may not be strong enough to offset an increase in oil demand brought about by the expected economic recovery in Europe and accelerated economic growth in the United States in 1982–83. We may therefore see the decline in oil demand temporarily halted or even reversed after this year. But when the economic improvement starts to level off, as it invariably does, the ongoing long-term process of oil conservation and substitution is likely to reassert its domination over demand. Thus, the 41.1 MMB/D historic peak for OECD oil demand reached in 1979 may very well remain unsurpassed throughout the 1980s.

In the less developed countries (LDCs) oil demand can be expected to grow at a rate which will approximately offset the decline in the industrial world. Thus, total NCW oil demand may be stagnant or, at most, increase minutely in the 1980s. The latest global energy forecasts by Exxon Corporation and by the Standard Oil Company of California both project an annual oil demand growth rate of 0.3 percent for the NCW from 1979 to 1990. The Petroleum Industry Research Foundation projects an NCW decline rate of 0.3 percent for the period 1979–90 (see Table 5.3). By comparison, in the eleven-year period ending in 1979 the NCW growth rate was nearly 4.0 percent per annum.

To complete our picture of an extended period with no sustained upward market pressure on OPEC prices, it should be pointed out that non-OPEC crude oil supplies, which increased on average by nearly 1 MMB/D in each of the last three years, are expected to continue to rise by around half this volume over the next ten years (see Table 5.4). Thus, it appears that for the foreseeable future no substantial long-term increase in the real price of oil will be required by *market* forces to keep demand from growing faster than technically and economically available supply.

Table 5.3 *Free World Oil Demand and Required OPEC Oil Production, 1978, 1979, 1980 and Projections to 1990 (in MMB/D)*

| | *1978* | *1979* | *1980* | *1985* | *1990* |
|---|---|---|---|---|---|
| *World oil consumption* | | | | | |
| United States | 18.85 | 18.43 | 17.01 | 16.47 | 15.62 |
| Western Europe | 14.63 | 14.87 | 13.75 | 13.78 | 13.73 |
| Japan | 5.42 | 5.50 | 5.00 | 5.40 | 5.57 |
| Other | 12.60 | 12.98 | 13.46 | 15.09 | 16.25 |
| TOTAL | 51.50 | 51.78 | 49.22 | 50.74 | 51.17 |
| Other adjustments[a] | −0.60 | +1.05 | +0.39 | +0.20 | +0.20 |
| Total free world oil requirements | 50.90 | 52.83 | 49.61 | 50.94 | 51.37 |
| Free world oil production outside OPEC countries[b] | 19.24 | 20.52 | 21.11 | 23.83 | 26.28 |
| Net oil exports from communist countries | 1.50 | 1.02 | 0.90 | 0.20 | – |
| Required OPEC oil production[c] | 30.16 | 31.29 | 27.60 | 26.91 | 25.09 |

[a] Includes crude oil stockpiling requirements, inventory changes, and unaccounted crude losses.
[b] Includes US processing gain.
[c] Crude and natural gas liquids.
*Source: BP Statistical Review* for 1978 and 1979; 1980 data and projections are those of PIRA.

This does not mean, however, that the possibility of such an increase in OPEC prices and, hence, world oil prices can be dismissed. By maintaining tight collective pricing discipline, together with production controls in the principal member countries, OPEC could in fact enforce such an increase at any time, given its share of world oil production. Or it may decide that a substantial increase brought about by a temporary reversal of the underlying market trend, such as a supply interruption caused by extraneous events, should be maintained when the long-term trend reasserts itself. One has become familiar with this type of OPEC price setting.

In the short run, say, about 5–6 years, OPEC would probably derive a net benefit from its action, since short-term price elasticity of

Table 5.4 *World Oil Supplies from Non-OPEC Areas 1978, 1979, 1980 and Projections to 1990 (in MMB/D)*

| | *1978* | *1979* | *1980* | *1985* | *1990* |
|---|---|---|---|---|---|
| United States | 10.77 | 10.66 | 10.76 | 9.90 | 10.00 |
| Canada | 1.58 | 1.83 | 1.74 | 1.60 | 1.75 |
| Other western hemisphere | 2.52 | 2.89 | 3.41 | 4.73 | 5.93 |
| Western Europe | 1.82 | 2.36 | 2.57 | 3.60 | 3.80 |
| Other eastern hemisphere | 2.56 | 2.73 | 2.63 | 4.00 | 4.80 |
| TOTAL | 19.24 | 20.52 | 21.11 | 23.83 | 26.28 |

*Note:* Includes natural gas liquids and processing gains in the United States.
*Source: BP Statistical Review* for 1978 and 1979; projections are those of PIRA.

oil is certainly below unity: the demand would fall by a smaller percentage than the increase in the price so that OPEC's export earnings would improve. But we have been told repeatedly that one basic difference between OPEC and the private multinational oil companies is that while the latter are guided largely by the goal of short-term profit maximization, the former's chief aim is to maximize oil's long-term contribution to its members' national economies. If that is OPEC's true aim, further significant real oil price increases are likely to prove counterproductive and not just in the very long run, particularly for those countries with high reserve/production ratios such as Saudi Arabia, Kuwait, Abu Dhabi, Iraq, and Venezuela, if that country's heavy oil reserves in the Orinoco region are included.

What these increases would do, and have already done on a remarkable scale, is to mobilize the entire technological and economic genius of the industrialized world for the task of reducing oil imports by another few million barrels per day over the next decade or so. The task is feasible but difficult at present oil prices. But if another $16–$18/bbl in real prices is added over the next 8–9 years[2] then its success is assured. For example, consider the case of synthetic fuels. Technologically and economically, this industry (particularly shale oil) is at the takeoff stage in the United States. But of late, several potential producers have had serious second thoughts about plunging ahead. One reason is that the new US administration appears for the time being less interested than the previous one in assisting with the birth of this industry. A second reason is that the current high interest rates on capital, combined with the long construction time for these projects, have lowered the potential attractiveness of the investment. Finally, looking at the declining market demand for oil, some companies are beginning to wonder whether conventional oil would not be available in sufficient quantities at lower cost than the synfuels. This does not mean that there will not be a synfuels industry in the United States;

but its birth will take longer and its growth will be slower than had been expected. All this could change within a few years, if the real oil price continues to rise significantly.

OPEC's current technically sustainable crude oil producing capacity is rated at 33.3 MMB/D.[3] Actual production in the first half of 1981 was nearly 10 MMB/D less. If real OPEC prices remain approximately where they are now, requirements for OPEC oil may increase slightly but will remain between 25 and 28 MMB/D on an annual average, as is shown in our projection in Table 5.3. Thus, in the absence of another major political supply interruption with long-term consequences, the organization will have significant spare capacity throughout the 1980s under any realistic market assumption.

If the real price should rise by, say, 50 percent between 1981 and 1990, it is not unreasonable to assume that the export demand for OPEC oil will drop by some 3.5–4.0 MMB/D, given the fact that the worldwide reduction in oil demand resulting from the price increase would be concentrated on imported oil and within the import sector on OPEC oil. This means that total OPEC oil demand could fall to the region of 20 MMB/D. OPEC would then be operating at 60 percent or less of its technical capacity. This would make it very difficult for the organization to continue to maintain its price cohesiveness. With 13 MMB/D of readily producible OPEC oil overhanging the market, some members may not be able to resist the temptation to sell more oil by offering hidden or open discounts to their customers. Once this process caught on it would rapidly undermine OPEC's floor price defense and cause prices to tumble, at least temporarily, since the actual production cost of most OPEC oil is only a very small fraction of its sales price. The potential for a price decline in the absence of any enforceable restrictions is therefore enormous.

Consequently, if OPEC is to continue to maintain a price level substantially in excess of its members' actual production cost, it will have to remain at or very near the present price (in real terms) of its marker crude throughout this period, and the prices of all other OPEC crudes will have to fall in line with the marker crude.

Probably OPEC's long-term survival as an effective price-setting organization will depend on its ability to maintain its crude output between 22 and 28 MMB/D. If production drops below the lower level of this band for more than a year, the organization's price cohesion, which is its *raison d'être*, is likely to be doomed for the reasons discussed above. This would be particularly true after the cessation of Iran-Iraqi hostilities and the consequent significant increase in OPEC's exportable supply. In fact, had there been no such hostilities in 1981, OPEC's price cohesion would already have been far more severely tested than it was. The organization's survival under these conditions may well have depended on Saudi Arabia's willingness to take a production cut of 2.5–3.0 MMB/D. This points up Saudi Arabia's dominant position as a price setter in OPEC whenever the group's collective production approaches the 22 MMB/D level.

At the upper end of the band - 28 MMB/D of crude - OPEC's remaining effective spare capacity would be quite small. Hence, market forces would be likely to provide encouragement for OPEC to raise its real prices once again at a rapid rate. Perhaps up to a demand level of 29 MMB/D of crude, the upward pressure on prices could be mitigated by an increase in Saudi Arabian production, provided the country is inclined to mitigate such a development. If requirements for OPEC oil should exceed 29 MMB/D for an extended period, a substantial increase in the real price of OPEC oil is probably inevitable, even in the face of active Saudi Arabian opposition. As was pointed out before, in the short run, such a price increase would of course benefit OPEC. In the longer run it would accelerate the trend away from imported oil and thereby hurt OPEC's interests.

I have limited my discussion so far largely to the impact on OPEC from changes in OECD oil import requirements. In 1979 80 percent of OPEC's exports went to OECD countries. Most of the balance went to less developed countries (LDCs). In addition, OPEC members last year domestically consumed about 2.8 MMB/D, or 10 percent their total output. Both of these, the LDCs and the domestic OPEC economies, are growth markets.

In fact, officials of some OPEC countries have in the past repeatedly warned their industrial customers that within a decade or so a large portion of the oil produced in these countries may no longer be available for export since it will be required domestically. While this would not be good news for OECD importers, it would be far worse news for the oil exporters that would have given up a hard currency foreign market at world prices for a soft currency domestic market at far lower local prices. A few OPEC members may have enough oil reserves to meet the requirements of both markets. Most oil exporters, however, will sooner or later be forced to curtail the growth rate in domestic oil consumption in order to protect their foreign exchange earnings. Thus, growth in domestic oil demand can hardly be considered an offset to a decline in exports to the OECD countries.

The growth in the import requirements of the LDCs presents a somewhat similar problem. These countries are already spending 40 percent of their total export earnings for oil imports. If the real price of oil continues to increase, their ability to import this commodity will decline, regardless of their underlying need for it. To maintain their LDC market outlets in the face of rising real prices, oil exporters would have to subsidize these sales through lower prices or preferential financing. To some extent this is already being done; it is desirable from the point of view of recycling OPEC's current account surplus - as long as there is one. But, again, it is not a substitute for the decline in exports into OPEC's prime hard currency market, the OECD area.

The argument made in this chapter that the longer run negative effect on OPEC members of any further significant real price increase would more than offset the short-term benefits to them is sometimes countered with the thesis that OPEC is collectively in a position to control world oil prices in both directions. Since the present price of OPEC oil is a high multiple of its actual production cost and will continue to remain so, it is argued that OPEC and certain other oil exporters can always protect their foreign markets simply by reducing their profit margins, if this should become necessary. This must be recognized as a valid argument. Certainly, the production cost of most OPEC exports is way below that of the new conventional and unconventional energy supplies developed to displace these exports.

However, the argument ignores the irreversible institutional changes brought about by OPEC's pricing policy. Substitution and conservation of oil is one such change. Since this is largely a function of changes in equipment design, substitution and conservation will continue relatively unaffected in the short to medium term by future price moderation. Another institutional factor is likely to be government protection of high-cost domestic energy production from low-cost foreign competition. There are plenty of precedents for this, such as the US oil import policy from 1957 to 1973, whose philosophic basis was the assumption that dependence on foreign oil presented a potential national security threat, independent of price, in view of the demonstrated unreliability of access to foreign oil.

Still another institutional factor is the change in life-style and value judgments brought about by the rise in energy costs. These changes may consist of a higher consideration than before of the transportation cost aspect of residential or industrial location and relocation, or they may take the form of a gradual move from energy intensive to nonenergy intensive leisure and other personal activities. Once such changes are made they tend to become divorced from their original cause (the rise in oil prices) and, hence, are not readily reversible if and when the original cause ceases to exist.

Since the above factors are most applicable to the industrial countries, institutional forces can be expected to play an important part in the long run irreversible reduction in oil import requirements in these countries if real oil prices should continue to rise significantly.

We do not know of course what pricing policy OPEC members will adopt, collectively or individually, for the remainder of the 1980s in the face of these developments. Their governments cannot be faulted for doubting the predictions of foreign oil companies. In the 1960s when the price of oil was consistently below $2/bbl they had predicted that the resource base would be adequate to meet a sustained, substantial demand growth well into the next century at approximately the then existing price level. In the 1970s when the price had soared to a multiple of its previous level the predictions were that oil was getting increasingly scarce and that the world would have to reduce its consumption over the remainer of this century in order to avoid further astronomic price increases brought on by economic and physical resource limitations.

OPEC, collectively and individually, is now increasingly making its own assessments of the future world oil market. These findings are not very different from those currently put out in the oil consuming countries. But they represent radical changes from OPEC's privately and publicly stated views prior to 1981. Thus, OPEC's most prominent spokesman, Saudi Arabia's Oil Minister, Sheik Ahmed Zaki Yamani, said in January 1981 in a widely publicized lecture in Damman:

> if we force Western countries to invest heavily in finding alternative sources of energy, they will. This would take no more than seven to ten years and would result in reducing dependence on oil as a source of energy to a point which will jeopardize Saudi Arabia's interests.

In a similar vein the United Arab Emirate's Oil Minister, Manna Saeed al-Otaiba, said in June 1981 at a conference in London that OPEC now must consider 'whether the existing price level . . . is, in fact, very close to the reasonable price for our crude and take it easy from now on'. Other OPEC ministers have made statements along the same line.

It may be assumed from these statements that OPEC's pricing policy in the 1980s will be more sensitive to market conditions than it was in the 1970s. If this is so, OPEC real prices will not rise significantly over the next nine years. If this assumption is wrong oil prices could continue to rise significantly for only a limited period before the organization's price structure would collapse under the onslaught of consumer conservation and producer competition.

## NOTES

1 I postulate as 'significant' a real average annual price increase in excess of 1.5 percent from 1981 to 1990.

2 This would represent about a 50 percent increase from the current (mid-1981) composite OPEC crude price. By comparison, from 1973 to 1980 the real OPEC crude price rose by 700 percent.

3 This assumes a sustainable capacity of 3.0 MMB/D in Iran, 2.8 MMB/D in Kuwait and 10.5 MMB/D in Saudi Arabia. All other capacity data are taken from the Central Intelligence Agency's publication, *International Energy Statistical Review* of July 28, 1981.

# 6 Recent Oil Price Escalations: Implications for OPEC Stability

GEORGE DALY JAMES M. GRIFFIN
HENRY B. STEELE

## I INTRODUCTION

Following the political upheavals in Iran of 1978–79 the world price of oil increased from $15 to $32 a barrel. A widespread belief in both the private and public sector, heavily reinforced by recent experience, holds that this increase will be permanent and, indeed, that the real price of oil may increase still further in the years ahead. This viewpoint is set forth in this volume by Morris Adelman in Chapter 2 and by Robert Pindyck in Chapter 7. Recently, the Energy Modeling Forum at Stanford University completed a survey of ten leading models. To quote the draft summary report by James Sweeney:[1]

> While there remains a high degree of uncertainty about future world oil prices, most of the uncertainty concerns not whether real prices will rise, but rather how rapidly they will increase . . . The overall real price trend will be upward.

According to this view, the price softness of 1981–82 was a temporary aberration due essentially to recessions in Europe and the U.S. Alternatively, are current price trends the result of long term supply and demand forces and thus a precursor of future price trends? Our view is that the magnitude of the 1978–79 price increase may ultimately be viewed as a watershed event which triggered substantial and fundamental changes in the long run supply and demand for oil.

Potential sources of such changes are numerous. It now appears that significant synthetic oil industries will develop in a number of nations including the United States, Canada, and Venezuela.[2] Saudi Arabia's plans to substantially enlarge productive capacity suggest that the Saudis now recognize the importance of reserve production capacity for stabilizing world crude prices. In addition, Saudi proposals for a mechanical pricing formula tied to exchange rates, inflation rates, and world economic growth reflect serious concerns with the crisis-triggered basis for past price escalations.[3] All of these developments suggest the appropriateness of reexamining some of the long-term issues associated with the future stability of the OPEC cartel. We propose to do this by utilizing a simulation model to compare cartel behavior of a post-Iranian revolution price path ($32/bbl real 1980 price) with a pre-revolution price path ($15/bbl real 1980 price) between 1980 and 2000.

In offering the results of still another model to the vast existing collection of models and forecasts, we note several distinguishing methodological characteristics. First, unlike many models which view OPEC as a monolithic wealth maximizer[4] or a satisficing monopolist,[5] the price of oil is set exogenously, allowing the model to be simulated under alternative price paths.[6] Monolithic optimizing or satisficing models may be useful as a pedagogical device but, as Moran's chapter (Chapter 4) indicates, they have had obvious deficiencies as predictive tools of OPEC price behavior. Our approach is to take the market price as given by whatever factors and to ask what are its implications for the long run supply and demand for crude oil. Second, the model features a disaggregated approach to OPEC supply. Supply responses were developed for each of the thirteen OPEC countries on the basis of actual and potential reserves, absorptive capacity, and political constraints. Each of these countries was then assigned to one of three groups designed to describe inherent differences in member countries' objectives and supply responses. Third, in contrast to previous studies which apply *ad hoc* price and income elasticities of demand, the results here utilize estimates of these key parameters based on the pooled intercountry analysis of energy demand in Griffin (1979).

Despite these distinguishing characteristics, our model shares several important similarities with its predecessors: (1) the analysis is partial equilibrium, focusing only on the oil market, thereby overlooking energy/macroeconomic interactions and financial market effects, (2) estimates of oil supply responses are essentially judgmental.

While we stop well short of predictions regarding the health and life expectancy of OPEC, we do believe that the analysis offers potentially useful insights into the issue of cartel stability. In particular, under certain highly plausible assumptions regarding key variables, a $32 real price path requires fairly drastic adaptations among OPEC members in order to balance supply and demand. This suggests, in turn, that it may be appropriate that we critically examine either the likelihood of such adjustments or, alternatively, reconsider the sustainability of such a price path.

Section II outlines the structure of the simulation model as well as the key supply and demand assumptions. Section III presents the comparison of the pre- and post-Iranian revolution price path simulations, emphasizing first the effects of price on world oil consumption and the supply response from non-OPEC countries over the period 1980–2000. The critical question then centers on the allocation of OPEC demand among the three types of OPEC producers. The magnitude and duration of the production cutbacks by the Cartel Core are central to the instability question. In Section IV, we examine the sensitivity of the above findings to alternative assumptions regarding world economic growth and the price paths of alternative energy forms. Section V explores how the model might be used to discover inconsistencies in the decisionmaker's assumptions. Section VI recapitulates our findings on the OPEC stability question.

## II MODEL DETAILS

### Model Structure

A fully dynamic simulation model is used to solve for non-communist world oil demand ($D$), non-OPEC production ($S_{no}$) excluding communist countries, and production from three respective OPEC production groups ($S_1$, $S_2$, $S_3$). The model assumes market clearing behavior at every period, that is,

$$D = S_{no} + S_1 + S_2 + S_3 \tag{1}$$

Note that we exclude communist areas under the assumption that future net imports or exports to non-communist areas are likely to be small.[7] Thus, as in the WAES study, we focus on the world outside the communist areas (WOCA) as the relevant market.

Econometric relationships form the basis for demand determination while supply relationships are based on judgmental estimates, which include considerations of present and anticipated reserves, absorptive capacity, and political and engineering constraints. Key exogenous variables to the model include the price of oil relative to other goods and an index of world economic activity. Since oil prices are treated as exogenous, the structure of the model is recursive, beginning with oil demand determination, then proceeding to supply determination.

The world demand (non-communist), $D_t$, for oil in period $t$ depends upon economic activity ($A_t$) in period $t$ and a distributed lag ($L$) on previous years' prices of oil relative to the other goods, ($P_o/P_a$), as follows:

$$D_t = F\left(A_t, \frac{P_o}{P_a}(L)\right) \tag{2}$$

Given assumptions about world economic growth and the price path of oil relative to other goods, equation (2) provides the solution for world oil demand. Implicit in this formulation is a long run oil price elasticity of −.73 and an elasticity of .75 with respect to economic activity.

Next, the model determines non-OPEC, non-communist oil production ($S_{no}$) as a function of the real price of oil ($P_o/P_a$) and existing institutional constraints ($Z_{no}$):

$$S_{no_t} = g\left(\frac{P_o}{P_a}, Z_{no_t}\right) \tag{3}$$

In this model, non-OPEC producers behave essentially as the competitive fringe producers outlined in Chapter 1. In addition we assume that non-OPEC production cannot exceed levels consistent with engineering limitations on reserves to production ratios, that is, production in a certain period must be equal to or less than a given fraction, $\alpha$, of previous year reserves ($R_{no_{t-1}}$):

$$S_{no_t} \leq \alpha R_{no_{t-1}} \tag{3a}$$

In turn, non-OPEC additions to reserves ($RA_{no}$) depend upon a distributed lag on past relative oil prices ($P_o/P_a$):

$$RA_{no_t} = f\left(\frac{P_o}{P_a}(L)\right) \tag{3b}$$

By the perpetual inventory formula, reserves at the end of period $t$ are obtained by the identity that they equal initial reserves ($R_{no_{t-1}}$) plus additions to reserves ($RA_{no_t}$) minus production ($S_{no_t}$):

$$R_{no_t} = R_{no_{t-1}} + RA_{no_t} - S_{no_t} \tag{3c}$$

Having determined non-OPEC production in equation (3) and oil demand in equation (2), we now turn to the question of how OPEC demand, defined as (2) less (3), is allocated among the producing countries. In doing this we make a departure from previous models[8] by dividing OPEC nations into three groups, each of which behaves in a different manner. The groups are: the Cartel Core (Saudi Arabia, Kuwait, Qatar, Libya, and the UAE), the Price Maximizers (Iran,

Algeria, and Venezuela), and the Output Maximizers (Iraq, Nigeria, Indonesia, Ecuador, and Gabon). The rationale for the individual groupings is provided subsequently, but for now we will just formally describe the assumed behavior of these three groups.

The Output Maximizers are assumed to behave as do the non-OPEC oil producers, taking oil price as given and allocating production so as to maximize their wealth. This behavior is analogous to the competitive fringe producers described in Chapter 1. As in the non-OPEC production case, production by the Output Maximizers ($S_1$) is a function of the real price of oil ($P_o/P_a$) and institutional constraints ($Z_1$), subject to a reserves to production ratio limit:

$$S_{1_t} = F\left(\frac{P_o}{P_a}, Z_{1_t}\right) \tag{4}$$

subject to

$$S_{1_t} \leq \alpha R_{1_{t-1}} \tag{4a}$$

As in the case of non-OPEC producers, reserve additions depend upon lagged real oil prices:

$$RA_{1_t} = F\left(\frac{P_o}{P_a}(L)\right) \tag{4b}$$

Reserves are obtained by the simple identity:

$$R_{1_t} = R_{1_{t-1}} + RA_{1_t} - S_{1_t} \tag{4c}$$

The supply response from the cartel group labeled Price Maximizers is similar to that indicated by the target revenue model set forth in Chapter 1 and advocated by Teece in Chapter 3. It is assumed that as long as this reserves to production ratio is below a certain threshold $\gamma_2^*$ (number of years of production at current production rates) there is a backward bending supply curve; that is, the Price Maximizers are willing to restrain output so as to raise price:

$$S_{2_t} = f(P_o/P_a) \tag{5}$$

where $\frac{1}{\alpha} \leq \frac{R_{2_{t-1}}}{S_{2_t}} \leq \gamma_2^*$ and

$$\frac{\partial S_2}{\partial (P_o/P_a)_+} < 0, \ \frac{\partial S_2}{\partial (P_o/P_a)_-} = 0$$

Alternatively, when the cutbacks in production necessary to sustain a high price result in large excess capacity, reflected in a reserves to production ratio in excess of $\gamma_2^*$, these producers are assumed to selectively cut price to increase production. In response to higher prices, they will no longer be willing to reduce output:

$$S_{2_t} = f^*(P_o/P_a) \qquad (5a)$$

where if $R_{2_{t-1}}/S_{2_t} > \gamma_2^*$, then $\dfrac{\partial S_2}{\partial(P_o/P_a)_+} = 0$ and

$$\frac{\partial S_2}{\partial(P_o/P_a)} < 0$$

Reserve additions are set exogenously, independent of price. Thus, reserves in period $t$ can be calculated as:

$$R_{2_t} = R_{2_{t-1}} + RA_{2_t} - S_{2_t} \qquad (5b)$$

We assume that the Cartel Core acts as a residual supplier, meeting all remaining OPEC demand at the market price. In effect, the Cartel Core acts as the dominant firm producer as outlined in Chapter 1 and advocated by Adelman (Chapter 2). Production by the Cartel Core then follows from a simple supply/demand identity:

$$S_3 = D - S_{no} - S_1 - S_2 \qquad (6)$$

As we discuss below, price paths leading to very high ratios of reserves to production restrict the ability of the Cartel Core to maintain price and suggest the possibility of cartel instability. As in the case of Price Maximizers, reserve additions are treated as exogenous. Reserves in each period can be determined as follows:

$$R_{3_t} = R_{3_{t-1}} + RA_{3_t} - S_{3_t} \qquad (6a)$$

To recapitulate, the supply representation of the model implicitly accepts Adelman's view that OPEC is a cartel, as evidenced by the existence of the Cartel Core, behaving as the dominant firm model hypothesizes. Clearly, if the Cartel Core did not act as the residual supplier, the market clearing equation (1) need not hold at the existing price level. At the same time, the presence of the Price Maximizers, exhibiting a backward bending supply schedule, incorporates, at least partially, elements of Teece's target revenue model. The presence of the Price Maximizers helps to explain cartel stability in an era of rising prices. Yet, as Teece emphasizes, this model implies greater instability in an era of declining prices as the Price Maximizers will increase output in order to maintain oil revenues.

While viewing OPEC as a cartel, the model stops short of postulating wealth maximizing behavior. Prices, which are exogenous, can be set to achieve economic and noneconomic goals. The model takes price as a datum and asks what adjustments are necessary to sustain such a price. The following two sections provide details on the supply and demand assumptions. Some readers may prefer to go directly to the discussion of measures of prospective instability.

## Crude Oil Supply Projections

Crude oil supply projections were developed for each of thirteen OPEC members and for twenty-seven non-OPEC countries outside communist areas. Projections were also made for other non-OPEC regions, taken as a group. These projections were made in the form of annual estimates of reserve additions, production, and year-end reserves for each country for each year, from 1980 through 2000.

In general, estimates of reserve additions were based upon geological information regarding both the discovered and undiscovered elements of a country's probable resource base. Not all of this material is available in published form. Interviews with government and oil company personnel proved helpful in estimating future reserve additions in a number of countries, of which Mexico, Iraq, Venezuela, Cameroon, Argentina, Brazil, Tunisia, Canada, Australia, Libya, Gabon, and of course Saudi Arabia are the most important, in terms of relative future discovery capability.

For some countries a well-informed estimate of the discoverable oil in the resource base is the most important data item, since in these regions large additional volumes of reserves will become available during the next twenty years at high prices. For countries with a more developed petroleum resource base, estimates of the additional amounts of oil that can be found and produced at higher prices depend more closely upon technology and on engineering estimates of increases in discovery, development, and production costs as known resources are more intensively developed. For countries with a mix of new and of developed regions in their resource bases, both geological and economic data are of considerable importance. Finally, political and cultural factors will in some countries be an important determinant of the rate at which the reserves in the resource base are discovered, developed, and produced. In this last respect we can distinguish between OPEC 'doves' and 'hawks', which prefer lower or higher prices, and higher or lower production limits, and non-OPEC reluctant dragons like Mexico, which might or might not develop an export industry commensurate with their reserves and productive capacity in accordance with their leaders' own idiosyncratic perceptions of the relationships between oil policy and international prestige.

The supply projections were divided into three categories: (1) OPEC members; (2) non-OPEC producers outside communist areas; and (3) oil producers in communist areas. OPEC members were divided into three groups: (a) Output Maximizers, (b) Price Maximizers, and (c) the Cartel Core. Future world oil market developments are foreseen to revolve around the relationship of a price determined at a high level by the OPEC cartel, and the increasing efforts over time, not only of non-OPEC producers, but also of the 'competitive fringe' within OPEC, to develop new reserves and productive capacity which will be more than normally profitable at the high OPEC price.

The Cartel Core consists of those OPEC members with vast oil reserves, relatively small populations, and more flexible economic development plans such that the relatively low production rates necessary to sustain oil prices at or above monopoly levels are both feasible and desirable. The non-OPEC oil producers are assumed to behave as a 'competitive fringe' in the world oil market, increasing output over time up to the rate at which production costs at the margin are equal to the OPEC price. The OPEC Output Maximizer group will act essentially like the non-OPEC segment of the market, increasing their output rates over time to the point where price equals marginal cost. The Output Maximizer subset of OPEC members consists of those countries with relatively lower total oil reserves, relatively higher populations, and greater pressures for internal economic development. Hence these countries are motivated to increase production at the OPEC-determined price in order to further their economic development. Unlike the Cartel Core members, they can efficiently invest the proceeds from much larger oil export volumes within their domestic economies without driving marginal investment returns to negative levels or causing unmanageable rapid inflation.

The OPEC Price Maximizers are in an intermediate position between the Cartel Core and the Output Maximizers. Behaviorally, the Price Maximizers are akin to the producers in the target revenue model. These members, like the Output Maximizers, have relatively large populations and considerable potential for economic development, but unlike other OPEC members their reserves are neither high relative to current production rates (as in the Cartel Core) nor do they appear to be capable of significant expansion in the future (as in the case of the Output Maximizers). During periods of short supply, the activities of the Price Maximizers aid the Cartel Core members since they can satisfy their target revenues at the higher prices by reducing output. While the Price Maximizers tend to produce close to full capacity, they do all that is in their power to avoid reducing the price of their oil and thus promote price stability. Since their total output is a minor fraction of that of OPEC as a whole, and since their expansibility of productive capacity is limited, they do not ordinarily exert downward pressure on OPEC prices because of their need to produce relatively close to capacity. But if non-OPEC supply increases, the activities of the Price Maximizers can become increasingly destabilizing to OPEC. Their output can become a larger fraction of OPEC's total production as the Cartel Core cuts its own production in order to prevent price declines, and if prices fall, the Price Maximizers try to increase output in order to keep oil export revenues from declining. Thus they can move from being a factor promoting cartel stability (like the Cartel Core) to a factor promoting instability (like the Output Maximizers).

The following OPEC members have been assigned to the Cartel Core: Saudi Arabia, Kuwait, Qatar, the United Arab Emirates, and Libya. All of these areas share the characteristics specified above: very large oil reserves, small populations, and a physical geography characterized by barren desert regions. Previously, researchers hypothesized that the absorptive capacity of these economies were quite limited and that consequently these countries, facing no internal development pressures, could accept much lower oil production rates to sustain OPEC's price. As Adelman points out in Chapter 2, the notion of a rigid absorptive capacity is contradicted by the phenominal growth in internal investments within Saudi Arabia. Our hypothesis is that while domestic investment potential is readily expansible, it is also quite flexible. Cartel Core members may cut back oil production, sustain declining oil revenues, and postpone domestic investment plans without creating the severe domestic problems experienced in other countries. The Arabian peninsula members generally prefer to maintain prices during periods of slack demand for OPEC oil by carrying more excess capacity. Their preferences are for relatively lower prices than are demanded by other OPEC members since, among other reasons, they stand to lose more in the long run, due to their large reserves, if economical substitutes for OPEC oil are developed in the future. Libya, however, has at various times in the past acted more like a Price Maximizer, insisting upon excessively high prices for its own oil with its advantages of higher quality and greater proximity to European markets. Libya is, however, included with the

Cartel Core since its own oil revenue uses for internal development have been very low, suggesting it can easily reduce output to help stabilize the cartel during periods of low demand.

The Price Maximizers consist of Algeria, Iran, and Venezuela. Ever since the beginning of OPEC, Venezuela has been the primary advocate of higher prices per barrel and restraint in production levels, due to its own low ratio of reserves to production and to its relatively low level of reserves per capita. With considerable potential for economic development, Venezuela is interested in high total annual oil export receipts; hence its desire to maximize prices for a relatively low level of exports. Algeria, like Libya, possesses high quality oil close to European markets and has in the past been a vigorous advocate of maximizing the price of its own oil. Algeria, however, has low oil reserves relative to its output rate, low reserves per capita, and promising prospects for internal development. Algeria has probably operated closer to full capacity in oil production than any other member of OPEC, and is a good example of a cartel member which desires to maximize both its price and its output. In the past, the same has been true of Iran, the third price maximizer member of OPEC. Before the 1978 revolution, Iran's policy was to maximize both oil prices and output in order to finance the very ambitious economic and military development programs of its former ruler. Although Iran has absolutely large oil reserves, its population is larger than that of the other Price Maximizers and its economic development potential correspondingly greater not only due to higher population but greater resources in other respects. In projecting Iran's future reserves and production it is assumed that Iranian oil resources will evolve under more rational and efficient management. It is further assumed that the oil resource base will not have been seriously damaged during the period of mismanagement.

The Output Maximizers consist of Iraq, Nigeria, Indonesia, Ecuador, and Gabon. This name is given to this group since logically these OPEC members should in the long run aim at maximizing their output, given their relatively large populations, extensive plans for economic development, and their relatively low but substantially expansible ratios of reserves per capita. As long as the other members of OPEC, in particular the Cartel Core, are willing to limit output in order to maintain high prices, the OPEC Output Maximizers should have the same incentive as non-OPEC producers to maximize output up to the point where price equals marginal cost. It must be conceded that to date only Iraq has appeared to be actively following the strategy of an Output Maximizer, by expanding output, even during periods of weak market demand, and by making price reductions when necessary. In part, Iraq's program of output expansion stems from its very large potential oil resources base - perhaps 300 billion barrels - relative to which its current output rate is quite low. Iraq is also expanding oil exports in order to finance ambitious internal development programs, and desires to have an expanded role in OPEC as a result of its greater share in the cartel's total output. While Iraq may in its official statements advocate policies of price stability and production limits, the actual opportunities and pressures faced by the country are such as to lead it increasingly into the role of an Output Maximizer. Only the unexpectedly rapid development of its vast resource base might temper its direction toward the Cartel Core, where it could bear the burden of excess capacity at the same time that it continues to develop its own economy. However, such a rate of reserve additions and development of productive capacity in Iraq is not seen in this study by the year 2000.

Indonesia may be the next OPEC member to follow a policy of output maximization, since its population is the largest of any OPEC member, its development plans depend critically on oil revenues, and its reserves, although not large, are thought to be expansible. Nigeria is the second most populous OPEC member and has larger and probably more expansible reserves than Indonesia. Gabon is essentially a smaller version of Nigeria with regard to these characteristics. Ecuador, which has perhaps the most problematic future of any OPEC member, still has the motivation to be an Output Maximizer due to low per capita oil revenues, an expansible resource base, and the capacity for internal economic development.

Table 6.1 shows the crude oil reserves estimates and reserve additions of individual OPEC members for 1980–2000 assuming a $32 real price path. For Saudi Arabia the assumption was made that at a high price level enough development activity would proceed to allow an increase in proved reserves of 2 billion barrels per year after netting out current production. (Higher rates of reserve additions would be possible, but there appears to be little motivation for this.) Kuwait's reported proved reserves have been stagnating for a number of years due to the imposition of an arbitrary production limit, but reserves are still high relative to production and could be increased substantially if necessary. It is projected that proved reserves in Kuwait will slowly decline to about 60 billion barrels by 1990 and then remain at that level through 2000. Reserves in Qatar are predicted to increase to a peak of about 4.5 billion barrels by 1990 and then decline slightly thereafter, while those of the UAE are projected to decline to about 25 billion barrels by 1993 and then remain at that level through 2000. Libya, on the other hand, is currently engaged in an active campaign to increase its reserves through new discoveries, and since the Libyan resource base is regarded as promising, Libyan reserves are estimated to increase from 20 to 40 billion barrels between 1980 and 1995, and then to decline slightly to 37.5 billion by 2000. Thus proved reserves in the Cartel Core rise from about 293 billion in 1980 to 325.5 billion in 2000, despite an enormous absolute level of production during those twenty years.

For the Price Maximizers, Algerian reserves are estimated to rise slightly to 9 billion barrels by 1982–85 and to fall to 8.5 billion in 1990 and to 7 billion in 2000. Even this performance is quite creditable given the strain on Algeria's limited resource base of producing over a million barrels per day during the remainder of the century. Venezuela's output is the most difficult to predict in this group. Higher prices should on balance be enough to stimulate the additional efforts needed to keep reserves roughly constant over the next two decades despite continuing high output rates and a resource base which (excluding the tar belt) is not extremely expansible. Iranian reserves are also difficult to predict, but enough is known about geological and cost conditions to project a moderate decline in reserves (from 57.5 billion barrels in 1980 to 50 billion barrels in 2000) by 2000 assuming that industry conditions improve and Iranian output is permitted to more closely approach its pre-revolutionary volume.

Among the Output Maximizers, Iraq is projected to be able to increase its reserves from 31 to 46.5 billion barrels between 1980 and 2000 while increasing its annual output rate appreciably over the same period. This effort should require the discovery and development of only a portion of Iraq's probably existent additional resources. Nigeria, like Libya, is trying to stimulate more exploration to increase its own oil reserves, and it appears that the resource base is there if the necessary arrangements can be made between the government and the oil companies. Accordingly, reserves are projected to increase appreciably. Indonesia is in the same general position as Libya and Nigeria, desirous of increasing its reserves, but with a smaller total resource base. A successful effort might increase reserves from 9.5 to 11.1 billion barrels between 1980 and 1994, with a decline to 10.5 billion occurring by 2000. Again, at the higher price level this rise in reserves would be compatible with increased output rates over two decades. Ecuadorean reserves, which stood at only 1.1 billion barrels in 1979, might be increased to 1.5 billion by 1990 and might then fall to 1.3 billion by 2000. Reserves in Gabon, however, which were about 5 billion barrels in 1978, could increase to 8 billion by 1995 before beginning to decline. The total reserves of the Output Maximizers increase from 64.6 billion in 1980 to 89.1 billion by 2000.

Table 6.2 shows the estimated crude oil reserves for non-OPEC members. Space limits do not permit detailed discussion of projections for each of the twenty-nine individual areas covered, but

Table 6.1 *Crude Oil Reserves Estimates (in MMB): OPEC Members ($32/bbl)*

| | *1979 reserves* | | *Projected proved reserves* | | | | *Gross reserve additions (annual rates)* | | | |
|---|---|---|---|---|---|---|---|---|---|---|
| | *Proved* | *Estimated ultimate recovery* | *1985* | *1990* | *1995* | *2000* | *1981–85* | *1986–90* | *1991–95* | *1996–2000* |
| Output Maximizers: | | | | | | | | | | |
| Iraq | 31,000 | 300,000 | 35,000 | 40,000 | 44,000 | 46,500 | 2,212 | 2,516 | 2,608 | 2,197 |
| Nigeria | 17,400 | 40,000 | 20,000 | 21,200 | 22,200 | 23,000 | 1,418 | 1,673 | 1,488 | 1,417 |
| Indonesia | 9,600 | 18,000 | 9,650 | 10,500 | 11,000 | 10,500 | 466 | 550 | 489 | 467 |
| Ecuador | 1,100 | 3,500 | 1,250 | 1,500 | 1,440 | 1,300 | 68 | 81 | 72 | 68 |
| Gabon | 5,000 | 12,500 | 6,000 | 7,500 | 8,000 | 7,800 | 315 | 372 | 327 | 315 |
| Group total: | 64,100 | 374,000 | 71,900 | 80,700 | 86,640 | 89,100 | 4,479 | 5,192 | 4,984 | 4,464 |
| Price Maximizers: | | | | | | | | | | |
| Algeria | 8,440 | 15,000 | 9,000 | 8,500 | 8,000 | 7,000 | 435 | 415 | 390 | 272 |
| Iran | 58,000 | 75,000 | 53,500 | 52,000 | 51,000 | 50,000 | 465 | 740 | 706 | 616 |
| Venezuela | 17,870 | 27,000 | 16,500 | 17,000 | 16,900 | 16,400 | 405 | 735 | 650 | 546 |
| Group total: | 84,310 | 117,000 | 79,000 | 77,500 | 75,900 | 73,400 | 1,305 | 1,890 | 1,746 | 1,434 |
| Cartel Core: | | | | | | | | | | |
| Saudi Arabia | 163,650 | 400,000 | 175,000 | 185,000 | 190,000 | 195,000 | 4,866 | 3,742 | 2,031 | 1,302 |
| Kuwait | 65,400 | 100,000 | 62,500 | 60,000 | 60,000 | 60,000 | 729 | 552 | 436 | 353 |
| Qatar | 3,760 | 7,500 | 4,000 | 4,500 | 4,000 | 3,500 | 146 | 111 | 87 | 71 |
| Libya | 23,500 | 50,000 | 33,000 | 39,000 | 40,000 | 37,500 | 739 | 529 | 410 | 328 |
| UAE | 29,400 | 50,000 | 27,300 | 25,600 | 25,000 | 25,000 | 695 | 552 | 444 | 367 |
| Neutral zone | 6,260 | 10,000 | 5,900 | 5,400 | 4,900 | 4,500 | 213 | 166 | 130 | 107 |
| Group total: | 291,970 | 617,500 | 307,700 | 319,500 | 323,900 | 325,500 | 7,388 | 5,652 | 3,538 | 2,528 |
| OPEC total: | 440,380 | 1,108,500 | 458,600 | 477,700 | 486,440 | 488,000 | 13,172 | 12,734 | 10,268 | 8,426 |

particular consideration should be given to several of the most important countries, of which Mexico is the most crucial. Mexican oil reserves stood at about 31 billion barrels in 1979 but an estimate of 100 billion in ultimate recovery seems reasonable at a $32/bbl real price over time, in the light of available data on Mexican petroleum geology. Given the desire of the existing and prospective Mexican government leaders to make Mexico a 'big power' in the world oil market, reserves have been estimated to increase at the rate of 6 billion barrels per year for 1979–83, 2.5 billion per year for 1984–87, 2 billion per year for 1988–92, and 1 billion per year for 1993–2000, reaching a total of 78 billion by 2000. While this projection may seem extravagant to many people, it is felt that the Mexican resource base justifies this forecast. It should also be noted that Mexican production is projected to expand less rapidly than reserves, largely for political reasons.

The projected increase in production and reserves in Cameroon is admittedly more speculative, and is based upon reports by geologists that the petroleum potential of Cameroon is roughly identical with that of its neighbor, Nigeria. Based on this information the projections for Cameroon are made on the basis of the analogy with the earlier production history of Nigeria, but allowing for the much higher prices for oil now available. Cameroon's reserves are estimated to increase from only 140 million barrels in 1979 to 25 billion by 1993–95, followed by a slight decline to 24.2 billion by 2000. Canadian oil reserves are projected to fall from 6.8 billion barrels in 1979 to 6 billion barrels in 1983, but then to rise slowly but steadily to 9.3 billion by 2000 as oil resources in Arctic regions are discovered and developed. Even at high prices, US proved reserves will fail to increase, declining from about 26.5 billion barrels in 1979 to about 20 billion by 2000. Even so, given the continued high production rates projected for the United States, the moderate decline in total reserves over a twenty-year period requires the discovery and development of many billions of barrels of new reserves during that time.

North Sea area reserves are projected to decline more rapidly than US reserves, while reserves in the other nine major prospective oil producing areas shown in Table 6.2 are estimated to increase significantly by 2000, although at different rates. Part of these reserve increases will result from more intensive drilling in the vicinity of regions already highly productive, as in Egypt, Syria, Oman, and Tunisia; other reserve increases are projected to come from exploratory drilling in newer regions, particularly offshore, as in Brazil, Argentina, Australia, and Malaysia.

### Crude Oil Demand Determination

The oil demand equation (2) is based on the long run elasticities

Table 6.2 *Crude Oil Reserves Estimates (in MMB): Non-OPEC ($32/bbl)*

| | *1979 reserves* | | *Projected proved reserves* | | | | *Gross reserve additions (annual rates)* | | | |
|---|---|---|---|---|---|---|---|---|---|---|
| | *Proved* | *Estimated ultimate recovery* | *1985* | *1990* | *1995* | *2000* | *1981–85* | *1986–90* | *1991–95* | *1996–2000* |
| United States | 26,500 | 45,000 | 23,400 | 22,500 | 21,000 | 20,000 | 2,751 | 2,970 | 2,840 | 2,777 |
| Canada | 6,800 | 20,000 | 6,500 | 7,600 | 8,600 | 9,300 | 423 | 464 | 626 | 809 |
| Mexico | 31,250 | 100,000 | 55,000 | 66,000 | 73,000 | 78,000 | 5,412 | 4,348 | 3,714 | 3,628 |
| North Sea: | | | | | | | | | | |
| UK | 15,400 | 20,000 | 14,000 | 13,000 | 11,700 | 10,200 | 913 | 817 | 866 | 760 |
| Norway | 5,750 | 10,000 | 5,100 | 5,500 | 5,100 | 4,450 | 330 | 336 | 377 | 331 |
| Others | 400 | 1,000 | 350 | 400 | 450 | 415 | 24 | 23 | 31 | 27 |
| Cameroon | 140 | 35,000 | 14,000 | 22,000 | 25,000 | 24,200 | 2,880 | 2,088 | 1,098 | 955 |
| Brunei-Malaysia | 4,600 | 15,000 | 5,600 | 6,000 | 5,800 | 5,400 | 360 | 366 | 429 | 421 |
| Egypt | 3,100 | 8,000 | 3,700 | 4,100 | 4,300 | 3,950 | 243 | 250 | 319 | 320 |
| India | 2,600 | 7,500 | 3,050 | 3,175 | 3,280 | 3,260 | 203 | 194 | 242 | 212 |
| Oman | 2,400 | 5,500 | 3,100 | 3,600 | 3,890 | 3,840 | 195 | 221 | 287 | 252 |
| Argentina | 2,400 | 10,000 | 3,300 | 4,050 | 4,300 | 4,290 | 269 | 295 | 255 | 287 |
| Tunisia | 2,250 | 7,500 | 2,900 | 3,400 | 3,850 | 3,965 | 288 | 207 | 283 | 248 |
| Australia | 2,130 | 6,000 | 3,000 | 3,700 | 3,900 | 3,500 | 182 | 227 | 287 | 252 |
| Syria | 2,000 | 5,000 | 2,700 | 3,100 | 3,250 | 3,200 | 170 | 188 | 242 | 216 |
| Brazil | 1,220 | 15,000 | 4,000 | 5,200 | 6,100 | 6,550 | 601 | 504 | 423 | 614 |
| Other non-OPEC | 7,250 | 28,350 | 11,520 | 13,865 | 13,455 | 13,020 | 964 | 666 | 532 | 543 |
| TOTAL non-OPEC | 116,190 | 338,850 | 161,220 | 186,940 | 196,975 | 197,540 | 16,208 | 14,164 | 12,851 | 12,652 |
| TOTAL WOCA | 556,570 | 1,447,350 | 619,820 | 664,640 | 683,415 | 685,540 | 29,380 | 26,898 | 23,119 | 21,078 |

obtained by simulations of the OECD Energy Demand Model developed by Griffin (1979). The model provides a separate sectoral characterization of energy demand for the manufacturing, residential and commercial, transportation, and electricity-generating sectors of eighteen OECD countries. Energy is in turn disaggregated into electricity, coal, oil, and gas (manufactured and natural). The model captures both energy/nonenergy substitution relationships as well as interfuel substitution responses. Economic activity is exogenous to the model.

Initially, it was planned to simulate a nine-country subgroup of the largest energy consuming economies, utilizing the model to determine oil demand directly. Preliminary work revealed that the model tended to indicate a too rapid rate of adjustment to long run equilibrium, yielding unreasonable short run price responses. It was decided to develop a single equation approximation of the aggregate model's long run elasticities with respect to price and economic activity. Simulations experiments with the OECD Demand Model indicated long run elasticities of .75 with respect to economic activity and − .73 with respect to crude oil price. These elasticities became the basis for the single equation approximation to the OECD Demand Model.

In order to provide a more plausible adjustment to the long run, we chose the simple geometric lag for the price effect and an instantaneous adjustment in response to economic activity. Assuming a log-linear specification, we obtain:

$$\ln D_t = \alpha_0 + \frac{\alpha_1}{1-\lambda L} \ln \frac{P_o}{P_{a_t}} + \alpha_2 \ln A_t \qquad (7)$$

where $\lambda$ is the speed of adjustment parameter and $L$ is the lag operator. To assure a slow speed of adjustment consistent with the turnover time of the capital stock of energy-consuming equipment, we let $\lambda = .9$. Letting $\lambda = .9$ implies that after ten years approximately 70 percent of the adjustment to the long run price elasticity has occurred. $A_t$ is simply an index of economic growth equal to unity in 1977, likewise $P_{a_t}$ is indexed to equal unity in 1977. The exact functional form for empirical application is:

$$\ln D_t = 1.338 - .073 \ln \frac{P_o}{P_{a_t}} + .753 \ln A_t - .678 \ln A_{t-1} + .9 \ln D_{t-1} \qquad (8)$$

Note that the long run price elasticity of − .73 is implied by $\alpha_1/(1-\lambda)$ and the long run income elasticity of .753 is given by $\alpha_2$ in equation (7). In subsequent simulation experiments, the critical nature of the price elasticity assumption is considered in greater detail.

## III MEASURES OF PROSPECTIVE INSTABILITY

In utilizing the results of this model to examine the issue of long run OPEC behavior and stability we place great emphasis on two general measures: (1) the market shares of the various producing groups, that is, non-OPEC, Output Maximizers, Price Maximizers, and the Cartel Core; (2) the reserves to production ratios for Price Maximizers and Cartel Core members.

The emphasis we place on market shares arises basically from the traditional importance of this variable to the analysis and description of cartel behavior. As emphasized in the market sharing monopoly model in Chapter 1, colluding members of a cartel will tend to share markets on a predetermined basis. It is our assumption that changes in market shares, particularly when they are not related to fundamental determinants of wealth-maximizing behavior such as reserve size, present substantial internal political, managerial, and equity problems for OPEC. This is particularly true of those changes which take place over relatively short time intervals. If large enough, such changes may require fundamental changes in the behavior of one or more OPEC members (e.g. an additional country adopting behavioral patterns of the Core members) in order to sustain the cartel. Thus, the greater the stability of market shares, the greater the likelihood of the continued health of OPEC, and the greater the instability, the less that likelihood.

Market shares alone, however, are inadequate as a proxy for an indicator of OPEC stability. This is because changes in such shares may occur due to changes in available reserves which reflect voluntary, wealth-maximizing behavior on the part of a nation whose production is declining and which, therefore, should not threaten cartel stability. For this reason, we use the ratio of reserves to production as a guide to excess capacity. That is, we assume that changes in market shares which reflect substantial upward departures from wealth-maximizing ratios of reserves to production imply undesired excess capacity and are indicative of threats to the stability of the cartel. Of course, there is no certainty regarding how or when ratios of reserves to production will prove destabilizing. Our hypothesis is simply that the probability of destabilizing actions is directly related to the magnitude of the undesired excess capacity as previously defined.

The role of reserves to production ratios in influencing cartel stability can be seen more clearly by reference to Figure 6.1 in which we plot that ratio on the vertical axis and time on the horizontal. The time horizon begins at $t_0$ and ends at $t_n$. The schedule $\gamma_3^*$ represents the maximum desired ratio of reserves to production ratio for the Cartel Core given the behavior of other suppliers which, as

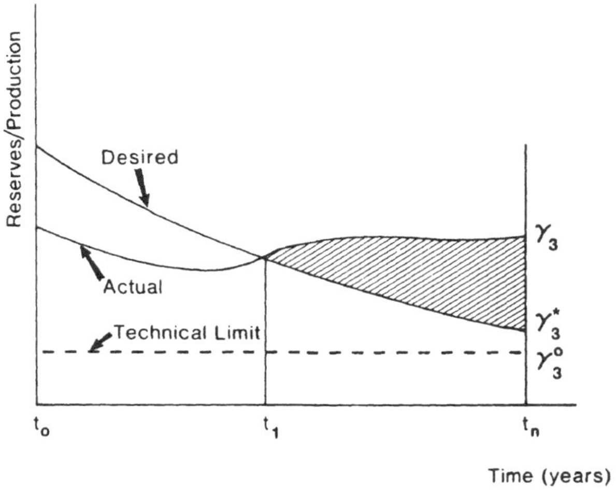


Figure 6.1 *Excess capacity as a destabilizing influence.*

noted above, depend on a variety of factors such as the real price of oil, technical and institutional factors, etc. Also, technical constraints determine a lower limit for this ratio at each point in time. This limit is depicted as the dotted schedule $\gamma_3^0$ in Figure 6.1 and is determined by a relationship identical to that expressed earlier in equation (4a). Finally, we draw the schedule $\gamma_3$ to depict actual (in the case of present or past) or expected (in the case of future) *actual* values for this ratio.

Any time that $\gamma_3 > \gamma_3^0$, excess capacity in some technical sense exists. However, as long as $\gamma_3 < \gamma_3^*$ any such excess capacity can be viewed as desired and is not a threat to cartel stability. For example, in Figure 6.1 excess capacity in the technical sense exists over the time interval $t_0$ to $t_1$. However, we view this as *desired* excess capacity over the interval $t_0$ to $t_1$ and, therefore, not a sign of instability. *Undesired* excess capacity exists whenever $\gamma_3 > \gamma_3^*$, that is, whenever the actual reserves to production ratio exceeds the maximum desired one, as is the case between $t_1$ and $t_n$ in Figure 6.1. Our hypothesis is simply that at any time $t$, the probability of cartel instability is primarily a function of the expected value of $\gamma_3^* - \gamma_3$ over the remainder of the time horizon.[9] For example, in Figure 6.1 a producer in year $t_1$ would anticipate the foreseeable future to be characterized by undesired excess capacity within the crosshatched area reflecting the probability of cartel instability.

## IV COMPARISON OF PRE- AND POST-IRANIAN REVOLUTION OIL PRICE PATHS

### Description of Model Results

In this section of this chapter we examine alternative price paths for the world price of oil during the 1980 to 2000 time interval using the model specified in Section II, and with special attention placed on the variables discussed in Section III. Table 6.3 contrasts the production rates for the period 1980 to 2000 that would occur at $15 and $32 real price paths. In both cases, world economic activity is assumed to grow at 3.5 percent annually, so that all differences in WOCA demand arise solely because of price differentials. At the $15 real price path, oil demand in the WOCA countries grows at a 3.2 percent annual rate, reaching 98 million barrels per day (MMB/D) in 2000. Even with non-OPEC supply growing from 18.1 to 30.7 MMB/D by 2000, OPEC's share of the market expands, as OPEC production rises from 36.4 to 67.3 MMB/D. Furthermore, it is anticipated that the Cartel Core would be the primary beneficiary of this demand growth. The Output Maximizers expand production modestly from 7.5 to 10.0 MMB/D by 2000. At the same time, the Price Maximizers opt for constant production rates. The Cartel Core experiences strong growth in output, with production rising from 22.5 MMB/D to 51.1 MMB/D by 2000. In sum, at the $15 real price path, OPEC would enjoy a rising share of world oil production; moreover, the Cartel Core members' share of OPEC production would increase significantly.

The $32 real price path in Table 6.3 emphasizes the extreme sensitivity to price increases over this range. In particular on the demand side, WOCA's annual growth rate is cut from 3.2 percent to 1.1 percent annually. Oil demand expands from a rate of 46.9 MMB/D in 1980 to 59.2 MMB/D in 2000. At the same time, higher oil prices result in non-OPEC oil production doubling by 2000. Under these conditions, OPEC production is forecast to decline over the next twenty years from 27.4 MMB/D in 1980 to 22.2 MMB/D in 2000. Despite the shrinking market for OPEC crude, the Output Maximizers respond to the higher oil prices by increasing output at a rate approximately 10 percent faster than in the $15 real price path. These production increases are roughly offset by the Price Maximizers who cut production modestly in response to the higher price path. With the Price and Output Maximizers virtually offsetting each other's production responses, the Cartel Core must absorb the brunt of the reduction in oil demand. Core producers experience a production decline from 14.4 MMB/D to 6.2 MMB/D by 2000. The interesting implication is that the Cartel Core's (residual) demand schedule turns out to be elastic over this range as oil revenues decline in the $32 real price path scenario. In contrast, both the Price and Output Maximizers are major gainers from the higher price path.

Table 6.3 *Market Clearing Production Rates: 1980 to 2000*

| | *1980* | *1985* | *1990* | *1995* | *2000* |
|---|---|---|---|---|---|
| | | | *$15 real price path* | | |
| OPEC: | | | | | |
| Output Maximizers | 7.5 | 8.1 | 8.7 | 9.3 | 10.0 |
| Price Maximizers | 6.4 | 7.3 | 6.8 | 6.5 | 6.2 |
| Cartel Core | 22.5 | 28.0 | 35.7 | 43.5 | 51.1 |
| TOTAL OPEC | 36.4 | 43.3 | 51.3 | 59.3 | 67.3 |
| Non-OPEC | 18.1 | 20.7 | 22.9 | 26.2 | 30.7 |
| WOCA | 54.5 | 64.0 | 74.2 | 85.5 | 98.0 |
| | | | *$32 real price path* | | |
| OPEC: | | | | | |
| Output Maximizers | 7.7 | 8.8 | 9.8 | 10.8 | 10.9 |
| Price Maximizers | 5.3 | 6.2 | 5.8 | 5.5 | 5.1 |
| Cartel Core | 14.4 | 9.2 | 8.9 | 6.2 | 6.2 |
| TOTAL OPEC | 27.4 | 24.2 | 24.5 | 22.5 | 22.2 |
| Non-OPEC | 19.5 | 22.5 | 26.2 | 30.9 | 37.0 |
| WOCA | 46.9 | 46.7 | 50.7 | 53.4 | 59.2 |

**Potential for Instability**

For reasons given above, it is necessary to investigate market shares and the ratio of reserves to production in order to assess the potential for conflict among OPEC producers. Table 6.4 reports the ratio of reserves to production (*R/P*) and Table 6.5 reports market shares for the respective producing groups. At the $15 real price path, the ratio of reserves to production declines for all producing groups, indicating that market conditions will improve for producers. Of particular significance is the decline in OPEC's overall *R/P* ratio from 36.3 years in 1980 to 19.5 years by 2000, resulting primarily from the sharp fall in *R/P* by the Cartel Core. These developments would clearly reinforce the stability of OPEC.

Market share trends also imply cartel stability at the $15 real price path. The largest gains in market shares are by the Cartel Core as their share of the market rises from 41.4 percent in 1980 to 52.1 percent in 2000. Since the Cartel Core serves as a residual supplier and since their market share rises while their *R/P* ratio declines substantially it is evident that cartel stability is not threatened in the $15 real price path.

Table 6.4 *Reserves to Production Ratios: 1980 to 2000*

| | *1980* | *1985* | *1990* | *1995* | *2000* |
|---|---|---|---|---|---|
| | | | *$15 real price path* | | |
| OPEC: | | | | | |
| Output Maximizers | 23.0 | 22.4 | 22.5 | 22.0 | 21.4 |
| Price Maximizers | 35.0 | 29.7 | 30.6 | 32.0 | 31.4 |
| Cartel Core | 42.0 | 28.9 | 23.6 | 20.2 | 17.7 |
| TOTAL OPEC | 36.3 | 27.9 | 24.5 | 21.7 | 19.5 |
| Non-OPEC | 17.9 | 18.2 | 18.1 | 16.4 | 14.1 |
| WOCA | 29.8 | 24.9 | 22.5 | 20.1 | 17.8 |
| | | | *$32 real price path* | | |
| OPEC: | | | | | |
| Output Maximizers | 23.0 | 22.4 | 22.5 | 22.0 | 22.4 |
| Price Maximizers | 43.0 | 35.0 | 32.7 | 37.8 | 39.5 |
| Cartel Core | 53.4 | 83.4 | 107.9 | 136.7 | 149.3 |
| TOTAL OPEC | 43.1 | 50.1 | 55.2 | 58.5 | 61.3 |
| Non-OPEC | 16.6 | 19.6 | 19.5 | 17.6 | 14.7 |
| WOCA | 32.3 | 35.7 | 36.5 | 34.7 | 32.0 |

Table 6.5 *Percentage Market Shares of Oil Suppliers*

| | *1980* | *1985* | *1990* | *1995* | *2000* |
|---|---|---|---|---|---|
| | | | *$15 real price path* | | |
| OPEC: | | | | | |
| Output Maximizers | 13.7 | 12.6 | 11.7 | 10.9 | 10.2 |
| Price Maximizers | 11.7 | 11.4 | 9.2 | 7.6 | 6.3 |
| Cartel Core | 41.4 | 43.8 | 47.7 | 50.8 | 52.1 |
| TOTAL OPEC | 66.8 | 67.8 | 68.6 | 69.4 | 68.6 |
| Non-OPEC | 33.2 | 32.3 | 31.4 | 30.6 | 31.3 |
| WOCA | 100.0 | 100.0 | 100.0 | 100.0 | 100.0 |
| | | | *$32 real price path* | | |
| OPEC: | | | | | |
| Output Maximizers | 16.4 | 18.8 | 19.9 | 20.2 | 18.4 |
| Price Maximizers | 11.3 | 13.3 | 11.8 | 10.3 | 8.6 |
| Cartel Core | 30.7 | 19.7 | 18.1 | 11.6 | 10.5 |
| TOTAL OPEC | 58.4 | 51.8 | 49.8 | 42.1 | 37.5 |
| Non-OPEC | 41.6 | 48.2 | 50.2 | 57.9 | 62.5 |
| WOCA | 100.0 | 100.0 | 100.0 | 100.0 | 100.0 |

Any tendency for oil prices to decline could easily be offset by reduced production by the Cartel Core.

The situation is quite different for the $32 real price path. Instead of the Cartel Core's market share expanding, it shrinks from 30.7 percent to 10.5 percent in 2000. At the same time, their *R/P* ratio rises from

53.4 years to 149.3 years. Clearly, this suggests the existence of substantial, undesired excess capacity in the Cartel Core. Another factor tending to inhibit cartel stability is the position of the Price Maximizers, who find their *R/P* ratio declining in the 1980s, then rising in the 1990s. Given their more-or-less constant production rate and thus constant real revenue stream, it is important to consider whether their rising absorptive capacity for oil revenues may exceed their income. If so, these producers may opt to selectively cut price in order to increase market share. Given the already low level of Cartel Core production, it seems unlikely that production increases by the Price Maximizers would be allowed by the Cartel Core, which would have only a 10.5 percent market share in 2000. Thus the $32 real price path places great pressures on the Cartel Core, but also may evince price cutting by the Price Maximizers.

To summarize: while the $15 real price path suggests considerable OPEC stability, the $32 real price path does not. In particular, the Cartel Core, which plays the critical role of maintaining the cartel, experiences dramatically different fates in the two scenarios. At the $15 real price path its market share rises while its reserves to production ratio falls. Both of these events clearly reinforce stability. On the other hand, at the $32 real price path the market share of the Core falls drastically while its reserves to production ratio rises to three times its current level. It is hard to imagine circumstances under which the Cartel Core would find these developments desirable and it is thus reasonable to suppose such events would seriously threaten cartel stability. In other words, the model raises serious doubts about the ultimate sustainability of the $32 real price path under the postulated OPEC behavioral assumptions. Under these conditions, the Cartel Core would be expected to call for major changes in cartel operations, including as possible options: (1) market prorationing with predetermined market shares or (2) production restraint by key Output Maximizers. Even though the concept of market prorationing would be an attractive device to assure cartel stability, we doubt its feasibility. Control over one's own oil production has long been held as a sovereign matter. On the other hand, efforts to expand the Cartel Core by moving some producers from the Output Maximizers to the Cartel Core seems more likely. In particular, Iraq's large resource base suggests its interests are akin to the Cartel Core; yet it is optimal from Iraq's perspective to act as an Output Maximizer as long as the Cartel Core is willing to support prices. There is also the question of whether threats by the Cartel Core would be taken seriously since they too would suffer initially from lower prices. Given these conflicting forces, the likely behavioral changes seem highly unpredictable, with the outcomes ranging from continued price stability to a collapse of prices.

## V SENSITIVITY OF RESULTS TO ALTERNATIVE ASSUMPTIONS

The results of the previous section indicate the likelihood of severe problems with cartel instability if the $32 real price path is maintained. If correct, these results are quite important. Yet, at the same time, one must adopt a healthy skepticism to any such outcomes. After all, previous models that analyzed the post-1973 crude price increase unanimously concluded that the long run price path lay below the post-embargo price.[10]

Ultimately, the validity of the predictions of any model must rest on the accuracy with which it depicts the phenomena it is attempting to analyze. Thus, it is appropriate that we critically examine the key components of our model and, further, ask ourselves how variations in critical assumptions influence outcomes. By performing such a 'sensitivity' analysis we can not only gain greater perspective on the prediction of our model but we can also determine which variables deserve greater scrutiny.

### The Demand for Oil

Without doubt, the single most critical assumption of the model is that of the price elasticity of −.73 for the demand for oil. It is this assumption which results in a difference in 2000 WOCA oil consumption of nearly 40 MMB/D in the $15 and $32 real price paths. Since supply responses for the two scenarios are rather similar (the difference is between 5 and 10 MMB/D), it is clear that the validity of demand assumptions is the crucial issue.

Implicit in the −.73 price elasticity of demand and the $15 versus $32 real price paths are two separate assumptions. First, there is, of course, the plausibility of the −.73 price elasticity. Second, there is the question of what magnitude of price responses in other competing fuels can be expected in response to a doubling of oil prices. To see the importance of induced price responses by other fuels, consider a simple five-factor model in which oil can be substituted against nonenergy inputs ($X$), coal ($C$), natural gas ($G$), and nuclear ($N$). Because the demand equation for oil is homogenous of degree zero in prices, the own price elasticity of oil demand ($E_{OO}$), can be written as the negative sum of the cross price elasticities:

$$E_{OO} = -(E_{OX} + E_{OC} + E_{OG} + E_{ON}) \qquad (9)$$

where, for example, $E_{OC}$ is the elasticity of oil demand with respect to a change in the coal price. Thus oil's own price elasticity of −.73 is the result of substitution possibilities measured by the magnitudes of the cross price elasticities ($E_{OX}$,$E_{OC}$,$E_{OG}$,$E_{ON}$).

Implicit in the comparison of the $32 real price path with the $15 real price path is the assumption that in response to the crude price doubling, all other prices remain constant. In effect, the long run supply schedules of other fuels and nonenergy inputs are assumed to be infinitely elastic so that increases in demand for these other factors does not increase their prices. Conversely, if the long run supply for other fuels and nonenergy inputs were perfectly inelastic, initial doubling of oil prices would not be sustained as other prices double in response to increasing factor demands, leaving the long run real price of oil unchanged and long run oil demand unaffected.

To the extent then that the supply elasticity of other fuels is not perfectly elastic, the 'effective' price elasticity of oil demand is reduced. Turning to the question of the likely long run supply elasticities of other fuels and nonenergy inputs, we note that it is not implausible to treat nonenergy inputs as available in an infinitely elastic supply at least over the relevant range of substitution *vis-à-vis* oil. The critical issue is the supply elasticity of other primary energy forms such as coal, natural gas, and nuclear fuel. Even though possibilities of indigenous supply expansions of coal in many European countries are quite limited, abundant US reserves are rapidly expansible for export markets at very modest price increases. Thus, because of the US coal resource base, the assumption of an infinitely elastic supply for coal does not appear to offer a gross distortion of reality. With respect to natural gas, it seems clear that natural gas supplies are expansible, but only at increasing prices. Thus, depending on the magnitude of $E_{OG}$ in equation (9) and the long run supply elasticity for natural gas, the $-.73$ demand elasticity for oil is overstated. With respect to nuclear fuel, reserve data suggest a very flat long run supply schedule; however, environmental objections to nuclear power seem likely to limit its supply response so that the long run supply schedule for nuclear fuel may be rather inelastic. Nevertheless, the issue appears moot since there is very little *direct* substitution of nuclear fuel for oil in electricity generation. In sum, $E_{ON}$ in equation (9) seems likely to be small.[11]

To recapitulate, the effective price elasticity of oil demand, $-.73$, probably represents an overstatement due to nonperfectly elastic supply responses for natural gas. In addition, it should be noted that the $-.73$ price elasticity obtained from the Griffin OECD Demand Model may itself be viewed as unrealistically large compared with other studies utilizing time series data. For example, the Energy Modeling Forum's comparison of the price elasticity of energy demand shows that studies utilizing pooled international data as contrasted with the time series intercountry data yielded substantially more elastic price elasticities.[12] In the Energy Modeling Forum's World Oil Project, the long run price elasticity was assumed to vary from −.375 to −.6.[13]

In view of these considerations, we explore the response to the model assuming an oil price elasticity of −.365, or one-half the value assumed previously. A long run elasticity of −.365 seems likely to provide a plausible lower bound.[14] Table 6.6 illustrates the sensitivity of the model to the lower price elasticity. In Table 6.6, oil demand in 2000 is 75.2 MMB/D at the $32 real price path as contrasted with 59.2 MMB/D assuming a price elasticity of −.73.

Table 6.6 *Sensitivity Results to Lower Price Elasticity of Demand at $32 Real Price Path*

| | *1980* | *1985* | *1990* | *1995* | *2000* |
|---|---|---|---|---|---|
| | | | *Production rates* | | |
| OPEC: | | | | | |
| Output Maximizers | 7.7 | 8.8 | 9.8 | 10.0 | 10.9 |
| Price Maximizers | 6.3 | 7.3 | 6.9 | 6.6 | 6.4 |
| Cartel Core | 16.9 | 15.4 | 16.8 | 18.4 | 20.9 |
| TOTAL OPEC | 30.9 | 31.5 | 33.5 | 35.0 | 38.3 |
| Non-OPEC | 19.5 | 22.5 | 26.2 | 30.9 | 37.0 |
| WOCA | 50.4 | 54.0 | 59.7 | 65.9 | 75.2 |
| | | | *Reserves to production ratios* | | |
| OPEC: | | | | | |
| Output Maximizers | 23.0 | 22.4 | 22.5 | 22.0 | 22.4 |
| Price Maximizers | 36.1 | 29.7 | 30.8 | 31.5 | 31.4 |
| Cartel Core | 45.3 | 49.3 | 47.5 | 45.3 | 42.1 |
| TOTAL OPEC | 38.0 | 37.8 | 37.3 | 35.6 | 34.7 |
| Non-OPEC | 16.6 | 19.6 | 19.5 | 17.6 | 14.7 |
| WOCA | 29.9 | 30.5 | 29.7 | 27.4 | 24.9 |
| | | | *Percentage market shares of oil suppliers* | | |
| OPEC: | | | | | |
| Output Maximizers | 15.3 | 16.2 | 16.4 | 15.0 | 14.5 |
| Price Maximizers | 12.5 | 13.5 | 11.6 | 9.9 | 8.5 |
| Cartel Core | 33.5 | 28.4 | 28.1 | 27.6 | 27.8 |
| TOTAL OPEC | 61.3 | 58.1 | 56.1 | 52.5 | 50.8 |
| Non-OPEC | 38.7 | 41.9 | 43.9 | 47.5 | 49.2 |
| WOCA | 100.0 | 100.0 | 100.0 | 100.0 | 100.0 |

The effect of the lower price elasticity is to allow the Cartel Core to expand output gradually from 16.9 MMB/D in 1980 to 20.9 MMB/D by 2000. Since the market shares and reserves to production ratios would remain relatively unchanged from the 1980 levels, it appears that the cartel would be relatively stable. At least, it would not appear less stable than it is currently. Predictions of instability in this case must rest on considerations other than market shares and reserve to production ratios.

One consideration, which is very difficult to quantify, is the growth in the absorptive capacities of the producing countries to productively invest at home.[15] Particularly in the case of the Price Maximizers, their absorptive capacity may exceed their relatively constant real income stream, promoting pressures to expand production. Furthermore, given reserves to production ratios of thirty years, production could easily be expanded from 6 MMB/D to 12 MMB/D, forcing the Cartel Core to make matching production decreases. In turn, the willingness of the Cartel Core to accept such output reductions depends on their own growing revenue requirements for domestic investment. A case can be made for increasing OPEC tensions in the low price elasticity scenario, but it must rest on growing absorptive capacities for domestic investment, rather than factors such as falling market shares or very large ratios of reserves to production.

## Growth Rates of World Economic Activity

The second factor to which the results of our model is highly sensitive is the growth rate of world economic activity and thus of the demand for OPEC oil. Because of the critical nature of this factor, it is appropriate that we examine it in somewhat greater detail.

The real rate of growth of OECD economic activity over the past two decades has averaged slightly over 4 percent per year, with considerably faster growth in the 1960s as compared to the 1970s. A wide variety of opinion exists regarding the probable value of this variable in the future. Some individuals, whom we might loosely describe as being of the 'limits to growth' perspective, foresee a sharp diminution in this rate for a variety of reasons including, in their view, likely reductions in energy availability. Others, especially economists of a neoclassical perspective, perceive no such likely trend and, indeed, might believe that the adoption of more reasonable, 'supply-side'-oriented policies could significantly raise this rate of growth.

As noted above, the elasticity of demand for oil with respect to world economic activity in our model is .75, that is, a doubling of world economic activity would increase energy demand 75 percent at unchanged real oil prices. The results reported in Tables 6.1 and 6.2 assume that the rate of real economic growth is 3.5 percent, or approximately .5 percent below historical trend. Our assumption of a .5 percent decline in the real growth rate can be traced directly to declining labor force growth rates in the major OECD countries. Barring major changes in labor force participation rates, the period 1980–2000 will be characterized by an approximate .5 percent per year decline in the growth of the labor force over the period 1960–80. Thus a 3.5 percent growth rate is consistent with labor productivity growth rates over the period 1960–80.

It should be noted that our 3.5 percent annual real growth rate assumption would be labeled optimistic by most forecasters as the current forecasters' consensus calls for a 3 percent annual growth rate. Since there is much uncertainty about this critical growth rate, sensitivity runs were made for a 4.5 percent annual real growth rate and a 2.5 percent real growth rate, giving plausible upper and lower bounds. The results of these simulations emphasize the critical link between economic growth and the growth in oil consumption. Clearly, if OPEC's situation would be tenuous at a 3.5 percent annual growth in economic activity, a 2.5 percent annual growth rate in economic activity signals severe mislocations, with world oil demand roughly constant over the period and negligible production rates in the Cartel Core.

On the other hand, a 4.5 percent annual growth rate would be a welcomed outcome for OPEC with WOCA oil demand reaching 70 MMB/D by 2000. This outcome implies similar results to those shown in Table 6.6 except that the Cartel Core's output would remain relatively constant over the period.

Let us now consider the most favorable scenario for OPEC, that is, a combination of rapid economic growth (4.5 percent annual growth) and a low price elasticity (– .365). Combining these two assumptions, we find that WOCA oil demand reaches 89 MMB/D by 2000. This scenario would result in a rising market share by the Cartel Core and the possibility of additional increases in the real price of oil. Nevertheless, even this scenario shows nothing of the 'energy gap' reminiscent of studies such as the WAES Report.

## VI TESTING FOR CONTRADICTORY ASSUMPTIONS: THE MODEL AS A PEDAGOGICAL DEVICE

Aside from the implications for OPEC stability, we believe that the type of model structure elaborated here can be a valuable tool to the decisionmaker. Irrespective of whether one accepts the particular price elasticity and economic growth assumptions utilized in the exercises here, models such as these offer a useful consistency check on the decisionmaker's view of the world.

Specifically, with such models decisionmakers can ask whether their assumptions about price elasticity of demand, economic growth, etc., are consistent with their assumptions about the future price of oil. Typically, we form expectations about future oil prices on the basis of recent price experience without explicitly forming opinions on the magnitude of key assumptions determining this price.

As a valid test of the decisionmaker's oil price hypothesis, one can consider the various sets of assumptions sufficient to yield the hypothesized price path. If the decisionmaker in turn accepts one of these sets of assumptions as highly likely, then he can conclude that his views on oil prices are consistent with his knowledge of factors determining the supply and demand for oil. In contrast, if the decisionmaker rejects all such sets of sufficient assumptions, he must either reject the model or his hypothesis about future oil prices.

For example, suppose the decisionmaker hypothesizes a continuing rise in the real price of oil, reaching $60 per barrel in 1980 dollars by the year 2000. By repeated simulation of the model, one can identify different sets of assumptions that would be sufficient to produce OPEC stability for the postulated price path. For example, suppose the following growth rate ($g$) and price elasticities of demand ($E_{OO}$) combinations are sufficient to produce stability at the postulated $60 real price path:

Assumption Set 1: $g = 3.5\%$ $E_{OO} = 0$
Assumption Set 2: $g = 4.5\%$ $E_{OO} = -.1$
Assumption Set 3: $g = 5.5\%$ $E_{OO} = -.2$
Assumption Set 4: $g = 6.5\%$ $E_{OO} = -.3$
. . .
. . .
. . .

The decisionmaker can then examine each assumption set. For example, he may reject Assumption Set 1 on the grounds that the oil price elasticity of demand cannot be perfectly inelastic, while Assumption Sets 3 and 4 assume unrealistically high growth rates in economic activity. Having ruled out all assumption sets other than set 2, our decisionmaker can then assess the plausibility of the hypothesized price path by examining his confidence in Assumption Set 2.

We note that in using the model in this manner, the end product is not 'the future price path of oil'; rather it offers a method of improving one's thinking about the problem. By testing the compatibility of one's hypothesized price path against the plausibilities of the assumptions sufficient to yield such a price path, the decisionmaker is at least forced to form logically consistent oil price expectations.

## VII SUMMARY AND CONCLUSIONS

Perhaps the most useful aspect of a model such as the one used in this chapter is that it allows one to structure a discussion of the phenomenon being analyzed, to link cause and effect in an explicit and apparent way. Among other things, such an approach allows us to isolate those factors which bear critically on the events being investigated. In addition, it can afford us the opportunity to work the problem backward, that is, given a predicted set of outcomes (oil prices) to ascertain the assumptions (critical elasticities) implied by those outcomes.

The results of this paper suggest that the Iranian political upheavals of 1978–79 and the subsequent doubling of crude oil prices may well have defined the limits of OPEC's monopoly power. A long run real price path significantly greater than $32 per barrel seems likely to evoke large supplies of synthetic fuels, coupled with substantial conservation effects - events which, taken together, make such a price path unlikely.

Indeed, it is by no means certain that a $32 real price path is sustainable in the long run. The results indicate that a price elasticity of oil demand of −.73 would result in intolerably low production levels by the Cartel Core. Even at the lower bound price elasticity estimate of −.365, cartel instabilities might result if future world economic growth rates fall 1 percent per year below historical trends. In view of economic growth rates in the 1970s, such a possibility is not to be dismissed. At the same time, there is little reason to believe that a real price of $15 or below could create conditions capable of producing instability in the cartel. In short, the two prices used in our analysis appear to bracket the range of likely long run prices, *given our assumptions.*

Some may, of course, take strong exception to those assumptions and the conclusion they yield. If nothing else, our research suggests that critics should focus their attention on particular sets of variables. On the supply side, our most critical assumptions relate to the technical, financial, and behavioral factors underlying our assumptions regarding OPEC actions. On the demand side, our most critical assumptions have to do with the supply elasticities of other forms of energy, particularly coal and synthetic fuels, the demand elasticities for petroleum, and the real growth rate of the world economy. In our analysis these are the variables which will, in fact, prove critical in determining the future behavior of OPEC and whose empirical estimation should be the key to future analyses.

We believe that our research is also suggestive of other issues that should be explored. One is to in fact 'work the problem backward', that is, to take existing and common assumptions regarding the future real price of oil (e.g. that it will increase 3 percent per year) and determine the combinations of values of key variables required to produce such a result in our model. The plausibility of these values should yield important insights.

A second avenue of inquiry relates to potential adaptations within OPEC in the event of a soft market. Based on the assumptions we have used, we believe that a price path substantially in excess of a $32 real price path would result in serious instability within OPEC *given current behavior patterns.* A reasonable question is this: What alternative configuration of nations into our tripartite behavioral classification would be necessary to remove this instability? Alternative configurations would appear capable of greatly attenuating the instability; yet achieving such a configuration is problematic. Under this scenario, the Cartel Core, in particular Saudi Arabia, would be expected to adopt a much more assertive posture. Whether or not other OPEC members accept this role appears to be one of the critical uncertainties.

## NOTES

The authors are professors of economics at the University of Houston. Griffin gratefully acknowledges the support of the Humboldt Foundation for work at the University of Köln in connection with this paper:

1 See Energy Modeling Forum (1981), pp. 4–5.
2 See *National Journal* (1980).
3 See OPEC (1980).
4 Examples include Pindyck (1977), Kalymon (1975), and Cremer and Weitzman (1976), pp. 155–64.
5 See Gately, Kyle, and Fischer (1977).
6 For other examples of simulation models in which oil prices are set exogenously, see Blitzer, Meeraus, and Stoutjesdijk (1975).
7 If instead one wishes to adopt the CIA (1979) assumptions of significant net imports into the communist bloc countries, the demand figures in Table 6.1 can simply be increased by these amounts.
8 While most models have treated OPEC as a monolith, Hnyilicza and Pindyck (1976) consider OPEC as a two-part cartel of 'saver' and 'spender' countries, each with separate objective functions.
9 Presumably, it may be appropriate to discount this difference for future years.
10 For review, see Fischer, Gately, and Kyle (1975).
11 See Griffin (1979), pp. 281–2.
12 See Energy Modeling Forum (1980).
13 See Energy Modeling Forum (1981), Table 1.
14 Note that the EMF study shows most time series econometric energy demand elasticities are approximately half the values reported by Griffin (1979) and Pindyck (1980). In addition, even if one assumes $E_{OG}$ is $+.25$ and the natural gas supply elasticity is perfectly inelastic, the reduction in the effective demand elasticity is from $-.73$ to $-.48$, or approximately one-third.
15 For a discussion see Ezzati (1976) and Griffin and Steele (1980), pp. 127–32.

# 7 OPEC Oil Pricing, and the Implications for Consumers and Producers

ROBERT S. PINDYCK

## I INTRODUCTION

In the past several years we have seen a plethora of models that describe 'economically rational' price formation by the OPEC cartel. The earlier examples of these models, including one of my own, were based on the notion of the cartel as a price leader, holding a fixed quantity of reserves, and facing competitive producers that produced according to some supply schedule. The problem for the cartel was then to determine a dynamically optimal trajectory for production over time, consistent with the behavior of world oil demand and of competitive supply. This in turn determines the pattern of world oil prices over time.[1]

Later models dealt with various issues involving cartel organization and optimal decision-making. In particular, such models addressed the ways in which cartel structure affects the optimal price, the price implications of dynamic optimization on the part of the competitive producers, and the problem of 'dynamic consistency' in the sense that simulated policies would be rational for all agents, and therefore would not be revised during the production horizon.[2]

Whether explicitly stated or not, most of these models tended to focus on predicting, at least subject to certain behavioral assumptions, the most likely future price path for oil. Now the time has come to assess these models, in terms of their value as predictors of world oil prices, and also in terms of their ability to explain the overall behavior of the world oil market. In particular, are better models of OPEC oil pricing now needed, and should such models be constructed and then used as a basis of predicting oil prices? (Such models could include a more detailed theoretical description of producer and consumer behavior, including such factors as the influence of financial markets, effects of uncertainty, etc., or could embody existing theoretical frameworks in disaggregated and statistically detailed empirical models.)

I will argue that improved models might be useful for examining various theoretical and empirical issues in the behavior of oil markets, but that they are not needed, and would not be very useful, for predicting world oil prices. Basically I will argue that future world oil prices are highly uncertain, and that for practical purposes point forecasts can be produced using some of the simpler versions of models that already exist. Furthermore, prudent policy formulation requires consideration of the alternative implications of a range of radically different price paths.

It is not surprising that there has been considerable interest in models of oil prices, and in the forecasts that such models elicit. Oil producers (in the United States and elsewhere) and oil consumers have an obvious interest in the possible evolution of oil prices over time. But I will argue that as far as decision-making is concerned, both on the part of oil producers and consumers, what is most important is not the point forecast of future oil price, but the *uncertainty* around that forecast. This inherent uncertainty over future oil prices cannot be eliminated by any economic model that I am aware of, and has important implications for consumer and producer decisions.

In the next section I briefly review the recent development of OPEC oil pricing models, and assess their use in predicting oil prices. I conclude (not surprisingly) that there is indeed a considerable amount of uncertainty over the future price of oil. Section III presents the consumer side of the market, and briefly discusses the implications of this uncertainty for energy policy in a country such as the United States. Section IV looks at competitive producers of oil, and in particular deals with the management of oil reserves. There I draw from some results in a recent paper in discussing the implications of oil price uncertainty for the production of oil from reserves.

## II THE LIMITATIONS OF MODELS FOR FORECASTING FUTURE OIL PRICES

Perhaps the easiest way to give the flavor of the earlier models of OPEC pricing is to briefly lay out the structure of a model that I used myself.[3] The basic model is specified to account for differences between short run and long run price elasticities both in demand and supply from 'competitive fringe' countries. Total demand (*TD*) for the resource in question would be of the form

$$TD_t = f_1(P_t, Y_t, TD_{t-1}) \tag{1}$$

where $P_t$ is real price and $Y_t$ is the measure of aggregate income or product. This specification of the demand function takes into account the substitution of other materials for this resource, and since we assume that the prices of competing materials are fixed, they need not be included explicitly in (1).

Net demand facing the cartel is

$$D_t = TD_t - S_t \tag{2}$$

where $S_t$ is the supply function for the 'competitive fringe', and is given by

$$S_t = f_2(P_t, S_{t-1}) \tag{3}$$

Resource depletion might be as significant a factor for the competitive fringe as it is for the cartel, in which case we can modify the supply function so that it moves to the left (rising marginal and average cost) in response to cumulative production $CS$:

$$S_t = f_2(P_t, S_{t-1})(1+\alpha)^{-CS_t/\bar{S}} \tag{3$'$}$$

with

$$CS_t = CS_{t-1} + S_t \tag{4}$$

where $\bar{S}$ is average annual competitive production and $\alpha$ is a parameter that determines the rate of depletion. Finally, an accounting identity keeps track of cartel reserves, $R$:

$$R_t = R_{t-1} - D_t \tag{5}$$

The objective of the cartel is to pick a price trajectory $\{P_t\}$ that will maximize the sum of discounted profits:

$$\max W = \sum_{t=1}^{N} \left(\frac{1}{(1+\delta)^t}\right) \left(P_t - \frac{m}{R_t}\right) D_t \tag{6}$$

where $m/R_t$ is average production cost (so that the parameter $m$ determines initial average cost), $\delta$ is the discount rate, and $N$ is chosen to be large enough (40–60 years) to approximate the infinite-horizon problem. Since average costs become infinite as the reserve base $R_t$

approaches zero, the resource exhaustion constraint need not be introduced explicitly. As a result, we have a classical, unconstrained discrete-time control problem for which numerical solutions can be obtained easily.

There are of course some problems with this model, both in terms of its theoretical underpinning, and in terms of simplifications that may not be appropriate in the light of the complexity of the world oil market. Perhaps the most serious problem is that the model assumes that OPEC acts as a single agent to maximize the equity value (i.e. the sum of present and discounted future profits) of its oil reserves. But in fact the different members of OPEC may have different objectives, and certainly operate under different constraints. For example, some countries, such as Saudi Arabia, have very large proven reserves and lower immediate revenue needs (so that their discount rate would be smaller), while other countries, such as Venezuela, have smaller reserve levels and higher revenue needs. Taking these differences into account requires a model that describes the process of bargaining and the formation of a 'cooperative equilibrium' within the cartel. Such a model was developed by Hnyilicza and myself (1976).

Even taking cartel structure into account, other problems remain. For example, in these models the cartel, whether viewed as a monolith or a set of members who must reconcile their different objectives and constraints, is assumed to behave in a dynamically optimal manner, but competitive producers in the model, although affected by depletion, do not pursue dynamically optimal strategies, and instead are represented by a supply function. Furthermore, if competitive producers indeed behave in a dynamically optimal manner, and if they also have rational expectations, then this imposes constraints of 'dynamic consistency' on the types of solutions that can result. *Theoretical* models that describe dynamically consistent price trajectories have been constructed by Salant (1976) and Newbery (1980). There is only one empirical model using this approach that I am aware of, and that is the one developed by Salant for ICF Inc. (1979), and that is not published.

Simulation models of OPEC oil pricing have also been constructed. Such models assume that OPEC members use various rules of thumb in determining their production levels, rather than dynamic optimization.[4] But simulation-type models have their own shortcomings, since the behavioral rules of thumb they incorporate are arbitrary, and may be 'reasonable' (or quasi-optimal) under certain conditions, but not under others.

Finally there is the problem of identifying the very objective of OPEC policy. The models that I surveyed above considered only *economic* objectives in the formation of oil prices. I believe that economic objectives are important, but clearly other objectives (political and military) are also likely to influence oil prices. This is a point discussed in some detail by Moran in his chapter of this book.

Recently, the Energy Modeling Forum at Stanford University has conducted a comparison of a number of different OPEC oil pricing models, both of the simulation and optimization variety. (See the survey paper by Beider (1980).) Not surprisingly, the EMF study found considerable differences in the forecasts for oil prices produced by these various models. These differences were partly a function of the theoretical framework of the model, but also a function of the assumptions used regarding price responsiveness of non-OPEC production and world oil demand. Clearly there are differences of opinion regarding these empirical assumptions, and that alone will imply differences of opinion regarding the future path of oil prices.[5]

It seems to me that from a theoretical point of view, models of OPEC oil pricing have reached a practical limit as tools of analysis. As far as empirical predictions of oil prices are concerned, some of these models have already exceeded that limit. The problem is a simple one; the real world is not as rational and dynamically optimal as economists would like to believe. And, economic rationality probably applies even less to OPEC producers than to many other real world economic agents.

On the other hand, the simpler versions of these models probably do have value in describing the limits of monopoly power, and the effects of resource exhaustion on pricing. Based on these models, it would probably be reasonable to assign a 2 to 4 percent real rate of growth to future oil prices as part of a 'most likely' forecast.[6] But at the same time it must be remembered that the confidence interval around that forecast is extremely wide, perhaps as large as 50 to 100 percent. *What should really matter in terms of the decisions of energy producers and energy consumers is not the 'best guess' forecast, but the fact that the uncertainty around that forecast is considerable.*

## III THE IMPLICATIONS FOR ENERGY POLICY

Again, the future of world oil prices is highly uncertain. It is quite conceivable, for example, that the world price of oil could *fall* in real terms over the next twenty years, or rise only slowly. During 1974–78, before the Iranian Revolution and the Iran–Iraq War, the economic objective of maximizing long run revenue seemed to dominate the setting of OPEC oil prices. I have calculated that a return to such a policy over the next two decades could lead to real oil prices that are actually below today's levels. Also, major new reserve discoveries and unexpected production increases in countries such as Mexico could help to push down world oil prices.

On the other hand, world oil prices might be sharply and unexpectedly accelerated by political turbulence in some of the major oil producing countries, as we saw recently with Iran. We must recognize that none of the major oil exporting countries today are bastions of stability, and the possibilities for supply cutoffs are numerous. Any country in that region, including Saudi Arabia, may face political upheaval during the next two decades which could considerably reduce or even terminate its production of oil. The potential for another Mideast war has been greatly reduced, but this possibility cannot be ruled out, and it would almost certainly lead to major production cutbacks by the Arab exporters. And military intervention by major powers could likewise lead to a supply cutoff.

The point here is that over the next twenty years the major oil consuming countries of the world must be prepared to face further increases in oil prices - and thus increases in the cost of energy in general. These increases may come about gradually, following the pattern predicted by many of the models discussed in the last section, but it is also quite possible that they will be sharp and unexpected as in 1974 and 1979. The strong possibility of future energy shocks has important implications for energy policy in a country like the United States.

An energy price shock, brought about by a sudden reduction in OPEC oil production, would have serious consequences for the economy of the United States, as well as the economies of most other industrialized nations. Of course any increase in the price of imported oil will reduce the real income of Americans (since we must trade more purchasing power for the same amount of oil), and it will cause some additional inflation. But the effect is much greater if the oil price increase is sharp and unexpected. A price 'shock' can cause a major increase in the rate of inflation, an increase in unemployment, and reductions in real output and real national income.

The adverse effects of an oil price shock are due largely to the important rigidities that characterize our economy - rigidities in prices, in the use of inputs to production, and in wages. For example, prices of goods other than energy do not fall rapidly to reflect changes in relative scarcities, and inputs to production cannot be shifted quickly given the new price of energy faced by industry. Perhaps most important, real wage rates often fail to fall quickly to the lower equilibrium level consistent with higher energy prices and the reduced real income level they imply. Labor thereby prices itself out of the market, full employment becomes uneconomical, and the unemployment rate rises and level of real output falls.[7]

This economic vulnerability adds a premium to the social value of a barrel of oil. Since the actions of no single firm or consumer can affect the economic impact of an energy price shock, it represents an external social cost that can only be reduced by government intervention. Furthermore, our current import level creates a political and strategic dependence that is undesirable.[8] Because of the economic consequences of a major cutback in OPEC production, we can become subject to blackmail by some of the oil exporting countries. This political cost further raises the premium on the value of oil.

For these reasons it would make good sense for the United States to further reduce its dependence on imported energy, and thereby reduce the potential economic impact of any sudden increases in world energy prices. In other words, it is desirable to raise the cost of energy, as seen both by producers and consumers, to its true marginal social value. Of course some people have argued that this justifies the subsidization of synthetic fuel development as an eventual substitute for oil. But this is not the case, and such subsidies would be an extremely inefficient way to deal with our import dependence.[9] Rather, the most effective way to deal with this problem is to impose a *tariff on imported oil.*

A tariff would raise the price for all oil in the United States, *both for consumers and for producers.* This would give consumers an added incentive to conserve, and it would give producers an added incentive to produce - *efficiently*, choosing those energy sources (oil or others) and those technologies that are most economical. The net result would be less domestic energy consumption, more domestic production, and a lower level of imports.

Unfortunately, in the short term the macroeconomic effect of a tariff is the same as that from an OPEC-induced increase in the price of oil - it is inflationary and recessionary. Therefore it is essential that two things be done to eliminate this adverse effect. First, the tariff must be phased in gradually, perhaps over a three- to five-year period. (Remember that gradual increases in energy prices are much less damaging than rapid increases.)

Second, the tariff must be matched dollar-for-dollar with cost-reducing tax cuts. The leading candidate for such cuts is the Social Security payroll tax. A decrease in this tax has exactly the same effect on prices and output as a reduction in the price of energy, and therefore can be used to perfectly offset the tariff. At the same time, revenues from the tariff would be earmarked for the Social Security Program, so that the only change would be in the source of its funding, and not the amount.

Related to the oil import tariff is the development of the strategic oil reserve, which should be another important component of energy policy. A strategic reserve can have two functions. First, in the event of an all-out war or military action that disrupted most shipping and trading of oil, the world oil market might cease to function as such, and shortages could occur in the sense that imports might be unavailable at any price. Strategic reserves could then be used to prevent such shortages.

Short of a major military conflict, strategic reserves are not needed to prevent shortages, since such shortages would not occur in the absence of government controls. But as was explained above, a *sharp* increase in energy prices resulting from an OPEC production cutback could be economically damaging to this country. The second function of a strategic reserve is its use to smooth out price increases in the wake of such a production cutback.

However, it is important to point out that strategic reserves are most effective when implemented multilaterally. The point here is that when a stockpile is released, no matter where it happens to reside, it adds to the supply of oil in the world market and thereby reduces the world price. As a result the benefits are enjoyed by *all* importing countries, even if they do not have stockpiles of their own, but the benefits to the country holding the stockpile are likewise reduced. If only the United States owned and released a stockpile in the wake of a crisis, its imports of oil would fall, but the impact on world oil prices, and prices faced by American consumers, would be small. But if most or all of the major OECD nations maintained large stockpiles of oil which, as part of an international agreement, flowed into the market during a major production cutback, this would significantly reduce any sharp price increases and resulting economic damage.

As our experience with the International Energy Agency has taught us, the likelihood of obtaining such an international agreement is extremely low. At the same time, the costs of physically implementing the strategic reserve have risen dramatically. (This might reflect inefficiencies in DOE's management of the program.) The entire program therefore needs to be carefully reassessed. It may be preferable to aim for a somewhat smaller stockpile, but at the same time impose a hefty tariff on imported oil.

As opposed to the decontrol of oil and natural gas prices, a tariff means more government intervention. This may make it unpalatable to the Reagan Administration as a component of energy policy. It would be unfortunate, however, if the President and his energy planners should underestimate the instability of world oil prices and the resulting threat that import dependence poses for our economy – and the benefit that a tariff would bring.[10]

## IV THE IMPLICATIONS FOR OIL PRODUCERS

If competitive oil producers (in the United States, for example) knew that oil prices were going to rise at a steady rate, their production decisions would be relatively straightforward. In particular, given a proved reserve level, and given a cost of production (perhaps a function of the rate of production as well as the reserve level), the optimal rate of production (in other words the 'decline curve') can be computed. Indeed, the methods that petroleum engineers and petroleum economists usually use to compute optimal production rates are based on the assumption that the trajectory for oil prices is known with certainly.[11]

But this production decision becomes much more complicated when the future price of oil is highly uncertain. Should future price uncertainty induce producers to speed up production (since the price might go down in the future), or to slow down production (since the price might rise)? And how should such uncertainty affect investment decisions for exploration for new reserves?

I examined this problem in a very preliminary way in a recent paper (1981a), the results of which I will briefly summarize here. I took the point of view of an oil producer who views the price of oil as following an exogenous growth path, but that is subject to stochastic variation around that path. I was not concerned with the determination of the expected price trajectory itself, nor with the reasons for stochastic fluctuations around that trajectory. In effect, I implicitly assumed that the price is controlled by a cartel, and both the expected and realized price trajectories reflect a mixture of rational and (to economists) irrational behavior on the part of the cartel.

I found that uncertainty over the future price of oil can affect the current production rate for two rather different reasons. First, if marginal extraction cost is a nonlinear function of the rate of production, stochastic fluctuations in price will lead (on average) to increases or decreases in cost over time. This means that cost can be reduced by either speeding up or slowing down the rate of depletion (depending on the non-linearity).

Second, in-ground reserves of a resource can be thought of as an 'option' on the future production of the resource.[12] If the future price of the resource turns out to be much higher than the cost of extraction, it may well be desirable to 'exercise' the option and produce the resource, but if instead the price falls so that production would be unprofitable, the option need never be exercised, and the only loss is the cost of discovering or purchasing the reserve. But this means that under future price uncertainty the current value of a unit of reserve is larger than the current price net of extraction cost, which in turn means that the greater the uncertainty the greater is the incentive to *hold back production*, and keep the option.

This also has implications for the value of exploration, and the amount of exploration that firms should undertake. Recall that the value of a call option on shares of stock rises as the volatility of the price of the stock rises. Again, the value of a unit of in-ground reserves rises as the uncertainty of the future price of the resource rises. This means that oil price uncertainty *increases* the economic incentive to explore for reserves and increase the proved reserve base. It also means that such uncertainty increases the value of offshore leases, and in fact can explain why over the past few years the bids for these leases have been so high.

## V CONCLUDING REMARKS

This chapter has dealt with a number of different problems. The unifying theme, however, is that the future price of oil is highly uncertain, and no economist or economic model can do much about that. This has implications for the construction and use of models, for the design of domestic energy policy, and for decisions to explore for and produce oil. I have dealt with these implications only briefly, and, I hope, not too superficially.

## NOTES

An earlier version of this chapter was presented at a conference on 'The Future of OPEC and the Long Run Price of Oil', University of Houston, May 8, 1981. Research leading to this paper was supported by the Center for Energy Policy Research of the MIT Energy Laboratory, and that support is gratefully acknowledged. The author also wishes to thank James Griffin for his careful reading of the earlier draft, and his detailed comments and suggestions.

1 See Pindyck (1978, 1979b), and the empirical study by Fromholzer (1980). One of the earlier theoretical models of the OPEC pricing problem was constructed by Schmalensee (1976).

2 For a model that deals with the problem of cartel organization and differing objectives among cartel members, see the paper by Hnyilicza and Pindyck (1976). Models that satisfy dynamic consistency were constructed by Salant (1976) and Newbery (1980). Also, see Gilbert (1978).

3 See Pindyck (1978, 1979b), Cremer and Weitzman (1976), Kalymon (1975), and Schmalensee (1976). For a (somewhat outdated) survey of models of OPEC oil pricing, see Fischer, Gately and Kyle (1975).

4 See, for example, Blitzer, Meeraus, and Stoutjesdijk (1975) and MacAvoy (1981).

5 A survey of some alternative estimates of demand elasticities is given in Pindyck (1979c).

6 This estimate comes out of the models in Pindyck (1978, 1979b), but is also consistent with many of the other models surveyed here.

7 For a detailed discussion of the macroeconomic impact of sudden increases in the price of energy, see Pindyck (1980) and Hall and Pindyck (1981a, b).
8 For a discussion of some of these problems, see Deese and Nye (1981).
9 Issues regarding synthetic fuel development are discussed in Pindyck (1981b).
10 For a general discussion of the energy policy (and economic policy) implications of unstable and/or rising energy prices, see Hall and Pindyck (1981b) and Pindyck (1981b).
11 See, for example, McCray (1975).
12 This notion was first suggested by Tourinho (1979).

# 8 Policies for Oil Importers

WILLIAM W. HOGAN

## I INTRODUCTION

The relationships among the various actors in the world oil market contain a mixture of opportunities for cooperation and confrontation. Due to the imbalance of effective power, the emphasis among oil importers has been on avoiding confrontations with the oil exporters. In this chapter we seek to stimulate a discussion of cooperative energy strategies for oil importers that might reverse this tendency and arrest further transfers of wealth and power to the oil exporters.

## II POLICY OBJECTIVES

A diagnosis of energy markets reveals two distinct problems that frame the agenda for policy action.[1] First, there is the long run requirement to stop the drain of wealth and replace expensive supplies of oil and gas with new sources of energy. Second, the oil importing countries must meet the threat of a sudden disruption of oil supplies.

Until recently, policymakers blurred the distinctions between these two broad challenges and fashioned policies that met neither satisfactorily. For example, propelled by the import threat, the United States adopted the misnamed Energy Security Act to create the Synthetic Fuels Corporation (SFC), which will contribute nothing to meeting security problems in this decade. But, being dominated by a sense of the immediacy of the import danger, the SFC may fail to make the technological contributions that could be so important in providing a later alternative to natural deposits of oil and gas.[2] At the same time the United States dallied in the creation of a strategic petroleum reserve and made a practice of rejecting serious preparations for energy emergencies.[3]

After years of analysis and debate, we now recognize that with foresight, ingenuity, and time, the resources and technology will be available to make the long run change in energy sources. The most important adjustments, through conservation and increased production, will come naturally in response to the formidable incentives created since 1972 by the nearly 500 percent increase in the real well-head price of oil or the greater than 100 percent increase in the real delivered price of energy. With relatively modest government support of public goods such as research and development, information programs, and subsidies for the disadvantaged, the long run adjustment could be no more than an energy problem - serious enough, but not a first-order political and security matter.

The wider concern with energy, particularly oil, stems from the great reliance on supplies which are vulnerable to major disruption at any time. If world supplies were distributed among many small producers, or if oil importers had a reserve of excess production capacity, there would be little danger in a high dependence on imports. But neither condition describes the state of the world today. Furthermore, the world oil market is an integrated system, and the security of any one country depends very much on the security of others in the market. For the United States, in particular, national oil import dependence is a poor measure of its security interest in its allies. During a severe supply interruption, the United States would have to share its oil with Europe and Japan.

In addition, the ability to manage the response to oil supply shocks could influence the long run price of oil. During 1979, for example, a sharp increase in the demand for world inventories led to fierce competition on the spot market. The spot price for oil leapt ahead of the long run contract price. This visible signpost alerted the OPEC hawks to an opportunity to push up the price of their oil. They may have been too avaricious, in which case everyone suffered. But it is not far-fetched to speculate that a different inventory policy on the part of oil importers could have lowered the long run price of oil. Failure to manage future oil supply disruptions could lead to even greater economic losses for oil importers.[4]

All oil importing countries share in this danger and all have been searching for strategies to lessen the risk or reduce their own exposure. But this recognition of the critical security problem has produced little more than rhetoric and non sequiturs like the synthetic fuels program. Recent agreement on the need for targeted energy policies to meet the supply vulnerability threat has not yet led to agreement on the substance of those policies.

Oil importers have made elaborate attempts to promote cooperation with oil exporters, producing a dramatic change in the structure of the world oil market as direct sales and government-to-government arrangements have expanded and the role of the international oil companies has contracted.[5] However, we have had only modest success at building cooperative arrangements among oil importers, with little more than the *de minimis* International Energy Program (IEP) or the so-far-unrestrictive import targets as the anemic products of our diplomatic labors.[6]

It takes only a glance at the narrow range of immediately available supply security options or the relative weakness of the oil importers to understand the failure to confront the oil vulnerability problem. Energy policymakers have tended to focus on the long term, when much more is possible. For the near term, political leaders have preferred to scramble for special arrangements with oil exporters, where security gains could be imagined by those desperate enough to ignore the fungibility of oil. No politician wants to sit at the international table with a bad hand and few chips; as a result, oil importers are losing the oil power contest by default.

Mistrust adds to the difficulty of promoting cooperative agreements among oil importers. Smaller countries fear that the United States can and will take care of itself, possibly through its special relationship with Saudi Arabia. The United States, on the other hand, injures itself by fretting over the possibility of exploitation by free-riders. This mistrust and concentration on relative status finds expression in the language of the IEP, with its concern for assuring 'supply rights' and enforcing 'sharing' agreements. Apparently the purpose of the IEP is to defend the signatories against each other during an oil emergency, not against the source of the problem. Slowing the enormous transfer of wealth from importers to exporters takes a back seat to garnishing a slightly larger share of a suddenly smaller pie.

We find the same strange lack of concern for the loss of wealth in the cycle of shortages and glut in the oil market. A contrived or accidental event precipitates a reduction in oil supply with a sudden surge in prices, and the Western economies reel from the shock. Slowly, however, the wrenching adjustments in demand begin and new sources of supply come forth. Production starts to exceed demand and prices soften, a little. Soon talk turns to the 'oil glut' and the weakening power of the oil exporters; complacency returns to the consumers.[7]

This is a theory that defines power only as the potential to inflict damage. Why, during the glut that follows the shock, do oil importers take comfort in accepting the suddenly greater drain of their collective wealth? The United States, for example, paid only 0.5 percent of its GNP for oil imports in 1973. During the pleasant 'glut' years of 1974–78, this figure held steady at about 1.8 percent. By the time of the 'soft' market of early 1981, this import bill was near 3 percent of GNP. In Japan, without the benefit of domestic oil production, the import bill rose from 1.4 percent of GNP in 1973 to 4.1 percent in 1980! Perhaps the greatest accomplishment of the oil exporters has been in making this abnormal transfer of wealth appear normal.

Fearing each other, and little concerned with the loss in wealth, oil importers are locked in a debilitating game where the individual at best defeats the collective good. The net effect is a policy vacuum which leaves an insecure market in which oil exporters are free to serve as tax collectors and importers pay to compete against each other. Surely this policy default deserves examination. Before abandoning ourselves to reliance on the benevolent restraint of oil exporters, we should look to the opportunities for cooperative action to lessen the danger of supply interruptions and to reduce the flow of wealth in payment for oil imports.

## III CONFRONTING VULNERABILITY

Capitulation is not the only option. Although weak, the oil importers are not powerless. There are individual and collective actions available to lessen the exposure to damage from the unstable world oil market. Unfortunately, the best we can hope for is the mitigation of damages; no true solutions have appeared on the scene. (This unpleasant fact may explain why little has been done so far to prepare for emergencies and develop effective cooperative strategies among oil importers. Most serious actions will impose real costs now - investing in storage capacity, imposing import restrictions - but offer no more than a softening of impacts in the future. Without immediate results, without certainty, without a panacea, energy security policy is a hard product to sell.) But when the potential costs are as great as they are for disruptions in the oil market, where comparisons can be made to the 1930s, even partial savings could be worth a great deal. We should turn to the agenda for cooperation to confront the threat of oil vulnerability and the loss of wealth.

The opportunities for action begin with a strengthening of the framework for international cooperation. Within the framework each country can take a variety of steps to prepare to manage oil supply interruptions. In parallel, oil importers can work with the exporters to lessen the likelihood, duration, or intensity of future supply emergencies. In addition to improving the resilience of the oil system, there are long run energy policy actions that will help with security problems while easing the transition away from oil and gas. Finally, these energy policies must be balanced by military and diplomatic efforts focused on the Persian Gulf.

## International Framework

The oil market is international. The fungibility of oil and the relatively low cost of transportation make it difficult for one country to insulate itself from the effects of changes in the market elsewhere in the world. During past supply interruptions, promises of special treatment for compliant countries have evaporated and the competition among oil importers has helped only the exporters. The first step in forging a program for cooperative action is to recognize the need for positive government initiatives to expand and use the international framework for cooperation.

In the domestic market, dissatisfaction with the distribution of income is arguable in principle and, in any event, subject to an array of alternative policy remedies. Hence, the role for government is to ensure efficient competition, and the policy of choice is to rely on private actors responding to market incentives. However, in the international market, the distribution of income, between oil exporters and oil importers, should not be a matter of indifference to governments. And only government intervention can compensate for the failure of the market to confront private actors with the full costs of their energy choices. Hence, the same logic that calls for the removal of government intervention in the domestic market identifies the need for government intervention in the international market.

### *International Energy Agency (IEA)*

This is a place to start. All the major oil importers are real or *de facto* members of the IEA, which has the administrative and information tools in place to provide the foundation for a significant expansion of the strength of cooperative policies. However, 'The agreement is opaquely technical . . . It is probably fair to say that many usually knowledgeable people . . . do not understand this critically important agreement'.[8] And for those who do understand the agreement, there is little confidence that it will help much in its present form. A few obvious reforms stand out, principally in the rules for sharing oil during supply interruptions.

For small shortages, the IEA sharing formula is based on total oil consumption, which should be compatible with the supply allocation that would result from competitive bidding on the spot market. But for large shortages, those above a 10 percent loss of expected oil supplies, the rule shifts to an import basis, which would work to the advantage of those countries with a large volume of domestic production, notably the United States. But in this circumstance, countries relying more heavily on oil imports would be able to obtain a larger share of the total oil supply by entering the spot market, and they would be under great pressure from their own consumers to ignore the IEA. Oil traders in Europe and Japan could not resist the temptation to pay high prices for small increases in their share of the market. The IEA agreement would collapse, prices would rise, and to the extent that all countries have about the same responsiveness of oil demand, higher prices would ration the oil in proportion to total oil consumption. Only the oil exporters stand to gain from this peculiar sharing formula, which could be revised best by making all allocations proportional to consumption.

For sub-crisis shortages, those below 7 percent of expected supplies, the IEA has no provisions for action. Yet in the early stages of an emergency, when the measured shortfall may be quite small, there is always the danger of precipitating a larger disruption by failing to take corrective action. Although informal mechanisms for coordination exist now, the IEA could be more effective if its members put in place procedures for joint response to subcritical emergencies. The chief policy tool, besides consultation and information exchange, would be to coordinate the use of inventories to prevent a sudden rush to the spot market, with its attendant price signal to the more militant oil exporters.

The IEA effectively ignores the question of the price for oil exchanged under its sharing agreement. Sudden changes in prices are a characteristic of oil supply interruptions, so pricing is sure to be a critical issue during implementation of the allocation formula. Without a definite rule, the debate over pricing may overwhelm the sharing arrangements. After all, there will always be a shortage of cheap oil, and everyone will want today's oil at yesterday's prices.

Sweden and Turkey have tried to use the IEA to gain access to oil at below-market prices, but no supplier wanted to support such a subsidy. The IEA needs a pricing rule and, just like the principle for designing a sharing scheme, the rule should formalize the incentives in the market while capturing the economic benefits for the importers. For example, countries with excess supplies could be required to share oil at a 'high-ten' price: the average price of the highest 10 percent of their other sales. This would provide security for the small countries who fear they will be frozen out by the giants, prevent the rush to the IEA as the source of protection from the reality of the new scarcity of oil, provide a realistic alternative to the price leapfrogging of the spot market, and preserve at least the minimum incentives for the haves to share with the have-nots.

These small changes in the IEA might help, but they would not expand the narrow scope of the present agreement. However, the oil importers need a further mechanism for cooperation that allows them to extend their horizons beyond just containing the putative voracity of their fellow importers. They need a policy to meet the observed voracity of the oil exporters.

*Summit Process*

Part of the explanation for the feeble state of the IEA agreement is found in the cumbersome nature of any process involving multilateral negotiation among twenty-one countries (with the twenty-second, France, standing in the wings). The IEA may be too large, and the demands of energy security policy too great, to expect this to be the forum for introducing fundamental changes in the objectives of international cooperation. The summit meetings offer an alternative mechanism that includes the major oil importers, should be small enough to arrive at any agreement that could be fashioned, and would be able to induce cooperation from others. Furthermore, the precedent for dealing with energy policy was set at the Tokyo Summit with the negotiation of oil import targets.[9]

The focus on import reductions and stanching the flow of wealth to oil exporters is the new initiative needed for international cooperation. By various calculations, the true cost of the extra barrel of oil imports is far above the price in the world market. Reduced oil imports by anyone would give everyone the benefits of both a lower price and reduced exposure to the damages of oil supply disruptions. During normal times this import premium could be at least 30 percent of the price of oil; during supply interruptions it could jump to 100 percent or more, reflecting the great transfer of wealth that high prices bring.[10] Evidently there are great gains to be had through cooperation to reduce import levels. The IEA has been reluctant to step up to this issue; the summit leaders have approached it gingerly, by adopting nonbinding import targets. With complacency on the rebound during the predictable oil 'glut' of the early 1980s, the summit countries should act to impose import controls that recognize the large premium not captured in the market price.

The choice of the optimal import reduction policy is problematic. The program must be visible and effective in each country or cooperation will not last long. And it must work within the context of an uncertain game of confrontation with the oil exporters. The two stylized extremes of tariffs and quotas illustrate the difficulties.

A collective oil import tariff would be highly visible. Every participating country would be able to see and measure the sacrifices being made by others and the tariff could be tuned to reflect the best measure of the import premium. A tariff would also be visible to the oil exporters. If we are lucky, they would recognize that further increases in oil prices would not affect the tariff, but would drive demand down even more. Faced with this prospect, they would lower prices to maintain demand. If we are not lucky, the oil exporters may develop unused market power or some belief about the high value of oil in the ground. They could interpret a tariff as evidence that importers could absorb even higher prices, and they would oblige us by raising prices and cutting production to maintain a tight oil market.

A quota would be visible, but not so clearly effective. Differences in the business cycle could make the same quota for any one country either irrelevant or a binding constraint. Without careful tuning, the agreement could collapse. Perhaps an even greater danger would follow from the change in incentives for the oil importers. Without the incentive of price, few countries would volunteer to import less than their quota, so the quota would become an effective prediction of the total demand for imported oil. Oil exporters would be free to raise their price without fear of losing their market, at least up to the price that makes the quota nonbinding. Oil importers could end up with the worst of both conditions: restricted supplies and higher prices.

Of course, these descriptions are not precise predictions of the result of applying either a tariff or a quota. Neither the exporters nor the importers could tune their policies well enough. Tariffs would not stay fixed in the face of a sudden jump in oil prices; in all likelihood they would be lowered. And quotas could not be met exactly; the oil importers could not change their policies fast enough to protect oil exporters from all loss in demand due to higher prices. But both sets of difficulties are serious enough to warrant a search for a compromise.

Politically, import targets, that is, general goals but not rigid constraints, have been more appealing than tariffs or strict quotas; witness the Tokyo agreements. A tariff may be too hard to explain at home since there is no disguising its price effects in domestic markets. A quota sounds a little too simplistic and, as we have seen, could be counterproductive. Import targets, on the other hand, leave a certain flexibility to the individual countries in designing the policies to meet the goal. This diversity of policies may make cooperation more possible for many countries and more difficult for the oil exporters to counter.

Perhaps the best strategy would involve a combination of the most attractive features of tariffs, quotas, and targets. One option is an agreement on oil-import-value-share targets. Under this proposal, each oil importing country would adopt a target for oil imports expressed as a value share of total GNP. As with quantity targets, the policies adopted to achieve the goal would be left to the preferences of the individual countries. There would still be the problem of choosing equitable targets that imposed a fair burden on each country, but the use of value shares would avoid at least two problems. First, countries whose economies suddenly expanded would be allowed automatically to increase their oil imports; similarly, those who were contracting would still share in the sacrifices at the margin. Second, although not confronted with the provocation of a tariff, oil exporters would face a strong incentive not to raise prices - higher export prices would precipitate lower demand for oil as the importers adjusted to meet the value share targets.

Once adopted by the summit countries, a policy of restricting the value share of oil imports could be extended to all the IEA members. In normal times, this might mean no more than an acceleration of programs already underway to control oil use and subsidize the production of import substitutes. (The United States, for example, through the decontrol of domestic oil prices, eliminated one of the chief sources of subsidies for oil imports.) Therefore, the summit nations may be able to avoid a confrontation with the IEA countries who did not participate in the negotiations to establish the targets.

This ability to select the participants and the forum for agreement will not extend into the realm of managing oil shortages. Here there seems to be an unavoidable conflict between using the more wieldy summit process and strengthening the IEA. Use of the IEA would have the advantages of exploiting an existing framework and staff for preparing for and coordinating emergency responses. But the IEA is limited by its narrow focus on oil policy. During a major interruption of oil supplies, military and political initiatives will be at least as important as the sharing of oil production and stockpiles. Hence, in a real crunch, the IEA will either implement the policies of the summit countries or it will be ignored.

A better course to follow might be to use the existing mechanism but to fashion new IEA policies to reflect the realistic priorities that will prevail during a major supply interruption. The summit countries should expand the scope of cooperation during emergencies, with a principal energy policy objective of stopping the drain of wealth caused by supply shortages. The form of the agreement during interruptions could be the oil-import-value-share targets, adjusted to reflect the expected size of the supply interruption. The delicate diplomatic effort should then follow to extend participation to include all the IEA countries.

## Demonstrating Commitment

Whether through the IEA, the summit process, or some other mechanism, the oil importers have much to gain from the development of cooperative energy policies. But no agreements will succeed if the principal players do not demonstrate a commitment to cooperation in actions that fall short of a crisis. There are many actions that oil importers could take to signal early an intention to join in collective actions during an emergency.

In the United States, for instance, at least two positive steps would help now. First, Congress should remove the restrictions on exporting Alaskan oil. The present limitation has a complicated history rooted in the early environmental debate over the need for the Alaskan pipeline. Today the restriction is maintained out of a false hope that keeping Alaskan oil in the United States somehow increases our security. But because of the international character of the world oil market, there is no security in such restrictions; they only add to the cost of using the oil, in this case because of the necessity to ship a large portion of the Alaskan oil to the Gulf of Mexico. It would be far more efficient to allow the Alaskan oil to go to Japan and to redirect Japanese imports to the United States. There would be no loss in real security, but the demonstration of willingness to share oil during stable times would make more credible the pledge to share oil during crises.

Second, the Congress could change the anti-trust laws to allow the major oil companies to participate more freely in IEA exercises and informal negotiations during periods of shortages too minor to trigger the full IEA sharing scheme. The oil companies have the critical information and expertise needed to manage oil supply shortages. As mentioned above, the IEA should be expanding its capability to deal with relatively small shortages. The United States could help by removing restrictions that now prevent taking action to nip emergencies in the bud.

All countries should consider more aggressive programs to monitor the behavior of their public and private oil traders, especially during the early stages of a supply emergency. Even a few companies rushing into the spot market and driving up prices can destroy confidence in the likelihood of cooperation. And each country must make the preparations for credible domestic programs that will give it the tools to live up to cooperative agreements for sharing during emergencies.

## IV EMERGENCY PREPAREDNESS

Individual countries, acting alone or collectively, should pursue the same list of energy policies for emergency preparation. The chief effect of cooperative action is to strengthen the incentives or increase the optimal scale for each action. Furthermore, a credible domestic program will be a prerequisite for building and implementing wider agreements across countries. Since further disruptions of world oil markets are likely to come, all oil importing countries should prepare the plans and capabilities to curtail demand, expand supply and manage the economy during an oil supply disruption.

### Demand Restrictions

A shortage in oil supplies means that some uses of oil must be forgone. The only policy choice is in selecting the mechanism. At one extreme, governments can do nothing and the price will rise until the reduced demand matches the available supply. But then the revenues from the higher prices go to the oil producers. Ideally, with a quick and effective response, governments could take steps to reduce demand and prevent the shortage from driving up the price of oil in the world market. If precisely the same demands are eliminated, then all the economic benefits might stay with energy consumers.

Perhaps the easiest way to imagine this government intervention is through the imposition of an emergency tax or tariff. Added to the price of oil, this would present the consumer with the same incentives as the free market in the presence of a suddenly reduced supply of oil and demand would drop. But then the revenues would go to the government instead of to the oil exporters. Unfortunately, the necessary tax or tariff during a major supply disruption could be very large. The price of oil more than doubled, to $33 per barrel, between 1979 and 1980 when Iran's output dropped about two million barrels per day, even though the curtailed production was quickly replaced by increased output from other sources. It is possible that a large interruption in the future could propel the market clearing price of oil to over $100 per barrel. It is hard to imagine a government with the ability to impose overnight a $2 per gallon tax on oil products, but this is what will be needed if the oil exporters are not to be left to impose the tax for us.

Such a tax or tariff may be the best policy in a country like the United States or Germany. Others, such as Japan or France, with a tradition of greater success in administrative control, may find it easier to design a system of direct restrictions on oil use as more effective in achieving a quick response. Lowered thermostat settings, curtailed driving, emergency van pooling operations, rapid conversion to alternative fuels, and rolling blackouts could combine to yield large and rapid reductions in the demand for petroleum products. The proposals for such plans in the United States are contained in the Emergency Energy Conservation Act (1979).[11]

Probably the best approach is in a pragmatic combination of tax incentives and administrative controls. The higher prices could reinforce the restrictions on use and induce many small adjustments that would be beyond the reach of direct controls. To the extent that anything less than a full price allocation system is used, government will face the problem of deciding on the allocation of scarce oil supplies. Part of the evidence of the credibility of the potential for cooperative action across countries will be in the preparation for the domestic allocation of supplies during a major interruption. For example, if a country has no more effective tools available than the universally derided gasoline rationing plan now on the books in the United States, it would be natural to assume that internal chaos would make it difficult for the government to cooperate in a program requiring sensitive coordination among countries. The United States, in particular, needs a realistic policy for dealing with its domestic energy problems during an oil emergency.[12]

In addition to preparing detailed allocation systems, investments in fuel switching facilities would improve both a country's capability and credibility to meet the threat of oil supply interruptions. Between crises, these emergency preparations should be managed by a standing organization with the visibility, stature, and resources to implement emergency plans. During the confusion of a supply interruption, there will not be time to pull together an effective team. A failure to prepare now will make it impossible to perform later. The foundation for a strong program of international cooperation among oil importers must be effective programs for domestic management of oil emergencies. Plans for these programs must be put in place now to complement the initiatives for coordinated action during the next major catastrophe on the world oil market.

**Supply Expansion**

Part of the preparations must include investments to provide the capability for a burst of new supply during an emergency. With the effective domestic price of oil doubling or tripling overnight, any source of emergency oil supplies would be a most valuable form of insurance. The source of new supplies could take many forms, ranging from a specially prepared strategic reserve of oil to surge production of coal or natural gas to replace oil through fuel switching programs.

The Strategic Petroleum Reserve is the first and most obvious source of emergency oil supplies. Estimates of the value of filling this reserve in the United States far exceed the companion estimates of the social cost of oil imports. Every country should be expanding its capacity to store oil and filling that capacity as rapidly as possible. A large inventory of oil would be one of the most visible and most credible tools for deterring supply interruptions or mitigating their effects. The need for effective policy is most urgent during the gluts that follow oil price shocks. Only an attention to the need for emergency preparedness could overcome the temptation to reduce oil inventories in a softening market. Reversing these incentives should be among the highest priorities for government action.

Part of the dilemma and policy debate surrounding the expansion of strategic reserves of oil has been the design of the appropriate ownership and use arrangements. Particularly in the United States, this debate has often inhibited action to acquire and store the oil. At present, with only a small reserve in place, the priorities should be clear. Each country should use whatever mechanisms it has to expand and fill its storage facilities. In parallel, the debate can proceed about long run mechanisms for private financing, a merger of the storage program and a futures market, the coordination of drawdown policies across countries, and the depoliticization of storage by the transfer of decision-making to private hands or independent public boards. But it is not likely that the outcome of this debate will much affect the size or disposition of the reserve that could be built before 1990. Therefore, these important decisions about what to do with a large strategic reserve should not be allowed to delay the creation of that large reserve.

The importance of the oil reserve often overshadows equally impressive opportunities for building surge capacity with other forms of energy. For example, both coal and natural gas are relatively easy to store in large quantities. In some uses, such as heating, natural gas can be a direct substitute for oil. When matched with companion programs for fuel conversion, even greater possibilities open up to accumulate supplies that can substitute for oil in an emergency. Studies by the National Petroleum Council and others suggest that with a little preparation, over one million barrels of oil per day could be obtained via substitution of stored natural gas.[13] And at the suddenly higher value of domestic oil, during an emergency, power wheeling from coal plants, and surge production of domestic oil and gas wells, may be both technically feasible and economically justifiable.

**Macroeconomic Preparations**

A dramatic jump in oil prices will change our perceptions of the policies that are economic. In addition, it will present entirely new problems that require coordination of energy policy and macroeconomic management. Unfortunately, we do not fully understand the interactions of the two, but a few examples can illustrate the need for viewing oil supply disruptions as macroeconomic problems.

Higher payments for oil will draw a substantial amount of purchasing power from the economy. Compared to 1978, for instance, oil payments in the United States during 1980 increased by $100 billion. During a future supply interruption, the figure could be much larger. The first challenge will be to manage the international banking system in order to handle the recycling of these dollars. Part of these revenues were recycled immediately as the domestic owners of oil began to spend their windfall, but at least half those revenues went to pay for imports and those payments will return slowly in the form of increased exports of goods and services.

If governments act wisely in the future, they will capture the rents from the shortages by using taxes and tariffs. In the United States, for instance, the windfall profits tax has been enacted to keep the rents from domestic producers. A product tax or an oil import tariff would add even more to government coffers. But these sudden accumulations of unspent surpluses would multiply throughout the economy to depress aggregate demand and output for all goods and services well below that necessary to accommodate the reduced oil supplies. Hence, part of the challenge for managing an oil supply interruption will be in maintaining full employment despite the sudden loss in consumer purchasing power.

At the same time, oil prices play a large enough role in the economy so that an oil supply interruption could again add a noticeable increment to inflation. This direct effect on the aggregate price level will present macroeconomic managers with the temptation to further depress the money supply in order to dampen the new burst of inflation. Combined with the potential recessionary effects of the fiscal drag caused by higher oil payments, the potential exists to create a major economic contraction, exacerbating the direct impacts of the new scarcity of oil. Such is the diagnosis of the counterproductive response to the oil shock of the 1973 oil embargo.[14]

If these two challenges are not enough, national leaders will face angry consumers on every side complaining about the inequities of the sudden redistribution of income caused by the higher prices on all oil. After the oil shocks of 1973–74, these distributional issues dominated decision-making on pricing in the United States and led to the subsidization of oil imports. The result, a combination of price controls and the entitlements program, increased the payments out of the country in order to slow the redistribution of payments within the country.[15]

One can speculate that a balanced program of taxes and income transfers could meet all of these three problems simultaneously. The taxes would be needed to capture the economic benefits for imports which would be real resource costs for the country. The income transfers would be targeted to the population hardest hit by the increase in oil prices, to avoid both the unnecessary reduction in standard of living and the fiscal drag. Depending on the institutional arrangements in each country, the form of the income transfers could be designed to compensate for the inflationary effect of the oil price increases. In the United States, for example, reductions in withholding for income taxes and Social Security payments could provide a quick transfer of income through existing institutions and provide a one time drop in the aggregate price level. Berman has shown that the potential exists in the United States to accommodate as much as $400 billion in annual transfers without creating a new administrative structure.[16] This could be large enough for all but the most extreme case of a supply interruption.

At least two problems have been suggested for this tax and income transfer package. First, those familiar with the practice of macroeconomic management blanch at the thought of hundreds of billions of fresh dollars making their way through government hands. No doubt this is a problem, but with the tax structure already in place it cannot be avoided, except for the revenues we are willing to give away to the oil exporters.[17] Therefore, unless we can design such efficient emergency responses that prices do not rise appreciably during a supply interruption, the only open issue is the degree to which we prepare for the complicated economic management task.

Second, and more disturbing, two analyses of the behavior of the US economy in the short run suggest that the timing of the taxes and payments is critical and, if our performance is no better than the average behavior in the past, disruption tariffs and massive rebates could be counterproductive, with the rebate coming too late to offset the negative effects of the inflation caused by the tariff itself.[18] While these are preliminary results, there are at least two potential resolutions of the difficulties. For one, there is no reason why the income transfers should be tied to the timing or scale of the government taxes on oil or related energy products. The income transfers could well be 'prebates', preceding the arrival of tax revenues and with a scale determined by the needs for macroeconomic management. Finally, the optimal policy will depend crucially on the state of the business cycle at the time of the oil supply interruption. More research must be done to illuminate attractive and robust economic management policies under a range of likely conditions. But in the interim all countries should be planning and preparing the taxing and income transfer authorities for coordinated management of energy and economic policy.

## V LONG RUN ADJUSTMENTS

The threat of an oil supply interruption will be a persistent short run problem. Although many of the policies needed to meet this challenge are not automatically required for the longer run adjustment to new sources of energy, there are many actions focused on reducing oil import dependence or stabilizing the longer run oil market that also reinforce preparations for dealing with emergencies.

### Import Restrictions

We have already examined import restrictions, both for the long run and during supply disruptions. The most attractive approach may be through the oil-import-value-share target that would leave flexibility for individual country action and present the oil exporters with a diversity of programs and incentives that would be about as difficult to counter as any program that could be put in place through multilateral negotiation.

### Excess Capacity

Oil importers will benefit from excess oil production capacity anywhere in the world. It would not be quite as beneficial to have the spare capacity in the oil exporting countries as elsewhere, but it could help in many cases. Although a production reserve in Saudi Arabia would not protect us in the event of the loss of Saudi Arabia, it proved to be valuable during 1980 in compensating in part for the loss of production from Iran and Iraq. For obvious reasons, construction of excess capacity is not likely to be part of an explicit arrangement with oil exporters. But it should be a continuing goal for quiet diplomacy and implicit bargains.

### Supply Diversification

Increased production outside the volatile Persian Gulf lessens the power of the oil exporters and reduces the threat and importance of a sudden disruption of oil supplies. The oil importing countries should be looking everywhere to promote the diversification of the total world oil supply. Of course, this is not the same as the scramble of individual countries to diversify their own import contracts. While rearranging existing contracts may help ease some of the adjustments during a disruption, the fungibility of oil makes this policy futile as a way to remove the systematic risk of a large total volume of unstable supplies. More appealing, for instance, are arrangements such as the original proposal for a World Bank affiliate to underwrite the private risk of expropriation of successful exploration ventures in developing countries.

Over the long run, diversification should include the expansion in the international trade in fuels that serve as an alternative to oil. Notably the trade in coal should expand greatly over the next decade. Fortunately, the inexpensive coal supplies are in different hands than the inexpensive oil supplies, so the increased availability of this new source of energy supply should serve to mute the power of the oil producers. And with the example of the vulnerability of oil supplies fresh in mind, coal importers are likely to take the precautions necessary to prevent falling into the energy-vulnerability trap a second time.

## Guaranteed Returns

One of the most perplexing problems which increases the likelihood of occasional disruptions of oil supply is the view in many oil exporting countries that the oil is more valuable if left in the ground. Cremer and Salehi-Isfahani have shown that restricted access to capital markets can validate this fear and rational behavior would call for reduced supply in response to higher prices.[19] In this circumstance, both the oil importers and the oil exporters would be helped by creating opportunities for investment in less liquid long-term assets with acceptable real rates of return. Given the size of the investments and the necessity to move the capital across national boundaries, such an ideal could be beyond our reach. But a better rate of return on petrodollars could result in a higher rate of oil production at a lower price. And entangling the oil exporters in long-term investments in other countries could be an effective stimulus for moderation in the oil market. For example, it might pay the IEA to offer the surplus Persian Gulf states a special rate on long-term bonds backed by the oil importing governments.

## Government-to-Governments Deals

Special production arrangements between governments seem much less attractive. At best the oil importer ends up making concessions in exchange for empty promises; for instance, the French seemed to have gained little from their Iraqi connection. At worst the arrangements might reduce the flexibility in the world oil market, making it more difficult to reallocate oil supplies during a major emergency; the direct involvement of governments in the oil trade would politicize every oil transaction. We should take heed from the example of President Carter's difficulty in filling his strategic petroleum reserve once the decision arrived on the diplomatic agenda between Saudi Arabia and the United States. All importing governments should benefit from maintaining their distance from the oil exporters when it comes to individual oil deals. In our confrontations with the oil exporters we need the nonconfrontational cover of a dispersed market.

## VI MILITARY AND DIPLOMATIC OPTIONS

New action on energy policy could improve the security of oil supply and slow the transfer of wealth to the oil exporters. But there is no hope that energy policy alone could be sufficient to eliminate the need for military and diplomatic efforts to protect the vulnerable oil supplies in the Persian Gulf. In the near term, the need is greater for action in these arenas, for even the best hopes for cooperation among the oil importers will produce only marginal gains in stabilizing oil markets.

These military and diplomatic options are discussed elsewhere in detail that goes beyond the scope of this chapter.[20] The oil importers need to accelerate the already growing efforts to project military power into the Persian Gulf. A land base within tactical air range of the oil fields is a prize worth a few risks. Failing this, the Rapid Deployment Force, advance positioning of supplies, expansion of oil field repair capabilities, bolstered aircraft carrier support, regular deployment exercises, and coordination with allies in the Middle East are items high on the agenda for improved defense of the Gulf. Of necessity, the balance will be precarious. For example, the military buildup needed to deter invasion of Persian Gulf countries may exacerbate the danger of disruptions by local radicals. There is no military option, including the option of doing nothing, that will be risk free. The oil is a great prize; there is no escaping the threat that competition for the oil could lead to a conflict in which everyone loses.

Just as delicate will be the fashioning of a diplomatic policy that threads its way through the thicket of local rivalries. Inevitably, every negotiation will encounter an entanglement with the Arab-Israeli issue. And oil importers must choose between heavy support of existing regimes and the dangers of later retaliation by their replacements. The primary objective of diplomacy should be to buy time and reinforce the military and energy policy initiatives needed to prepare us for the inevitable disruptions that no one can expect to prevent.

## VII CONCLUSION

Our expensive experience in the world oil market has taught us of the importance of the oil-vulnerability problem as a first-order security

Table 8.1 *An Agenda for Cooperation*

- International framework
  - Reforming the IEA
    - Sharing proportional to consumption
    - Subcrisis cooperation
    - Pricing according to high-ten rule
  - Summit nations
    - Focus on wealth transfers
    - Oil-import-value-share targets
    - Provide lead for IEA
- Demonstrating commitment
  - Share all oil supplies
  - Remove anti-trust restrictions
  - Control trading companies in spot market
- Emergency preparedness
  - Demand restrictions
    - Tax/tariff
    - Administrative controls
    - Fuel switching investments
    - Allocation programs
    - Emergency management teams
  - Supply expansion
    - Fill strategic oil reserves
    - Expand storage capacity
    - Develop management plans
    - Natural gas and coal stockpiles
  - Macroeconomic management
    - Tax policies
    - 'Prebates'
    - Recycling
- Long run adjustments
  - Import restrictions
  - Excess capacity construction
  - Supply diversification
  - Guaranteed returns
  - Avoid unilateral oil deals
- Military and diplomatic options
  - Protect oil fields
  - Buy time for energy options

threat and the evidence at the pump is a constant reminder of the drain in our wealth caused by periodic supply interruptions or sustained high oil prices. After an early blush of optimism about the imminent demise of the new reality in the oil market, importing nations lapsed into the doldrums of despair about their ability to counter the power of the exporters.

Although there is no doubt that the exporters hold the highest cards, the importers are not so weak that they need concede every hand at the oil poker table. There are opportunities for collective action to protect ourselves against the instability in the Persian Gulf supplies and the continued drain of exorbitant payments for oil imports. This agenda for cooperation, summarized in Table 8.1, will require bold action and immediate sacrifices by the oil importers. But the investment could pay healthy dividends. Without initiatives to promote a cooperative defense, we will be subject to extortion alone.

## NOTES

1 The present chapter continues the discussion along the lines of Rowen and Weyant (1981). For a summary of many diagnostic studies, see Alm (1981) or Rowen and Hogan (1981). An earlier version of this paper was discussed at the joint European American Institute/Security Conference on Asia and the Pacific Workshop, Kronberg, Germany, June 4–6, 1981.

2 The original proposals called for the creation of an Energy Security Corporation; the last minute name change corrected the most embarassing misnomer; see Energy Security Act, PL 96-294, June 1980.

3 After years of delay, oil purchases were mandated by Congress in the Energy Security Act. One year later, the problem changed to finding a way to expand the limited storage facilities. See *National Journal* (1981).

4 See Alm (1981) for a summary of the economic damages of oil supply interruptions.

5 Neff (1981).

6 The IEP contains the formal emergency oil sharing agreement of the International Energy Agency.

7 Silk (1981), Tucker (1981).

8 Deese and Nye (1981b). For a description and analysis of the IEA, see Krapels (1980) or Weiner (1981).

9 Leaders of the seven summit nations met in Tokyo in June 1979. President Carter called for ceilings on oil imports and announced a target for the United States of 8.5 million barrels per day. In his January 1980 State of the Union address he modified this to 8.2 million barrels per day. The ceiling has never been binding, due to the high price of oil. Working through the IEA, the other oil importers adopted similar ceilings.

10 See, for example, Deese and Nye (1981a), Chapter 9.

11 Berman (1981a).

12 With the expiration of the Emergency Petroleum Allocation Act, in September 1981, the United States has only the most general emergency authorities deriving from the national security powers. Emergency response programs, therefore, will likely be developed during the heat of a crisis.

13 National Petroleum Council (1980), Pan Heuristics (1980).

14 For example, see Landsberg *et al.* (1981), Chapter 4.

15 Kalt (1981).

16 Berman (1981b).

17 Berman (1981a).
18 Mork (1981) and Hubbard and Fry (1981).
19 Cremer and Salehi-Isfahani (1980).
20 Rowen (1981c) Deese and Nye (1981a).

# 9 Conclusions

JAMES M. GRIFFIN and DAVID J. TEECE

## INTRODUCTION

This book has brought together, in the various contributing chapters, a rather diverse collection of views on OPEC behavior and the long run price of oil. Despite some obvious differences, which we have not attempted to eliminate, there is a remarkable congruence of views on several important matters. We will exercise our editorial prerogatives to the fullest in order to develop what we believe are some provocative conclusions.

## I IS OPEC A CARTEL AND DOES IT MATTER?

Let us summarize the views presented with respect to this matter. We observe, at the outset, that while there is disagreement on the importance of wealth-maximizing motives, there is consensus on the following critical issue: the world price of oil since 1974 has been considerably above the level that would prevail if prices were competitively determined with producers using 'reasonable' discount rates and reserves and demand forecasts. This conclusion follows from Professor Adelman's dominant producer model, from Professor Teece's target revenue perspective, and from Professor Moran's political model. Likewise, this view is either explicitly or implicitly given in the chapters by Mr Lichtblau, by Professors Daly, Griffin, and Steele, by Professor Pindyck, and by Professor Hogan. All recognize the existence of economic rents and the presence of discretionary power over price. This is an important conclusion in that it confirms that the enormous transfer of wealth which has taken place from consuming to producing nations is far greater than it would have been had the multinational oil companies kept control of production decisions. It also implicitly rejects the property rights interpretation of the world oil market, which would posit that present price levels are competitively determined.

Whether OPEC is garnering economic rents because of *cooperative* behavior is not a matter upon which there is agreement. Professor Adelman characterizes OPEC as a loosely cooperating oligopoly, while Professor Teece postulates that a (moving) target revenue perspective explains OPEC behavior. The target revenue model suggests that OPEC's gains in the past have not been cooperatively attained, and if cooperation is needed to protect monopoly rents in the future, it may not be forthcoming. Clearly, identifying the type of cartel in operation is of some importance.

## II FUTURE MARKET CONDITIONS FACING OPEC

Traditional economic factors related to supply and demand suggest that OPEC's production levels and market share may well decline throughout this century. The principal reason is that high prices are reducing consumption levels below those generally considered possible just a few years ago. In the major non-communist industrialized countries, 1980 oil consumption was about where it was in 1973 (see Table 9.1). Despite the fact that 1980 aggregate national product in the industrialized world was about 25 percent above 1973 levels, total energy per unit of national income has declined, with a small degree of substitution away from oil. Since oil and energy consumption are closely tied to the stock of energy using capital, substantial future gains in conservation are to be expected as the capital stock is turned over. In response to higher energy prices, those capital types that are relatively efficient in energy use will expand at the expense of inefficient energy-using capital configurations. The time frame required to achieve a complete turnover of the capital stock varies widely, depending on the life of the capital equipment and the rate of growth of the capital stock. In addition, energy-saving technological change will continue to have an impact on the capital stock even after it has all turned over. For these reasons, the authors in this volume believe that the world economy has by no means fully responded to the 1973–74 price shock, let alone the 1979 shock. To use the words of John Lichtblau, the price increases we have experienced have 'mobilized the entire technological and economic genius of the industrialized world for the task of reducing oil imports' and oil consumption. The result, quoting Professor Adelman, is that 'for the first time in 120 years, oil is no longer a growth industry and is probably a declining industry'.

Accordingly, it would be correct to identify most of the contributing authors as elasticity 'optimists'. Professors Daly, Griffin, and Steele employ long run oil demand elasticities ranging from $-.365$ to $-.73$, a range that was tacitly accepted by most of the contributing authors. This analysis suggested that substantial

Table 9.1 *Petroleum Consumption for Major Non-Communist Industrialized Countries (Thousand barrels per day)*

| | *Canada* | *France* | *Italy* | *Japan* | *United Kingdom* | *United States* | *West Germany* | *Other OECD* | *Total OECD* |
|---|---|---|---|---|---|---|---|---|---|
| 1973 | 1,597 | 2,219 | 1,525 | 5,000 | 1,958 | 17,308 | 2,693 | 4,069 | 36,370 |
| 1974 | 1,630 | 2,094 | 1,521 | 4,872 | 1,829 | 16,653 | 2,408 | 4,047 | 36,050 |
| 1975 | 1,595 | 1,925 | 1,468 | 4,568 | 1,633 | 16,322 | 2,319 | 3,905 | 33,740 |
| 1976 | 1,647 | 2,075 | 1,503 | 4,786 | 1,601 | 17,461 | 2,507 | 4,265 | 35,850 |
| 1977 | 1,661 | 1,973 | 1,476 | 5,015 | 1,655 | 18,431 | 2,478 | 4,214 | 36,900 |
| 1978 | 1,701 | 2,077 | 1,551 | 5,115 | 1,683 | 18,847 | 2,596 | 4,387 | 37,960 |
| 1979 | 1,766 | 2,107 | 1,607 | 5,173 | 1,690 | 18,513 | 2,664 | 4,487 | 38,010 |
| 1980 | 1,730 | 1,965 | 1,602 | 4,680 | 1,420 | 17,006 | 2,360 | 4,402 | 34,970 |

*Source:* US Department of Energy, *Monthly Energy Review*, August 1981.

production cutbacks would be necessary at the −.73 price elasticity by the cartel core. Serious pressures on OPEC could even occur at the −.365 price elasticity assuming economic growth rates well below historical levels. While it is by no means certain that sustained slow growth in world oil demand, particularly in the 1980s, will materialize, this is a likely outcome. Consumption has stabilized and the supply of non-OPEC oil is inching upward, which means that OPEC exports must decline or the price must fall.

## III OPEC PRICING AND STABILITY WITH A PROLONGED SOFT MARKET

One's predictions about price and OPEC stability in the face of a soft market turn out to swing rather importantly upon the behavioral model one decides is the more accurate representation of OPEC.

### Dominant Producer

According to this view, each OPEC member is quite aware of the mutual interdependencies that exist among producers and, for the common good, producers are willing to share the burden of output reductions by adhering to some kind of formal or informal prorationing scheme. In any event, widespread cheating is unlikely since all participants are aware of the disastrous outcomes if cartel discipline were to evaporate. Accordingly, a collapse of the cartel price seems unlikely and modest (real) price increases, even in the face of flat or declining OPEC exports, are quite possible.

This seems close to Professor Adelman's view that OPEC will attempt to raise the price even higher, because of internal pressures within OPEC from producers outside the Persian Gulf. As these producers begin to run budget deficits, they will demand that the Saudis and others in the Gulf core go along with higher prices. While the Saudis are anxious to avoid these pressures and are seeking agreement on long range pricing objectives on this account, they are nevertheless likely to submit to these pressures because the 'nuisance value' of the OPEC states outside the Gulf is considerable. Providing the real price increases were not large and production in the cartel core does not fall below certain thresholds, this model would seem to predict price stability and continued OPEC vitality. There is, however, the problem that political events might trigger still another leap in oil prices. An attempt by the cartel to ratify and sustain such a price could ultimately result in such low production in the cartel core and elsewhere that widespread cheating could undermine the whole price structure and OPEC stability. Barring this last outcome, this model of OPEC behavior suggests that the prospects for constant price or modest real price increases (averaging 1 to 2 percent) are quite good despite a prolonged soft market environment.

**Target Revenue Perspective**

The target revenue approach rests on the assumption that absorptive capacity is limited in the short run and that artificially low discount rates are used, at least implicitly, in production planning. Both factors result in very conservative production policies, so long as oil revenues meet budgetary requirements (which in turn depend on absorptive capacity), and so long as low real returns on liquid financial assets reinforce (myopic) expectations that oil in the ground is a better investment than money in the bank.

However, a prolonged period of soft crude prices can permit the growth in absorptive capacity to outstrip current revenues. This will induce a tendency toward output expansion. Additionally, if real returns on foreign financial assets continue at historically high levels, many countries may decide that foreign assets are a desirable component of one's investment portfolio, and will expand production simply to build foreign assets. Both factors will tilt production decisions toward expansion, with additional capacity being added if necessary.

Since production policies are considered matters of national sovereignty, it will not be easy for OPEC to hold the line through collective action. The Saudis might well be pressed to cut back production, at least until production is down to about 7 MMB/D. However, Saudi resistance to further reductions would be met at about this level. Since OPEC will have difficulty achieving formal prorationing, the price might very well fall dramatically. This is all the more likely if a pro-development regime is restored in Iran, and relations with Iraq are improved. Such a development would create budgetary demands in both countries. While this rather optimistic scenario could of course be upset by political turmoil, the implication is clear: the target revenue model suggests that substantial downward price movements are likely in the event of a prolonged soft market.

**Political Models**

As discussed in Chapter 1, political models have weak predictive abilities, in that the political process is exceedingly difficult to model. Accordingly, it is very difficult to contrast Professor Moran's political model of OPEC with the economic models outlined in the other chapters. Just as political factors are an integral part of Professor Teece's target revenue model, so too are economic factors a part of Professor Moran's political model. While political and security concerns may 'wag the economic tail', most political scientists agree that the wagging can be performed with greater alacrity if economic concerns are not of great immediacy. Thus, one way to contrast political models with the economic models is to recognize that when economic variables fall within some acceptable and rather broadly defined range, then political factors will receive full play.

However, if economic variables are not within this comfortable range, producers must recognize critical tradeoffs between economic and political goals. Thus a prolonged soft market will surely attenuate OPEC's ability to use the oil weapon for political purposes. In short, even if political objectives are recognized to be of paramount importance, the market conditions that we expect to prevail in the future may result in economic factors wagging the political tail at least on some matters. Thus, consumers should be reluctant to give favors today in exchange for price decreases which market forces might very well bring about in any event. Hence, future market conditions indicate that 'linkage' might be made to work in reverse - the United States and other consumers might continue to purchase OPEC output in exchange for political favors in the Mideast. If the Saudis can make linkage work for them in a tight market, perhaps the consuming nations can make it work in reverse when the market is slack!

## Reaching a Consensus

With the possible exception of Professor Pindyck's Chapter 7, all contributors indicate, with greater or lesser conviction, that OPEC may well have reached its zenith with respect to its ability to increase the price of crude oil faster than the rate of inflation. As John Lichtblau explained in Chapter 5, market forces do not support any significant further real price increases, where significant is defined as a real average annual price increase in excess of 1.5 percent from 1981 to 1990. This is not to say that there will not be an increase in price because of a political disruption.

Furthermore, it was indicated by Professor Adelman in Chapter 2 that miscalculation may well trigger a price overshoot by some producers. The consensus of the authors appears to be that if a large price hike occurs in response to some political disruption, it will not be sustainable in the long run, unless such political upheavals permanently take appreciable capacity out of production.

Indeed, several authors imply that a $32.00 real price path may not be sustainable in the long run. The editors are perhaps further down this road than several of the contributors. The results of Professors Daly, Griffin, and Steele's modeling exercise indicates that under realistic elasticity and economic growth assumptions, OPEC production in the year 2000 will not be significantly higher than at present even if the real price of oil does not rise above 1981 levels. This suggests potential trouble for OPEC in the mid-1980s if not before, particularly if one accepts the target revenue model.

Thus OPEC, having discovered how to employ short run demand elasticities to great advantage, might well be hoisted on its own petard in that there is both upside and downside demand inelasticity. The principal difference, however, is that the downside inelasticity may be greater both in the short run and in the long run since, in the face of precipitously falling prices, we would fully expect most consuming nations to engage policies to protect domestic energy investments. There are several reasons why this is likely. The most obvious is the political power of vested interests to protect capital intensive investments in various energy producing and energy saving technologies. Tariffs or quotas on imported oil are likely for this reason alone. These factors will be reinforced by national security considerations, with importers being reluctant to increase dependence on foreign oil, after struggling so hard to reduce dependence.

We anticipate, therefore, that precipitously falling prices would be greeted in consuming nations with tariffs and quotas designed to prevent domestic prices from falling. This means that the demand curve facing OPEC will become extremely inelastic; powerful incentives will be created for OPEC to engineer production cuts since price reductions will not open up consuming nations' markets to significant additional OPEC imports.

**Departures from the 'Conventional Wisdom'**

The conventional wisdom with respect to crude oil prices and availabilities runs something as follows: the consuming nations should expect about a 4 percent average annual increase in the real price of oil through to the year 2000, with some possible temporary softness. To summarize the findings of Stanford's Energy Modeling Forum, 'The unmistakable overall message is that the world price of oil, in real terms, can be expected to rise during the next several decades . . .[1] The clear upward trend (in constant 1981 prices) is evident even with the variation among the models. In 1985, oil price projections in the reference case range from a low of $30 per barrel (1981 dollars) for the IPE model to a high of almost $50 for OILTANK with a median of $35. By the year 2000 the range is from $42 to $90 per barrel, with a median of $70. The median real price increases by 2 percent annually between 1980 and 1985, by 6 percent annually for the next five years, and by 4 percent annually over the last ten years of the decade.[2] Figure 9.1 illustrates the reference case oil price projections through the year 2000 for the ten models in question. The basic rationale for this position derives from 'projections that oil supplies will grow more slowly than world economic activity. Even considering the delayed demand adjustments motivated by the pre-1980 price increases, world oil demand could be expected to grow more rapidly than supply if prices were to remain constant. Therefore, world oil price must continue to rise, slowing demand growth and increasing supply growth so as to clear the world oil market'.[3]

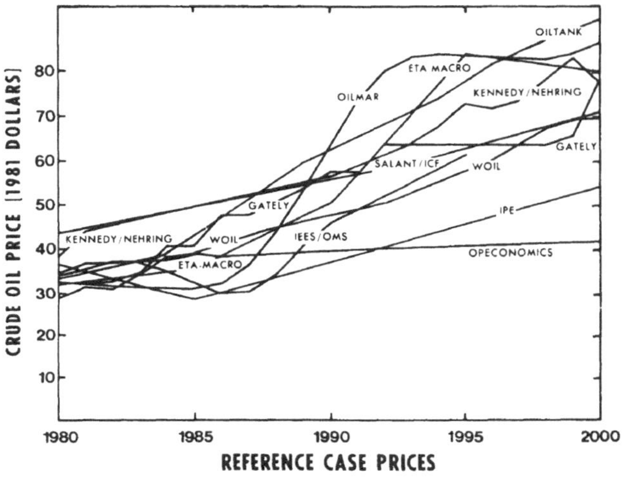


Figure 9.1 *Ten energy models – Stanford University Energy Modeling Forum.*
*Source:* Energy Modeling Forum (1981).

The Energy Modeling Forum's participants expect conventional supplies of oil to begin to decline during the 1980s. Declining OPEC oil reserves, at best modest increases in oil production from the non-OPEC, non-OECD world, and an assumption of relatively constant OPEC oil production capacity imply drops in the overall production rates. With none of the models is there projected to be any significant growth in OECD production.

The principal differences between the views presented here and Stanford's Energy Modeling Forum appear to stem from assumptions about OPEC's behavior and the non-OPEC supply response. The differences are not principally due to the price elasticity of demand assumptions even though the Daly, Griffin, and Steele estimate of $-.73$ exceeds the maximum value of $-.6$ assumed by the Energy Modeling Forum. In the EMF simulations, OPEC production is set exogenously at 34 MMB/D. We believe this assumption is excessively conservative. As shown in Table 6.6 of Chapter 6, even if OPEC production reached 38.3 MMB/D in the year 2000, reserves to production ratios in the Cartel Core would not be appreciably different than in 1980. Given the absence of geological constraints, internal development programs are likely to lead to a more accommodative view of production. Additionally, Daly, Griffin, and Steele (in Chapter 6) foresee rising non-OPEC production, expanding from 19.5 MMB/D in 1980 to 37 MMB/D by 2000.

However, since there are many factors at work in the oil market which can upset the best predictions, we concur with conventional views that it is appropriate to emphasize uncertainty. Professor Pindyck is quite correct in emphasizing that planners consider a range of possible price paths. The important point is that now it would appear that not all of the risk is on the upside. In our view, there are good theoretical and empirical reasons for stressing the possibility that real prices might fall because of competitive output expansion by OPEC producers in the absence of an increase in the demand for OPEC oil.

## Public Policy Implications

The preceding analysis has important policy implications to which there is broad agreement. Accordingly, consumer country policies should be geared to two principal objectives: (1) transforming the possibility of a price reduction into a certainty by the imposition of policies to reduce the demand for OPEC crude, and (2) instigating policies which reduce the costs of a supply disruption, should one occur. These two policy objectives are related but it is important to analyze them separately. Policymakers tend to blur the distinctions between the two, adopting policies which meet neither very well. The consuming countries face a unique situation in which policies to promote security mutually reinforce programs to reduce long run oil prices and vice versa.

### *Economic Power Considerations*

Consuming nations should immediately institute a tariff on imported oil to take advantage of the buying power wedge which is implicitly postulated to exist by several of the authors in this monograph. With the possible exception of Professor Moran's political model, all of the models advanced recognize that reduced demand for OPEC oil will tend to restrain further price increases and may well bring about a significant drop in prices. Even the United States acting alone is likely to have an impact since roughly one-fourth of OPEC exports are consumed in the United States. However, in view of the 'public' nature of price de-escalation, coordinated action by consuming countries is desirable both on grounds of efficiency and equity.

A tariff on imported oil and petroleum products is likely to be the most efficient instrument for exercising buyer power. In order to encourage competitive output expansion as well as to internalize the security costs associated with imported oil, an *ad valorem* tariff of say 30 percent could be implemented. The important advantage of an *ad valorem* tariff as opposed to a fixed tariff is that the amount paid per barrel rises and falls with the OPEC price. This would serve to make the demand curve facing OPEC more elastic, thereby providing incentives for OPEC countries to lower prices in order to increase exports.

The important advantage of a tariff over a simple oil tax is that it focuses maximum incentives on reducing oil imports, thereby attenuating upward price pressures. At the same time, the reduction in imports improves the security position of the consuming countries as the price of imported oil now reflects its true social cost. Either reason in itself would be sufficient justification for a tariff, but the first rationale deserves particular consideration in view of the evolving soft market conditions we anticipate. Reduction of oil imports by an additional one or two million barrels could significantly reduce world oil prices. Moreover, the consuming nations could wrest some of the tax receipts away from the OPEC countries even if the decline in world oil prices does not exceed the tariff.

Such an *ad valorem* tariff will be unappealing to domestic producers if it is perceived to increase the probability that the world price will fall, thereby reducing the value of their investments. The more likely event is that the price decline would not exceed the increase in domestic prices due to the tariff, thereby leaving domestic producers in a net advantage. Should the price reduction substantially exceed this, the *ad valorem* tariff might require alteration to a standard tariff level sufficient to reflect the greater insecurity premium occurring at lower oil prices.

It must be recognized that success by consuming nations may spell near disaster for OPEC. A burgeoning glut and falling prices may provoke political action by certain producers to take competitive oil off the market. The sabotaging of facilities in the Gulf by radical states like Libya is not out of the question. Saudi Arabia is the obvious target for such incursions and this may explain why the kingdom is itself contemplating a strategic petroleum reserve with access to the Red Sea.

*Minimizing Disruption Costs*

The second problem framing the agenda for policy action is the need to meet the immediate threat of a sudden disruption in oil supplies. This concern remains to a greater or lesser degree, no matter the particular behavioral model of OPEC that one finds the most appealing. So far, agreement on the need for targeted energy policies to meet the supply vulnerability threat has not led to agreement on the substance of those policies. Attempts at cooperation among consumers have yielded pathetic results like the *de minimis* International Energy Program of the IEA or the import targets agreed to in Tokyo.

As Professor Hogan's chapter emphasizes, there are individual and collective actions available to lessen the exposure to damage from a disruption. International cooperation among consumers is a prerequisite since the market for crude is international. The high degree of fungibility of oil and the relatively low cost of its transportation mean that it is extremely difficult for any one country to insulate itself from the effects of changes in the market elsewhere in the world. The implication is that cooperative efforts among consumers are essential.

The International Energy Agency (IEA) provides the infrastructure within which meaningful cooperation can begin. However, as explained in Chapter 8, the sharing formulas have a deficiency which needs to be rectified. For small shortages, sharing is based on total oil consumption, but for large shortages (those above a 10 percent loss of expected oil supplies) the rule shifts to an import base, which works to the advantage of those countries with a large volume of domestic production, notably the United States. This structure provides a temptation for other countries to obtain a larger share of total oil supply by entering the spot market. The sharing arrangement would then be in danger of collapsing to the benefit of the oil exporters. The sharing formula should therefore be revised by making all allocations proportional to consumption and establishing a price formula in advance.

However, even a strengthened IEA is too modest for the task at hand. It is too large and cumbersome (twenty-one members) in relation to the demands for security. Professor Hogan advocated summit meetings among the major oil importers as a more sturdy vehicle for obtaining the degree of cooperation that is needed. The focus of these meetings should be to obtain cooperation in reducing imports and restraining entry into spot markets during periods of potential shortage. Hogan emphasizes that international agreements should focus on a target, leaving each country free to select the policy instruments necessary to achieve that target. He suggest that an upper limit be placed on the dollar expenditure on imports as a percentage of GNP. Individual countries are then free to choose tax, tariff, or administrative sanctions as instruments to achieve the target.

For the United States during times of supply disruptions, we recommend the price mechanism as the best method of reducing imports to achieve a percentage share import target. For example, the United States could put in place a variable rate *ad valorem* tariff. The tariff rate could increase from the, say, 30 percent floor in response to the magnitude of the supply disruption. With very severe disruptions, the tariff rate might rise to 100 or even 150 percent. At the same time, matching reductions in other government tax programs such as withholding taxes or social security contributions could offset the deleterious macroeconomic effects of the massive tariff receipts. The important advantage to such a variable rate *ad valorem* tariff is that it would automatically trigger higher prices, which would restrain oil consumption. Additionally, with a tariff, there is the advantage that the economic rents resulting from the disruption accrue to the consuming governments rather than the oil exporters. Moreover, with a return to normal, the tariff rates would return to the floor level and world oil prices would be lower than they would have since the tariff impeded the rise in world oil prices.

Besides reduced imports, Hogan emphasizes the importance of programs to provide the capability for a burst of new supply during an emergency. With the effective domestic price of oil doubling or tripling overnight as a result of a major disruption, emergency supplies have enormous value. The source of new supplies might take many forms ranging from a strategic petroleum reserve to surge production of coal or natural gas to replace oil through fuel switching programs. Every country should be expanding capacity to store oil as a large inventory of oil would be one of the most visible and credible tools for deterring supply interruptions or mitigating their effects.

## IV CONCLUDING REMARKS

The world petroleum market has yielded unpleasant surprises in abundance through the decade of the 1970s. Higher prices riveted attention on the Middle East and transformed economic and political relationships between producers and consumers. It is common to expect history to repeat itself, and public and private policy are often fashioned accordingly.

One of the principal objectives of this monograph is to indicate that the 1970s was a very unusual decade. The economic and social fabric of industrial societies was strained by a quantum leap in the relative price of energy. We expect the price uncertainty experienced in the 1970s will continue into the 1980s and beyond, but we counsel that reductions in the real price are as likely as further increases.

This prediction by no means implies that complacency is in order. Indeed, there is some danger that a period without severe price increases may lull consumers into a sense of false security. Unfortunately, however, any softening of OPEC's economic power will not be accompanied by the elimination of strategic dependence of the West on Middle East oil. For these reasons, we believe that it is of utmost importance for consumers to move forward with plans to increase energy security. A tariff on imported oil is a good place to start.

## NOTES

1 See Energy Modeling Forum Report 6.
2 Sweeney (1981), p. 20.
3 Sweeney (1981), pp. 21–2.

# Bibliography


Adelman, M. (1972), *The World Petroleum Market* (Baltimore: Johns Hopkins University Press for Resources for the Future).

Adelman, M. (1973), 'The Impact of the Tehran–Tripoli Agreements on US oil policy and prices', *Journal of Petroleum Technology* (November), p. 1256.

Adelman, M. (1977), 'The changing structure of big international oil', in F. Trager (ed.), *Oil, Divestiture, and National Security* (New York: Crane Russak).

Adelman, M. (1978), 'Constraints on the world oil monopoly price', *Resources and Energy*, vol. 1, pp. 3–19.

Al-Sabah, Y.S.F. (1980), *The Oil Economy of Kuwait* (London: Kegan Paul International).

Allison, G. (1971), 'Essence of a Decision: Exploring the Cuban Missile Crisis' (New York; Little Brown).

Alm, A. (1981), 'Energy supply interruptions and national security', *Science*, vol. 211 (March 27).

Baumol, W. J. and Quandt, R. E. (1964), 'Rules of thumb and optimally imperfect decisions', *American Economic Review*.

Beider, P. (1980), 'Comparison of the EMF 6 models', Working Paper, Energy Modeling Forum, Stanford University (January).

Ben-Shahar, H. (1976), *Oil: Prices and Capital* (Lexington, Mass.: Heath).

Berman, J. (1981a), 'A summary of contingency planning for energy emergencies', Discussion Paper, Energy and Environmental Policy Center, Harvard University (January).

Berman, J. (1981b), 'Rebate strategies for an oil emergency', Discussion Paper, Energy and Environmental Policy Center, Harvard University, (November).

Blair, J. M. (1976), *The Control of Oil* (New York: Vintage Books).

Blitzer, C., Meeraus, A. and Stoutjesdijk, A. (1975), 'A dynamic model of OPEC trade and production', *Journal of Development Economics*, vol. 2, no. 4, pp. 319–55.

Bohi, D. R. (1980), 'Price elasticities of energy demand: an introduction', *Resources* (Summer).

Bohi, D. R. and Russell, M. (1978), *Limiting Oil Imports: An Economic History and Analysis* (Baltimore: Johns Hopkins Press for Resources for the Future).

Brown, W. M. and Kahn, H. (1980), 'Why OPEC is vulnerable', *Fortune* (July 14).

Central Intelligence Agency (1977), 'The international energy situation: outlook to 1985' (April).

Central Intelligence Agency (1979), 'The world oil market in the years ahead', ER-79-10327U (August).

Choucri, N. and Ferraro, V. (1976), *International Politics of Energy*

*Interdependence: The Case of Petroleum* (Lexington, Mass.: Lexington Books).
Cremer, J. and Salehi-Isfahani, D. (1980), 'Competitive pricing in the oil market: how important is OPEC?', Working Paper, University of Pennsylvania, Phil.
Cremer, J. and Weitzman, M. L. (1976), 'OPEC and the monopoly price of world oil', *European Economic Review*, vol. 8 (August), pp. 155–64.
Dasgupta, P. S. and Heal, G. M. (1979), *Economic Theory and Exhaustible Resources* (Cambridge, England: Cambridge University Press).
Deese, D. A. and Nye, J. S. (eds), (1981a), *Energy and Security* (Cambridge, Mass.: Ballinger).
Deese, D. A. and Nye, J. S. (1981b), 'Energy and security', *Harvard Magazine* (Jan.–Feb.).
Dikko, M. Y. (1981), *Middle East Economic Survey*, June 1.
Eckaus, R. S. (1972), 'Absorptive capacity as a constraint due to maturation processes', in J. Bhagwati and R. Eckaus (eds), *Development and Planning* (London: Allen & Unwin).
Eckbo, P. L. (1976), *The Future of World Oil* (Cambridge, Mass.: Ballinger).
Enders, T. (1975), 'OPEC and the industrial countries: the next ten years', *Foreign Affairs* (July).
Energy Modeling Forum I (1977), *Energy and the Economy*, Stanford University, Palo Alto (September).
Energy Modeling Forum IV (1980), *Aggregate Elasticity of Energy Demand*, Stanford University, Palo Alto.
Energy Modeling Forum VI (1981), *World Oil*, Stanford University, Palo Alto (April).
Ezzati, A. (1976), 'Future OPEC price and production strategies as affected by its capacity to absorb oil revenues', *European Economic Review*, vol. 8, pp. 107–38.
Feith, D. J. (1981), 'Saudi production cutback an empty threat?', *Wall Street Journal*, March 30.
Fischer, D., Gately, D. and Kyle, J. F. (1975), 'The prospects for OPEC: a critical survey of the models of the world oil market', *Journal of Development Economics*, vol. 2, no. 4, pp. 363–86.
Friedman, M. (1974), *Newsweek*, March 4.
Friedman, M. (1980), *Newsweek*, September 15.
Fromholzer, D. R. (1980), 'The impacts of demand dynamics and consumer expectations on world oil prices', PhD dissertation, Department of Engineering-Economic Systems, Stanford University (December).
Gately, D. (1980), 'Simulating OPEC pricing behavior in the world energy market', Discussion Paper, International Energy Program, Stanford University (January).
Gately, D., Kyle, J. F. and Fischer, D. (1977), 'Strategies for OPEC's decisions', *European Economic Review* (December).
Gilbert, R. (1978), 'Dominant firm pricing in a market for an exhaustible resource', *Bell Journal of Economics*, vol. 9 (Autumn).
Griffin, J. M. (1979), *Energy Conservation in the OECD: 1980 to 2000* (Cambridge, Mass.: Ballinger).

Griffin, J. M. and Steele, H. (1980), *Energy Economics and Policy* (New York: Academic).
Grossling, B. (1978), 'A long-range outlook of world petroleum prospects', Joint Economic Committee, Subcommittee on Energy, US Congress (March 2).
Hall, R. E. and Pindyck, R. S. (1981a), 'Oil shocks and the Western economies'. *Technology Review* (May).
Hall, R. E. and Pindyck, R. S. (1981b), 'What to do when energy prices rise again', *The Public Interest* (Fall).
Herfindahl, O. C. and Kneese, A. V. (1974), *Economic Theory of Natural Resources* (Columbus, Ohio: Merrill).
Hersh, S. (1978), 'White House and Aramco at odds on oil: officials in Administration allege mismanagement of Saudi fields', *New York Times*, February 8.
Hnyilicza, E. and Pindyck, R. S. (1976), 'Pricing policies for a two-part exhaustible resource cartel: the case of OPEC', *European Economic Review*, vol. 8, pp. 139–54 (September).
Hotelling, H. (1931), 'The economics of exhaustible resources', *Journal of Political Economy* (April).
Houthakker, H. (1976), *The World Price of Oil: A Medium-Term Analysis* (Washington, D. C.: American Enterprise Institute).
Hubbard, G. and Fry, R. (1981), 'Macroeconomics and oil supply disruptions', Discussion Paper, Energy and Environmental Policy Center, Harvard University (June).
Ibbetson, R. G. and Sinquefield, R. A. (1979), *Stocks, Bonds, Bills and Inflation* (New York: Financial Analysts Research Foundation).
ICF Incorporated (1979), 'Imperfect competition in the international energy market: a computerized Nash-Cournot model', Report to the Office of Policy and Evaluation, US Department of Energy (May).
*International Energy Annual* (1980), USDOE/E1A-0219(79) (September).
Johany, A. D. (1978), 'OPEC is not a cartel: a property rights explanation of the rise in crude oil prices', unpublished doctoral dissertation, University of California, Santa Barbara.
Kalt, J. (1981), *The Economics and Politics of Oil Price Regulation* (Cambridge, Mass.: MIT Press).
Kalymon, B. A. (1975), 'Economic incentives in OPEC oil pricing policy', *Journal of Development Economics*, vol. 2, no. 4.
Kanovsky, E. (1980), 'On Saudi oil policy', *New York Times*, December 19.
Koreisha, S. and Stobaugh, R. (1979), Appendix in R. Stobaugh and D. Yergin (eds), *Energy Future: Report of the Energy Project of the Harvard Business School* (New York: Random House).
Krapels, E. (1980), *Oil Crisis Management* (Baltimore: Johns Hopkins University Press).
Krasner, S. (1973), 'Business-government relations: the case of the international coffee agreement', *International Organization* (Fall).
Landsberg, H. *et al.* (1981), *Energy: The Next Twenty Years* (Cambridge, Mass.: Ballinger).
Lovejoy, W. F. and Homan, P. T. (1967), *Economic Aspects of Oil Conservation Regulation* (Baltimore: Johns Hopkins University Press).
MacAvoy, P. W. (1981), 'World crude oil prices: the role of OPEC and

market fundamentals', Working Paper No. 21, Yale School of Organization and Management (June).
MacDonald, S. L. (1971), *Petroleum Conservation in the United States* (Baltimore: Johns Hopkins University Press).
Manne, A. (1979), 'International energy supplies and demands: a long term perspective', Stanford University International Energy Program Report (November).
Manne, A. (1980), 'Demand elasticities poll', memo., Energy Modeling Forum VI, Stanford University, Palo Alto (May 28).
McCray, A. W. (1975), *Petroleum Evaluations and Economic Decisions* (Englewood Cliffs, N. J.: Prentice-Hall).
Mead, W. J. (1979), 'The performance of government energy regulations', *American Economic Review* (May).
Misner, S. (1979), 'A comparison of energy forecasts: 1977–1979', unpublished discussion paper, International Energy Program, Stanford University, Palo Alto (October).
Modigliani, F. (1958), 'New developments on the oligopoly front', *Journal of Political Economy* (June).
*Monthly Energy Review* (1981), DOE/E1A-0035(81/08) (August 20).
Moran, T. H. (1974), *Multinational Corporations and the Politics of Dependence: Copper in Chile* (Princeton, N. J.: Princeton University Press).
Moran, T. H. (1982), 'The Middle East and the Gulf: what is the linkage for US policy?', forthcoming.
Mork, K. (1981), in J. Plummer (ed.), *Energy Vulnerability* (Cambridge, Mass.: Ballinger).
*National Journal* (1980), 'You know that synfuels are for real when the big boys enter the picture', September 13, pp. 1508–11.
*National Journal* (1981), 'No room in the caverns – U.S. running out of storage space for oil reserve', October 31.
National Petroleum Council (1980), 'Emergency preparedness for interruption of petroleum imports into the United States', Washington D.C. (April).
Nau, H. (1980), 'US oil and security policies in the Middle East: links between energy and defense', xerox, George Washington University, Washington, D.C. (June).
Neff, T. (1981), 'The changing world oil market', in D. Deese and J. Nye (eds), *Energy and Security* (Cambridge, Mass.: Ballinger).
Nehring, R. (1978), *Giant Oilfields and World Oil Resources* (Rand Corporation for the Central Intelligence Agency) (June).
Newbery, D. M. G. (1980), 'Oil prices, cartels, and a solution to dynamic consistency', unpublished Working Paper, Churchill College, Cambridge, England (May).
Nordhaus, W. D. (1973), 'The allocation of energy resources', Brookings Papers, vol. 3.
Oppenheim, V. H. (1976–77), 'Why oil prices go up: the past: we pushed them', *Foreign Policy* (Winter).
Pahlavi, Mohammad Reza (1980), *Answer to History* (New York: Stein & Day).
Pan Heuristics (1980), 'Persian Gulf and Western security', Marina del Rey, Calif. (November).

Peterson, F. and Fisher, A. (1977), 'The exploitation of extractive resources: a survey', *Economic Journal* (December).
Pindyck, R. S. (1977), 'The economics of oil pricing', *Wall Street Journal*, December 20.
Pindyck, R. S. (1978a), 'Gains to producers from the cartelization of exhaustible resources', *Review of Economics and Statistics* (May).
Pindyck, R. S. (1978b), 'OPEC's threat to the West', *Foreign Policy* (Spring).
Pindyck, R. S. (1979a), 'The cartelization of world commodity markets', *American Economic Review* (May).
Pindyck, R. S. (1979b), 'Some long-term problems in OPEC oil pricing', *Journal of Energy and Development* (Spring).
Pindyck, R. S. (1979c), *The Structure of World Energy Demand* (Cambridge, Mass.: MIT Press).
Pindyck, R. S. (1980), 'Energy price increases and macroeconomic policy', *The Energy Journal* (October).
Pindyck, R. S. (1981a), 'The optimal production of an exhaustible resource when price is exogenous and stochastic', *Scandinavian Journal of Economics* (June).
Pindyck, R. S. (1981b), 'Energy, productivity, and the new US industrial policy', in M. Wachter and S. Wachter (eds), *A New U.S. Industrial Policy* (Philadelphia: University of Pennsylvania Press).
Quandt, W. B. (1980), 'Saudi Arabia's foreign and defense policies in the 1980s', Brookings Institution, Washington D.C. (June).
Riefman, A. (1975), 'U.S. energy policy: a perspective on major immediate issues', Library of Congress, Congressional Research Service (July 24).
Rosenstein-Rodan, P. N. (1961), 'International aid for underdeveloped countries', *Review of Economics and Statistics*, vol. 43, no. 2 (May).
Rowen, H. (1981a), 'A letter to the Secretary of State', *Washington Post*, March 22.
Rowen, H. (1981b), 'Oil importers wonder: can glut continue?', *Washington Post*, June 28.
Rowen, H. (1981c), 'How the West should protect Persian Gulf oil - and insure against its loss', presented at the Joint European American Institute/Security Conference on Asia and the Pacific Workshop, Kronberg, Germany (June 4–6).
Rowen, H. and Hogan, W. (1981), 'The Persian Gulf and the Western economies: energy issues', presented at the Security Conference on Asia and the Pacific Workshop, Tokyo (January 23–25).
Rowen, H. and Weyant, J. (1981), 'Improving international cooperation on energy', presented at the Tokyo Workshop of the Security Conference on Asia and the Pacific (January 23–25).
Salant, S. W. (1976), 'Exhaustible resources and the industrial structure: a Nash–Cournot approach to the world oil market', *Journal of Political Economy* (October).
Salant, S. W. (1980), 'Imperfect competition in the international energy market: a computerized Nash–Cournot model', unpublished paper.
Samore, G. (1980a), 'Determinants of oil policy', Kennedy School of Government, Harvard University, unpublished draft, p. 14 (May).
Samore, G. (1980b), in D. A. Deese and J. S. Nye (eds), *Energy and Security* (Cambridge, Mass.: Ballinger).

Sant, R. W. *et al.* (1980), *The Least-Cost Energy Strategy.*

Schelling, T. (1960), *The Strategy of Conflict* (Cambridge, Mass.: Harvard University Press).

Schlesinger, J. (1978), 'Don't count on Saudi Arabia to produce more than 12 MMB/D says Schlesinger', *Middle East Economic Survey,* January 30.

Schmalensee, R. (1976), 'Resource exploitation theory and the behavior of the oil cartel', *European Economic Review*, vol. 7, pp. 257–79.

Silk, L. (1981), 'The slippage in OPEC power', *New York Times,* May 13.

Singer, S. F. (1978), 'Limits to Arab Oil Power', *Foreign Policy* (Spring).

Smith, J. P. (1978a), 'CIA trims Saudi oil estimates; experts are skeptical', *Washington Post*, February 5.

Smith, J. P. (1978b), 'CIA again revises estimates of Saudi oil output potential', *Washington Post*, February 11.

Solow, R. M. (1974), 'The Economics of Resources or the Resources of Economics', *American Economic Review* (May).

Stiglitz, J. (1976), 'Monopoly and the rate of extraction of exhaustible resources', *American Economic Review* (September).

Stocking, G. W. and Watkins, M. W. (1946), *Cartels in Action* (New York: Twentieth Century Fund).

Sweeney, J. (1977), 'Economics of depletable resources: market forces and intertemporal bias', *Review of Economic Studies* (February).

Sweeney, J. (1981), Energy Modeling Forum VI, *Draft Summary Report*, Stanford University, Palo Alto (April).

Tourinho, O.A.F. (1979), 'The option value of reserves of natural resources', Working Paper No. 94, Graduate School of Business, University of California, Berkeley (September).

Tucker, W. (1981), 'The energy crisis is over!', *Harper's* (November).

Turner, L. and Bedore, J. (1979), *Middle East Industrialization* (Wheatmead, Hants.: Saxon House).

US Senate (1979), 'The future of Saudi Arabian oil production', Staff Report to the Subcommittee on International Economic Policy of the Committee on Foreign Relations (April).

Weiner, R. (1981), 'The oil import question in an international context: institutional and economic aspects of consumer cooperation', Discussion Paper, Energy and Environmental Policy Center, Harvard University (June).

Willett, T. D. (1979), 'Conflict and cooperation in OPEC: some additional economic considerations', *International Organization* (Autumn).

Workshop on Alternative Energy Strategies (1977), Energy: Global Prospects, 1985–2000 (New York: McGraw Hill).

Yamani, Sheik Ahmed (1981), 'Yamani takes a look at the future for oil', Lecture at the University of Petroleum and Minerals, Damman, January 31. Reprinted in *Middle East Economic Survey.*

# Conference Participants on 'The Future of OPEC and the Long Run Price of Oil' Sponsored by: Center for Public Policy University of Houston May 8, 1981

JOSEPH E. BURNS
Federal Reserve Bank of Dallas
Dallas, Texas

P. J. CARROLL
Shell Oil Company
Houston, Texas

LEONEL CASTILLO
Castillo Interests
Houston, Texas

MARSHALL CLOYD
Brown & Root, Inc.
Houston, Texas

MARVIN CLUETT
Houston Natural Gas Corporation
Houston, Texas

B. M. COX
Pennzoil Exploration & Production
Houston, Texas

LES DEMAN
Texas Eastern Corporation
Houston, Texas

RON DURANT
Exxon Company, USA
Houston, Texas

JOHN GARRETT
Gulf Oil Exploration and Production Company
Houston, Texas

DONALD GOLDSTEIN
Ofice of Economics and Energy Affairs
Department of Defense
Washington, D.C.

HERBERT E. HANSEN
Gulf Oil Exploration and Production Company
Houston, Texas

ROGER HEMMINGHAUS
United Gas Pipeline Company
Houston, Texas

HANS HEYMANN, JR.
Central Intelligence Agency
Washington, D.C.

ALVIN HILDEBRANDT
University of Houston
Houston, Texas

MILTON HOLLOWAY
Texas Energy and Natural Resources Advisory Council
Austin, Texas

DON HORN
Harris County AFL-CIO Council
Houston, Texas

WILLIAM A. JOHNSON
Tenneco, Inc.
Houston, Texas

PAUL L. KELLY
Zapata Corporation
Houston, Texas

FRITZ KLAUSNER
Exxon Company, USA
Houston, Texas

JOE LAHEY
Pullman Kellog
Houston, Texas

SHEL LAMBERT
Shell Oil Company
Houston, Texas

ALICE LEBLANC
Texas Commerce Bank
Houston, Texas

THOMAS J. MANNING
Pace Company
Houston, Texas

THOMAS H. MAYOR
University of Houston
Houston, Texas

CARL NEWBROUGH
Union Texas Petroleum Corporation
Houston, Texas

LUCIAN F. PUGLIARESI
Department of Energy
Washington, D.C.

J. P. ROBERTS
Houston Lighting and Power Company
Houston, Texas

SARGON E. RUSTUM
Bechtel Petroleum, Inc.
Houston, Texas

JOHN SAUER
Conoco, Inc.
Houston, Texas

RAYMOND J. SNOKHOUS
Gulf Refining and Marketing Company
Houston, Texas

FRAN STECKMEST
Shell Oil Company
Houston, Texas

R. N. TENNYSON
Fluor Engineers and Constructors, Inc.
Houston, Texas

R. WILLIAM THOMAS
Institute for Defense Analysis
Arlington, Virginia

L. R. THOMPSON
Gulf Refining and Marketing Company
Houston, Texas

S. G. VASTOLA, JR.
Exxon Company, USA
Houston, Texas

SCOTT WILLIS
Hughes Tool Company
Houston, Texas

# Index

N.B. References in **bold** type refer to major sections
References in *italic* type refer to tables, figures etc.